Hardboiled Hollywood

Max Décharné

HARDBOILED HOLLYWOOD

No Exit Press

2003

This edition published in October 2003 by

No Exit Press
18 Coleswood Road
Harpenden
Herts
AL5 1EQ

www.noexit.co.uk

ISBN 1 84243 70 X Hardboiled Hollywood

Printed & bound by CPD Wales

Text design and typesetting by Able Solutions (UK) Ltd

For my mother

Acknowledgements

To Sven Severin, Mark Rubenstein and J J Rassler for helping out and putting a lot of good crime material my way. To Ion and everyone at No Exit for having faith in this book, to Lisa and Claire and Floss and Peter for helping put it together, to Damon Wise for inspiration, James Johnston for letting me rummage around in his basement, and James Hollands for plying me with drink and letting me harangue the public at the Horse Hospital.

Thanks and much love to Katja for support and for putting up with a year of endless stories about mobsters, hit-men and wiseguys.

Finally, special thanks and a raised glass of Tullamore Dew to the late Mike Hart who died just as I was completing this book, for all the drinks, the good times and the advice at Compendium and Murder One, for being the first person to ever show any interest in my books back in the late 1980s, but mostly just for being one of the very best.

Contents

Opening Shot

When Robert Aldrich, the director of *Kiss Me, Deadly* (1955), was asked by *Sight & Sound* magazine about Mickey Spillane's source novel of the same name, he replied: 'The book had nothing. We just took the title and threw the rest away.' Alfred Hitchcock also adopted pretty much the same attitude towards Robert Bloch's novel *Psycho*. In all the controversy surrounding the release of Arthur Penn's *Bonnie and Clyde* (1967), questions were asked about the film's relation to the real-life killers whose story had inspired it, but here again, the director felt that it wasn't particularly important what kind of people they'd been, or how the actual facts might relate to the movie he'd made. In many ways, this is fair enough. Films are films, and their sources of inspiration are another thing entirely. However, there's been a distinct tendency to take the film director's word as gospel when discussing many of these pictures, largely as a result of the popularity of the *auteur* theory, in which the director is God and sole author of everything, and the writer is an irrelevance and probably never existed at all. This is all very well, but it's worth remembering that this theory was first put forward by a group of would-be film directors who then went on to become... film directors. Quelle surprise, as the French would say.

The object of this book is to examine the events leading up to the making of various classic films of the crime genre, taking into account the conditions and constraints in place at the time, and then to follow them through the various stages of shooting and release. Crime films and the novels which inspired them were usually seen as cheap, low-class entertainment for the masses, many of them dismissed out of hand by the upmarket magazines and supposedly 'serious' film publications of the past. Mostly, they were dealt with in the pages of the popular film magazines such as *ABC Film Review, Picturegoer* and *Photoplay*, which is where the overwhelming majority of their original audience would have been likely to read about them, and it seemed relevant to give equal space to material drawn from these sources. Many of the books which have been written about crime films, and *film noir* in particular, have been written from the point of view of university film studies courses and attempt to psychoanalyse the films from a modern perspective far removed from that of the people who actually made the movies themselves. Again, fair enough, but that wasn't what interested me.

Most of these films are world famous. Often, but not always, their sources are much less well known. This is an attempt to illuminate a little more of their background. As a character in Charles Williams' 1953 hardboiled novel *Hell Hath No Fury (aka The Hot Spot)* remarks:

> When you break the law you can forget about playing the averages because you have to win all the time. Who ever won all the time? Yeah, but the thing which always trips'em is association with other criminals, and I don't know any, talkative or otherwise. An amateur's got a better chance than the pro because nobody knows him and he hasn't got any clippings in the files.

Hollywood's been associating with criminals for decades now. Here are a few of the clippings they left in the files.

Max Décharné
Berlin, December 2002

Scene of the Crime

'I was forty-five years old and tired of being an artist. Besides, I owed $20,000 to relatives, finance companies, banks and assorted bookmakers and shylocks. It was really time to grow up and sell out as Lenny Bruce once advised. So I told my editors OK, I'll write a book about the Mafia, just give me some money to get started.'

Mario Puzo, The Making of *The Godfather*

Crime films, like crime fiction, were never 'respectable'. At the beginning, neither was Hollywood. The movies started out as a sideshow attraction a hundred years ago, a quick way to part you from whatever small change you had in your pockets. A novelty, a racket, a hustle – and once they got bored showing you simplistic flickering scenes of idiots in gardens with hosepipes or workers milling around outside factory gates, they soon learned that if you slung together a few shots of some tough-looking characters waving artillery around and attempting to steal something, then the public was going to start lining up around the block. Which short film from 1903 is generally held to be the first to really make an impact in terms of dramatic storyline? It was called *The Great Train Robbery*, and it was produced by the Edison Company in response to the success of a film from England that had been knocking out New York audiences. A *Daring Daylight Burglary* was a tasty item featuring a thrilling police pursuit and a guest appearance from the Sheffield Fire Brigade. Note the last word in each title.

As Raymond Chandler famously remarked about his days of writing stories for pulp magazines like *Dime Detective* and *Black Mask*: 'When in doubt have a man come through the door with a gun in his hand.' As far as Hollywood is concerned, the guys with the guns in their hands have been a regular money-spinner and source of inspiration for as long as the Dream Factory has been in existence, but, for most of that time, there's also been a steady stream of pressure groups, legislative bodies, concerned citizens and a fair number of certifiable cranks attempting to influence, censor, suppress or merely hurl abuse at the crime films that Hollywood has produced. This is an enjoyable game, and almost anyone can play, regardless of their qualifications. Of course, this genre of films, and movies in general, are hardly unique in this respect. Pretty much anything worthwhile in the way of books, paintings and music that has appeared over the centuries has usually had a rough ride from the press, the politicians and the self-appointed guardians of public decency. In

1888, at a time when the Lumière Brothers and Edison were preparing to unleash the magic of cinema upon the world, the magazine *Temple Bar* was also warning its readers about some new evil threatening to corrupt the great British public:

> Those shameless purveyors of garbage . . . This new school has imagined the impossible. Hyenas, delighting in carrion, they have lost touch with humanity.

The hyenas in question (condemned here in terms remarkably similar to those used by British politicians and the press during the artificially-generated 'video nasties' debate in the early 1980s), were the novelist Émile Zola and others of the Naturalist school. These days it's accepted that they were writing some of the classic texts of nineteenth-century literature, but at the time, even the MPs in the House of Commons were being warned by fellow member Samuel Smith about these Gallic filth-merchants:

> Nothing more diabolical had ever been written by the pen of man; they were fit only for swine, and those who read them must turn their minds into cesspools.

It took several decades – and, crucially, the coming of sound – before films were considered enough of a threat for the censorship lobby to really mobilise and crack down on Tinseltown. As moving pictures became the new mass market entertainment, out-stripping the influence of the written word among the 'lower orders' whose moral welfare has concerned so many interest groups over the years, the censors moved in with all kinds of restrictions upon which subjects were fit to be depicted onscreen. Sex would have to go, for a start (that smacked far too much of people enjoying themselves) and as for violence – well, let's just pretend it doesn't exist. It wouldn't do to have the riff-raff attempting to imitate those mobsters they've seen at the cinema. These two basic principles have remained in force in varying degrees throughout the history of the crime film genre, during which time censorship of books has all but disappeared, leading to the current anomaly where, until 2002, consenting adults who could read Gordon Williams's novel *The Siege of Trencher's Farm* any time they liked were forbidden by the British Board of Film Classification from watching Sam Peckinpah's 1971 adaptation of the same story, *Straw Dogs*.

If it was evil filth, designed to corrupt and deprave, then how come it's on sale now (and how come the original cinema audiences didn't riot in the streets, looting and pillaging?). On the other hand, if it's a great film from one of the twentieth century's greatest directors, then why lock it in a cupboard for thirty years?

The first tentative American attempts to protect the public from what self-appointed watchdog Mary Whitehouse would later term 'a tidal wave of filth' came in 1908, with the setting up of the National Board of Censorship, established by the film industry in response to criticisms that their early one-reel short films were awash with immorality. In general, this failed to stem the rising tide of complaints, and so in 1922 they established a self-regulating censorship body called the Motion Picture Producers and Distributors of America (MPPDA) under the command of Postmaster General Will H Hays. This organisation, which later changed its name to the MPAA (Motion Picture Association of America), became generally known as the Hays Office, which in 1924 introduced a set of movie regulations called *The Formula*. These were only suggested guidelines however, and Hays lacked the power to enforce their judgements, so in 1927 he introduced a new list entitled *Don'ts and Be Carefuls*. Included here were some things which 'shall not appear in pictures . . . irrespective of the manner in which they are treated', such as: 'any licentious or suggestive nudity – in fact or in silhouette', 'the illegal traffic in drugs', 'ridicule of the clergy' and 'sex relationships between the white and black races'. Subjects requiring 'special care' included 'the use of firearms', 'theft, robbery, safe-cracking', 'sympathy for criminals', 'technique of committing murder by whatever method' and 'excessive or lustful kissing, particularly when one or the other is a 'heavy''. As can be clearly seen – kissing a mobster is officially more lewd than kissing a law-abiding citizen.

Unsurprisingly, this list was far too short to satisfy Hays for long (a public servant so convinced of his own worth that he was only persuaded to step down from office in 1945 when offered $500,000, payable over five years, as a golden handshake). His next move was certainly the most far-reaching; greatly affecting the course and nature of film production for the next quarter of a century. This was the establishment of the Production Code of 1930 – a year in which Al Capone was still a force to be reckoned with in Chicago, the newspapers were full of stories of mobsters, bootleggers and bankrobbers, and movie hoods like Edward G Robinson and Jimmy Cagney were in the process of filming *Little Caesar* and *The Public Enemy* (both released 1931). The new code, which, with various revisions, became the stick that was used to beat a significant number of the landmark crime movies of the golden age of the gangster and *film noir* genres, was announced as follows in the pages of the

15

New York Times, on April Fool's Day, 1930:

> CODE OF CONDUCT FOR FILMS REVISED
> Crime Details Are Ruled Out and Respect for Flag Demanded in Movies
>
> A new code of conduct was adopted by the Motion Picture Producers and Distributors Association at a meeting of the board of directors of that organisation yesterday at their offices, 469 Fifth Avenue . . . The new code is generally considered an outgrowth of severe criticism by prominent churchmen, who charge that the moral character of audiences is being undermined by the sort of action they see on the screen.

The Production Code, drawn up with the confidence of the democratically unelected, by the Reverend Daniel A Lord and Martin Quigley (publisher of the *Motion Picture Herald*), was careful to stress that 'methods of crime shall not be presented in explicit detail on the screen'. The newspaper report summed up its three main points as follows:

> Every effort shall be made to reflect in drama and entertainment the better standards of life.
>
> Law, natural or human, shall not be ridiculed.
>
> Sympathy shall not be created for the violators of the law.

The small print of the full text of the Code blatantly acknowledges that films are to be judged in a different way from books, largely because that fearsome element which the Victorians used to call the 'Great Unwashed' might be affected by them. Under the heading *Moral Obligations* it says:

> Most arts appeal to the mature. This art appeals at once to every class, mature, immature, developed, underdeveloped, law abiding, criminal. Music has its grades for different classes; so has literature and drama. This art of the motion picture, combining as it does the two fundamental appeals of looking at a picture and listening to a story, at once reached every class of society.

16

So there you have it – the unbreachable gulf between the art of the mature and the art of Victor Mature, and heaven help us all if art should fall into the hands of the lower classes. All of which recalls the patronising words of prosecutor Mervyn Griffiths-Jones, who famously asked the jury at the 1960 obscenity trial for D H Lawrence's *Lady Chatterley's Lover*, banned since 1928: 'Is it a book you would wish your wife or your servants to read?'

There was a lengthy section of the Code entitled *Special Regulations on Crime in Motion Pictures*, which stated, among other things:

> There must be no display, at any time, of machine guns, sub-machine guns or other weapons generally classified as illegal weapons in the hands of gangsters, or other criminals, and there are to be no off-stage sounds of the repercussions of these guns.

> There must be no scenes, at any time, showing law-enforcement officers dying at the hands of criminals. This includes private detectives and guards for banks, motor trucks, etc.

> No picture shall be approved dealing with the life of a notorious criminal of current or recent times which uses the name, nickname or alias of such notorious criminal in the film, nor shall a picture be approved if based on the life of such a notorious criminal unless the character shown in the film be punished for crimes shown in the film as committed by him.

Given that the full document continues in this same vein at some length, it's remarkable that anyone managed to make a crime film at all in the 1930s, let alone some of the classics of the genre. Still, not everyone who was criticising the output of Hollywood was doing so out of any particular concern for the moral health of the public. In November 1930 the novelist Theodore Dreiser threatened to sue the studio that was in the process of adapting his book *An American Tragedy* for the screen if he didn't approve of the end result. 'Motion Pictures,' he said, 'are making the American mind smaller than it is, if that is possible. I am not interested in what they are doing to the children of America. I am not interested in children. But motion pictures are making the kind of people one sees in motion pictures.' This attitude wouldn't have impressed the likes of Charles H Martens, the Mayor of East Orange, New Jersey, who in June 1931 was moved to write to Will Hays himself in an effort to bring about the banning of gangster films, saying, 'I do not wish Hollywood to dictate the morals of the youth of East Orange.'

In the early 1930s, it was clear that many film-makers were not sticking exactly to the guidelines laid down in the Code, and the Hays Office still lacked any real power to enforce their decisions. Millionaire movie producer Howard Hughes had a well-publicised fight with individual state censors in 1932 over the release of Howard Hawks's *Scarface*, a thinly-veiled biography of Al Capone. New York's censorship board refused to pass the film, so Hughes announced that he would show it only in such states where there was no local censor, and he sought public endorsements from bodies such as the California State Crime Commission to back him up. Nevertheless, he still wound up releasing the film with a moralistic subtitle, so that it was called *Scarface: The Shame of a Nation*. In the event, millions queued up to see Paul Muni in the title role, and to watch George Raft flipping coins, but it's doubtful if any of them left the cinemas feeling particularly ashamed.

However, in 1934 – the year in which many of America's real-life gangsters such as John Dillinger, Pretty Boy Floyd and Clyde Barrow met their ends – a major campaign was launched which was to have a far-reaching effect on Hollywood's ability to make crime pictures, when Cardinal Dougherty of Philadelphia urged a wholesale boycott of motion pictures for members of the Catholic Church: 'A vicious and insidious attack is being made on the very foundations of Christian civilization,' he told the press on 9 June. 'A very great proportion of the screen productions deal largely with sex or crime. The usual theme of these moving pictures is divorce, free love, marital infidelity and the exploits of gangsters and racketeers.' This was the opening salvo in a war about to be waged by a new organisation known as the Catholic Legion of Decency, an organisation formed after a Monsignor Cicognani had impressed the previous year's annual American Bishops Convention with a ringing denunciation of the evils of motion pictures. By 18 June 1934 papers were reporting that 50,000 Catholics in the Cleveland Stadium in Ohio had taken the pledge of the Legion, which maintained that films were 'corrupting public morals and promoting a sex mania in our land'. The pledge read, in part:

> I shall do all I can to arouse public opinion against the portrayal of
> vice as a normal condition of affairs, and against depicting criminals
> of any class as heroes and heroines, presenting their filthy philosophy
> of life as something acceptable to decent men and women.

This campaign was hugely effective, and a frightened movie industry ensured that the Hays Office set up a department called the Production Code Administration Office (PCA), under a man named Joseph Breen who was to be backed up for the first time with real powers: any studio which released a film without a certificate of approval from the PCA would be fined the then considerable sum of $25,000. From this point forward, the movie producers were very careful to submit treatments, scripts and story ideas long in advance of production, rather than take the risk of putting money into a film which might then prove to be deemed unreleasable on account of its proposed subject matter. One immediate result of these changes was that author James M Cain, whose new book – a taut, economical crime story of murder and adultery entitled *The Postman Always Rings Twice* (1934) – had been optioned for the movies, found that it was thrown in a drawer marked unfilmable until censorship restrictions eased over a decade later. Then, in 1936, with his new novel *Double Indemnity* in the middle of a five-way movie rights bidding war and his agent poised to sell them for $25,000, there was just the little matter of the report from the Hays Office on the book's suitability as a subject for a movie. As Cain later recalled:

> That afternoon the Hays Office report came in, and it started off: 'Under no circumstances . . . ' and it ended up, ' . . . way, shape or form.' My agent asked me if I wanted to hear what was in between, and I told him I could guess.

As it turned out, when Hollywood finally got permission to film *Double Indemnity* in 1944 – in a fine version directed by Billy Wilder and co-scripted by Raymond Chandler – it proved to be the breakthrough picture which taught the studios that it was now safe to approach more hardboiled crime subjects, and paved the way for the whole post-war *film noir* boom. The censorship climbdown on the part of the Hays Office happened at a time when the US was involved in a world war, and the mood of the times was naturally more down-to-earth and realistic, and more willing to admit the existence of things such as crime, guns and adulterous relationships. The Hays Office once again fell foul of Howard Hughes, this time over his methods of marketing his new discovery, Jane Russell, in his film *The Outlaw,* which he released in 1943 without Production Code approval. It was shortly after this skirmish that Joseph Breen at the PCA gave his approval for the adaptation of *Double Indemnity,* and the following year he agreed in principle to the idea of a film version of *The Postman*

Always Rings Twice, as long as this involved the removal of 'all scenes of physical contact – hugging and kissing' between the two lead characters. When the film finally appeared, James M Cain wrote an article in the *New York Times,* 21 April 1946, telling the story of how *Double Indemnity* had finally been sold to the movies for $15,000, which was $10,000 less than he'd originally been offered in 1936 before the report from Joseph Breen's office had killed the sale:

> Now what I would like to know is, who pays me this $10,000? In my simple scheme of things, I think this jolly Irishman [Breen] owes it to me, and if he should happen to read this I would like him to know I still want it, and the passage of time hasn't mellowed my feeling about it in any way whatever.

Double Indemnity's co-screenwriter Raymond Chandler evidently sensed that a change in attitudes was on the way: in a letter written on 18 December 1944 he remarked, 'An adult, that is a dirty or plain-spoken art of the screen, could exist at any moment the Hays Office [...] and the local censorship boards would let it.' The picture proved a big commercial and critical success and was nominated for several Oscars, while some reviewers noted that the story had its origins in a real-life murder case of the 1920s. As *Variety* put it:

> There are unmistakeable similarities between the Paramount pic and the famous Snyder-Gray murder wherein Albert Snyder was sash-weighted to death 17 years ago in his Queens Village, N.Y. home by his wife Ruth, and her lover, Judd Gray. Both the fictional and the real murders were for the slain men's insurance. Both were committed by the murdered men's wives and their amours.

If a picture so obviously patterned on a genuine murder case and featuring characters involved in an adulterous relationship could not only gain a Production Code seal but go on to be nominated for the industry's highest awards, then things had obviously changed a great deal, and the way was clear for Hollywood producers to have much more leeway in their presentation of crime on the screen – including the making of films specifically named after well-known criminals, such as Max Nosseck's *Dillinger* (1945). James M Cain, the man whose novels had hitherto been considered 'unfilmable', now found himself the subject of three very high-profile adaptations in as many years: *Double Indemnity* (1944), *Mildred Pierce* (1945) and *The Postman Always Rings Twice*

(1946). He was interviewed in August 1945 for a *New York Times* article about this new trend in pictures which carried the headline: 'Crime Certainly Pays on the Screen – The growing crop of homicidal films poses questions for psychologists and producers':

> The reason Hollywood is making so many of these so-called hard-boiled crime pictures,' he explains, 'is simply that the producers are now belatedly realizing that these stories make good movies . . . It's just that producers have got hep to the fact that plenty of real crime takes place every day and that it makes a good movie. The public is fed up with the old-fashioned melodramatic type of hokum. You know, the whodunit at which the audience after the second reel starts shouting 'We know the murderer. It's the butler. It's the butler. It's the butler.'

The Hays Office may have been finally becoming a little more liberal, but local censorship boards could still cause trouble, as was the case in Boston in the summer of 1946, when Laurence Olivier's much-praised adaptation of Shakespeare's *Henry V* (1944) hit town, causing the city's Department of Public Utilities to put the boot into the Bard – but only on Sundays. Weekday showings were unaffected, but, on religious grounds, a censored print was screened every Sunday, in which, it was reported, 'three 'hells' are deleted and the lines '…but bastard Normans, Norman bastards' are blacked out.' Local difficulties aside, the pressure from the Production Code office was declining (and Will Hays himself was finally persuaded to step down in 1945), but another heresy – apart from the depiction of mobsters or sex – was soon discovered: the 'Communist conspiracy'. In the decade immediately following the war, some of Hollywood's finest picture makers were to have their careers cut short or seriously damaged by the anti-red witch hunts of the House Un-American Activities Committee and Senator Joe McCarthy. The atmosphere of suspicion and paranoia this engendered may have done wonders for the creation of many classics of the *film noir* genre, but it's doubtful whether many of the people whose livelihoods were being destroyed were grateful. J Edgar Hoover, head of the FBI, was convinced that the Communist menace was the great evil facing America – much more so than the Mafia; an organisation whose existence he initially denied. Even as late as 1959, there were over four hundred operatives in the FBI's New York office alone working on fighting the 'Communist conspiracy', as opposed to just four responsible for organised crime. Hoover himself apparently tried even more direct methods of influencing the content of movies, according to screenwriter Bernard Gordon, who himself was a victim of the anti-Communist witch-hunts. In his book, *Hollywood Exile or How I Learned to Love the Blacklist* (1999), Gordon says he found a file during his time at Paramount containing 'original story material' written by J Edgar Hoover: 'None of this story material had ever been used, but the files showed he'd been paid for his contribution to our cultural resources, not once but a number of times.'

Hoover may have downplayed the existence of the mob, but the public was unlikely to have been fooled. Quite apart from the evidence presented in the daily newspapers, there was also the gripping spectacle of Senator Estes Kefauver's Senate Crime Investigating Committee hearings, broadcast to the nation through the new medium of television between 10 May 1950 and 1 May 1951. The senator, who liked to pose for the press wearing a Davy Crockett-style coonskin hat, then published his findings in a book entitled, *Crime in America – Trial Before Television of America's Leading Thugs* (1951), in which he stated:

> Behind the local mobs which make up the national crime syndicate is a shadowy, international criminal organisation known as the Mafia, so fantastic that most Americans find it hard to believe it really exists.

One reason for this disbelief might just have been the fact that Hollywood had long been forbidden to depict much of the mob's activities onscreen. Malvin Wald (scriptwriter for *Al Capone* (1959) and the CBS TV show *Albert Anastasia: His Life and Death* (1957)) wrote to *Sight & Sound* in Summer 1968 to say that when he had worked on the mob film *Undercover Man* (1949), 'we were forbidden by the American censors to mention Al Capone by name, and were forced to refer to him obliquely as 'The Big Fellow'. As the 1950s drew to a close, however, following the huge success of television shows such as *Dragnet* and *The Untouchables,* there was a new willingness on the part of film-makers to put fictionalised versions of real-life criminals' life stories up on the screen. This cycle of pictures included *Baby Face Nelson* (1958), *The Bonnie Parker Story* (1958), *Machine Gun Kelly* (1958), *Al Capone* (1959) and *Pretty Boy Floyd* (1959). Mostly these films originated at the low-budget end of the market, and the average bankrobber or hood would have to wait another decade for the big studio treatment, but all this activity caused the FBI chief to issue a public statement in 1958 protesting about the 'ominous trend of crime glorification'. Quoting the recent example of two brothers from Oklahoma, aged 10 and 12, who had gone on a shooting spree which left one person dead and two others wounded, he wrote that they told the police that they 'got the idea from watching television and movie crime stories'. Hoover called for new stories to be made which would show criminals in their proper light 'as wretched unglamorous leeches who bring nothing but degradation to themselves and human suffering to their fellow men'.

One wretched unglamorous leech who'd hit the headlines earlier that year was a teenage thrill-killer named Charlie Starkweather, who took off across Wyoming and Nebraska with his 14-year-old girlfriend, Caril Fulgate, leaving a trail of bodies in his wake. According to a report headline entitled 'Eleven Lay Dead' (*Newsweek*, 10 February 1958), he told the police: 'I shot all these people in self-defence. People kept coming at me and I had to shoot. What else would you do? I wanted to be a criminal, but I didn't know it would be like this.' In the event, it seemed as if Starkweather's James Dean-fixated dress code and would-be hepcat lifestyle offended the newspapers almost as much as his crimes: 'He got a reputation among his classmates for knife-fighting. He affected cowboy boots and leather jackets; he wore his hair long and grew sideburns; he was a voracious reader of comic books and a devotee of hot-rod automobiles.' Charlie drew the death penalty, but his story wound up as the basis for Terrence Malick's stunning 1974 debut feature *Badlands*, by which time films such as *Bonnie and Clyde* (1967) and *Bloody Mama* (1970) had proved that it wasn't necessary for your criminal subjects to have been particularly loveable in real life in order to form the basis of a good film.

One of the first significant attempts to document the mindset of a killer onscreen using actual names and places was Richard Brooks's 1967 film of Truman Capote's bestselling book *In Cold Blood*, which detailed the senseless murder of the Clutter family in 1959 by Dick Hickock and Perry Smith. Brooks managed to obtain permission to film his recreation of the murders in the actual house where they had taken place, even though he had been warned by many that he would be stirring up bad memories by attempting to film in the close-knit rural community so soon after the actual events had occurred. 'People told me to go to Nebraska or Iowa,' Brooks told the press. 'They said there would be a lot fewer problems. But how can I go to Nebraska to film something that happened here? People would say 'That's Hollywood for you. It happened in Kansas and they make it in Nebraska."' During filming he carried around with him various items that had belonged to the two killers, including a copy of a book, *Man and Nature: Excerpts from Thoreau*, inscribed 'PROPERTY OF PERRY SMITH DEATH ROW', which had been given by one of the killers to the prison chaplain just before his execution. Brooks had earlier told the press of his plan to move into a cell in the penitentiary at Lansing, Kansas, where the two were hung, in order to finish writing the script and 'get a feel for my material'. Upon its release, the film split critical opinion right down the middle: Joseph Morgenstern in *Newsweek* wrote that it had made the book 'suitable for audiences with weak stomachs and weaker minds. They have de-horrified the horror so cleverly that nothing is missed but the point,' whereas reviewers from magazines such as *Time* and the *Saturday Review* were generally full of praise. However, the picture had emerged in a year when a full-blown controversy developed in the media about violence in films – mostly centred on Arthur Penn's *Bonnie and Clyde* (1967).

The violence debate was so fierce during 1968, particularly in the wake of Robert Kennedy's assassination, that even Roger Corman's backers, American International Pictures displayed a momentary loss of nerve, issuing the following press statement in June 1968: 'American International Pictures has cancelled August production plans for filming of *Bloody Mama*, dealing with the life of the notorious Ma Barker, due to the excessive violence inherent in the story.' In the event, this decision was short lived, and Corman was free to develop his film based on the life and bullet-riddled death of Ma Barker and her boys – a woman memorably described in Herbert Corey's 1936 book *Farewell, Mr Gangster! – America's War on Crime* as 'a red-eyed, wattle-necked harridan, fond of hanging cheap beads and ten-cent-store gimcrackery on her bulging person. She was as vicious as a Gila monster, and yet she was able to pose as a nice old woman when in the presence of strangers.' Corman's film featured a first-rate cast, including a glue-sniffing Robert DeNiro as the youngest son, and Shelley Winters giving a barnstorming performance in the title role. However, Shelley managed to confuse producer Sam Arkoff by simultaneously adding her name to a series of adverts placed in the trade press by a pressure group called the Alliance Against Violence in Motion Pictures, calling for film-makers to reduce the amount of violence onscreen. As Arkoff later wrote, he rang up Shelley to ask her why she'd put her name to such a thing when she was also appearing in a film like *Bloody Mama*, only to be met with the reply, 'Sam, *Bloody Mama* isn't a violent picture. It's *against* violence!'

If violence was being shown on the screen in ever more graphic ways, the new cycle of gangster and mob pictures which followed in the wake of the virtually simultaneous release of *Bonnie and Clyde* and Roger Corman's *The St*

Valentine's Day Massacre (1967) ran headlong into the objections of yet another interest group, except that this time it wasn't the clergy or the moralists, but rather an organisation alleged to have the backing of the mob itself: The Italian-American Civil Rights League. This body enlisted the help of such well-known figures as Frank Sinatra in its campaign to protest about the fact that many film and television portrayals of gangsters featured characters with Italian names, claiming that their entire community was being insulted. The difficulty was that the League had been founded by Joseph Colombo Snr, who, as Nicholas Pileggi has pointed out, was at that time the Godfather of one of New York's 'Five Families' – the dominant Mafia organisations in the city. However, with the aid of pressure from sympathetic politicians and newspapers, the League managed to make the US Justice Department agree to stop using the words 'Mafia' and 'Cosa Nostra' in their press releases, and in March 1971 it was announced that the giant ABC-TV network would no longer use these two words in their hit series, *F.B.I.* The League's biggest battle, however, came with a book and a film entitled, appropriately enough, *The Godfather.*

Mario Puzo's 1968 novel was a genuine publishing sensation. Written by a cash-strapped 45-year-old with Southern Italian ancestors but no direct knowledge of the Mafia life, it set a new record when its paperback rights were sold for $410,000 – of which Puzo received half – and in the single year 1970-71 it sold an estimated six million copies. As the author himself has pointed out, at that time, owing to the relative box office failure of Martin Ritt's *The Brotherhood* (1968), the prevailing wisdom around Hollywood was that films about Mafia dons were unlikely to be a hit with the public, and that it was really only *The Godfather's* phenomenal run in the lists of bestselling books which finally caused the studio to believe fully in the project and give it the finance it deserved. Certainly, the protests of the Italian-American Civil Rights League were only one of the many problems which assailed the picture from the outset, and throughout the filming, Francis Ford Coppola, its young and relatively inexperienced director, wasn't even sure if he had the backing of his own studio, as he told Stephen Farber in the Autumn 1972 issue of *Sight & Sound:*

> I was getting 'fired' every other week. The things they were going to fire me over were, one: wanting to cast Brando. Two: wanting to cast Pacino. Wanting to shoot in Sicily; wanting to make it in period. The very things that made the film different from any other film.

Brando had been Puzo's original suggestion for the role, but his last few pictures had hardly set the box office alight, and it was only when Coppola himself stood up to the studio and insisted that the actor was perfect for the part of Don Corleone that the casting was approved. In preparation, Brando and Coppola studied recordings of Mafia boss Frank Costello testifying before the Kefauver Committee, and were particularly impressed with his quiet, distinctive voice. As Richard Hammer wrote in a 1975 description of Costello: 'Afflicted early with throat trouble – the result of a slipshod operation to remove tonsils and adenoids when a child – he never spoke much above a rasping whisper and that soft voice seemed to lend added authority and importance to whatever he had to say.'

If Brando was observing the Mafia, then the Mafia made it clear that they were certainly watching him. In his 1994 autobiography, *Songs My Mother Taught Me*, he wrote:

> From the start, the real Mafia took a strong interest in our depiction of the fictional one, much of which was filmed on its turf in Little Italy in New York City. It sent a delegation to [Paramount chief] Bluhdorn and, I was told after the picture was finished, he agreed to meet certain conditions to obtain its cooperation, including a promise not to mention the word 'Mafia' in the picture. I'm sure they let him know that it wouldn't be too difficult for their friends in the New York labour unions to tie up shooting, and as partial payment I suspect that Paramount promised them some jobs on the picture. Several members of the crew were in the Mafia and four or five mafiosi had minor parts.

In an on-set report which appeared in the 15 August edition of the *New York Times* written by Nicholas Pileggi, whose 1987 book *Wise Guy* was to become the basis of Martin Scorsese's *Goodfellas* (1990), the real Mafia are seen hanging around watching as Brando filmed scenes on Mott Street in Little Italy, criticising his dress sense:

> A man of that stature . . . would never wear a hat like that. They never pinched them in the front like that. Italian block, that's the way they wore them. Italian block.

Shortly after this it is revealed that real-life Godfather Carlo Gambino is having coffee in a café around the corner on Grand Street:

> It was his custom as well as his duty as head of a Mafia family, to hear at regular intervals the endless woes of racketeers, dishonoured fathers and deplorable husbands. They were ushered before him, one at a time, from a waiting area in a restaurant across the street. He was the final judge to people still willing to accept his decisions as law.

The Godfather crew had obtained permission to film in the heart of Little Italy, not just from city officials, but also as a result of a deal struck by Paramount executive Al Ruddy with Joseph Colombo Snr, his son Anthony and the Italian-American Civil Rights League. The deal secured a smooth ride for the film company, and also ensured that – since there were so many Mafia people hanging around the production – the actors had the benefit of observing real-life mobsters at first hand. James Caan in particular became quite friendly with several of them, and commented that it had helped enormously in his characterisation of Sonny Corleone: 'They've got incredible moves,' he told Pileggi. 'I watched them with each other and with their wives and girlfriends. It's incredible how affectionate they are to each other . . . When we'd go to a bar or somewhere, they were always known. They didn't go where they were not known. They always bought a bottle, too. They didn't buy drinks by the glass. Always a bottle.'

The influence worked both ways, and some mobsters became interested in showbusiness, while others, impressed by the sales of Puzo's book, thought about publishing their own stories. Much-feared mob gunman Crazy Joe Gallo announced to the press in March 1972 that he had done a deal to write his memoirs – an ambition cut short a mere two weeks later when he was gunned down in Little Italy.

After a difficult two-year struggle, *The Godfather* finally hit the cinemas to largely favourable reviews, not least from the Mafia, who seemed to love the version of themselves which appeared on the screen, and went on to attract a wildly enthusiastic public and a slew of Oscar nominations. That October, the film even opened in the Sicilian Mafia's own heartland, Palermo, dubbed into the local dialect – a version in which the language was reported to be 'more forceful and the nuances were less subtle'. According to press reports, most of the local Mafia godfathers turned out to see it, and some were allegedly slightly envious of the life of Don Corleone as depicted onscreen. Puzo's fictional godfather had taken his surname from the Sicilian town of Corleone, which in more recent times has returned the compliment by selling a local after-dinner liqueur named after Don Vito Corleone. The character's first name also has something of a history in Mafia folklore – it was the real-life Sicilian godfather Don Vito Cascio Ferro who, in the early 1920s, was credited with introducing the extortion racket known as 'fari vagnari a pizzu' ('wetting the beak'), which has been used ever since both in Sicily and America, and which also features in Puzo's novel.

While the Mafia, the Production Code or the religious campaigners may have affected the course of crime film production over the years, another factor which can't be discounted is the influence of major Hollywood stars, particularly in instances where they happen also to be the movie's producer, as was the case with Warren Beatty in *Bonnie and Clyde* (1967) and with Steve McQueen in *The Getaway* (1973). In the case of the latter film, which was directed by Sam Peckinpah and adapted from the classic 1958 Jim Thompson novel of the same name, what emerged was something much more tailored to the requirements of the star and his new girlfriend Ali McGraw, rather than anything particularly close to the book. The most obvious change was in the final scenes, where Thompson's bleak, pessimistic ending has been completely altered, so that the two star bankrobbers happily drive off into the sunset with their loot. Although it is known that McQueen essentially took the film away from Peckinpah after shooting and re-edited it (throwing out Jerry Fielding's entire music score against the director's wishes and reducing Al Lettieri's part so much that the actor in question threatened physical violence at a preview screening as a result), Peckinpah was on record as saying that he himself hadn't liked the book's original ending. Sam had spoken to Jim Thompson himself eight years previously, attempting to get an earlier version of the film made, and later said: 'I'd read *The Getaway* before they ever brought it to me. But I always thought the original ending was wrong.' Nevertheless, McQueen's influence during shooting was very pronounced, and he made himself extremely unpopular with the crew as a result. Garner Simmons, in his 1998 book *Peckinpah: A Portrait in Montage*, quotes one un-named technician as follows: 'To work with Steve McQueen [was] to work with a complete and thorough child . . . McQueen [was] just in everybody's case, giving contrary orders and changing lines.' When the film appeared in December 1972, even *Variety's* reviewer was moved to comment: 'whose 'cut' the film is ranks as another current trade speculation.' As it turned out, it was the most commercially successful film of Peckinpah's career, but certainly one of his least personal, and as a Jim Thompson adaptation, it pales beside Bertrand Tavernier's masterful 1981 *Coup de Torchon*, based on the 1964 novel *Pop. 1280*.

By contrast, when Dustin Hoffman became interested in filming Edward Bunker's stunning 1973 novel *No Beast So Fierce*, which had been based on the author's experiences as a newly-paroled ex-convict and the difficulty of ever being allowed by society to fit back into the 'normal' world, he not only cared enough to invite the author to co-write the script, but also gave him a small part in the film, which was called *Straight Time* (1978). Hoffman was originally intending to direct, but, like Warren Beatty with *Bonnie and Clyde*, he decided that it was better not to attempt to be in front of the camera as well as behind, and in the event handed over the reins to Ulu Grosbard. This meant that the film had an on-set technical adviser with all the right qualifications – being a former bankrobber and convict, as well as the original author of the novel under adaptation and also co-scriptwriter. Hoffman's sympathetic attitude didn't end there, as Bunker later wrote in his 1999 autobiography, *Mr. Blue: Memoirs of a Renegade:*

> Dustin optioned the rights to [Bunker's novel] *Animal Factory*, not because he wanted to make it, but because he wanted to help me out.

The film itself was evidently too realistic and downbeat for some tastes, in particular the reviewer who commented that 'one leaves the theatre hoping the character will die painfully and slowly in a hail of bullets', but it probably said more about the lives of real criminals than most crime movies ever accomplish. The fact that these people, even mobsters, actually have private lives and everyday concerns, was something which impressed the late Quentin Crisp when he saw Martin Scorsese's *Goodfellas* (1990), a dramatisation of the life of Mafia footsoldier Henry Hill. In a piece for *Neon* magazine entitled *Quentin Crisp's Ten Wonderful Gangster Movies,* he remarked that '*Goodfellas* was nice because it gave you a glimpse of what gangsters' wives did'. For Scorsese, the story was made-to-order. He'd grown up in New York's Little Italy, and had seen characters who behaved like Henry Hill ever since he was a small kid playing out in the street. In an interview given to Guy Flatley at the time of *Mean Streets* (1973), he said of his childhood days:

> It was unheard of for any of us to call a cop, unless it was to give

him some graft. Cops were always Irish, always drinking, and always had their hands out. We used to bribe them so we could play stickball out in the street.

Goodfellas was very much a return to the territory that he had first explored in *Mean Streets*, a film which Henry Hill had apparently encouraged his own crime boss to watch in 1974, so it had evidently struck some sort of a chord. Certainly, the wealth of inside information given to writer Nicholas Pileggi by Henry Hill himself, once he was away from the criminal life and living under an assumed name on the Government's witness protection programme, ensured that the daily life of the mob as depicted in the film rings very true. The scenes in which actor Paul Sorvino lovingly cooks up an Italian meal while in prison, describing his recommended way of slicing garlic, are reminiscent of the behaviour of legendary mob informer Joe Valachi while in jail in Washington DC, as recounted in Peter Maas's 1968 book *The Valachi Papers*:

> [Valachi had] a hot plate on which he could turn out a meal of his own. His foodstuffs, stored in a small refrigerator, were furnished by a couple of his special guards, an occasional visitor from the Organized Crime and Racketeering Section, or an FBI agent who wanted more information about a particular racketeer. Valachi was such a good cook that his guards asked him to write his recipes for their wives. He entitled his most popular creation 'Joe's special recipe for Spaghetti Sauce and Meatballs'.

In the end, it's the day-to-day details which give such a picture its power. Certainly, there's a lot of violence in the film, but it's depicting a violent world. Back in 1968, at the height of the *Bonnie and Clyde*-inspired violence-in-cinema controversy, Renata Adler wrote an article for the *New York Times* entitled *The Movies Make Heroes of Them All,* arguing that by their very nature, films which showed graphic violence couldn't help but depict it as entertainment, and turn criminals into heroes. However, anyone seriously considering a career in the Mafia would probably be better off watching a film like *Goodfellas* first, rather than *Little Caesar*, if they're after an accurate representation of the kind of life they might expect.

The passage of time has eventually smoothed over pretty much all of these censorship controversies, leaving behind a series of crime films which can be judged on their own merits as pictures. It's instructive to see just how much critical and popular opinion can shift over the years even in respect to what is one of the greatest films of the genre, *The Godfather*, as viewed in the pages of the magazine *Time Out*. In the issue dated 4-10 May 1973, at a time when the film had just been nominated for a fistful of Oscars and was selling out all over town, they wrote it off in three words: 'Leaden mafia caper.' Moving forward to the issue dated 15-21 December 1978, they published a negative review of Coppola's follow-up, *The Godfather Part II*, commenting that it wasn't nearly as good as the original. By the time of the 1998 edition of the *Time Out Film Guide*, drawn from 30 years of the magazine's reviews, *The Godfather* is rated number two (after *Citizen Kane*) in their list of the 'Top One Hundred Best Films' of the last hundred years.

As for Mario Puzo, whose novel helped bring about this new-found respectability for the gentlemen of the 'Honoured Society':

> I'm ashamed to admit that I wrote *The Godfather* entirely from research. I never met a real, honest-to-god gangster. I knew the gambling world pretty good, but that's all. After the book became 'famous', I was introduced to a few gentlemen related to the material. They were flattering. They refused to believe that I had never been in the rackets. They refused to believe that I never had the confidence of a Don. But all of them loved the book . . .

Little Caesar

The Power-Mad Monarch of the Murder Mobs!

Film: Little Caesar
Director: Mervyn LeRoy
Leading players: Edward G Robinson, Douglas Fairbanks Jr., Glenda Farrell,
Stanley Fields
Year of release: 1931

Book: Little Caesar
Author: W R Burnett
Year of publication: 1929

Real-life events: Chicago mob wars and city corruption in the 1920s, the rise
and fall of the Sam Cardinelli gang, the kingdom of Al Capone.

*Chicago, 1927 – Capone was king. Corruption was rampant. Big Bill Thompson, the
mayor, was threatening to punch King George of England in the 'snoot'. Gangsters were
shooting each other all over town . . .*
W R Burnett, introduction to the 1959 paperback edition of *Little Caesar.*

For William Riley Burnett – a 28-year-old former statistician newly arrived
from Springfield, Ohio – Chicago in the wild days of Prohibition was bound
to be something of an education. At that time, 'Scarface' Al Capone's personal
yearly earnings were estimated at somewhere around the $5,000,000 mark
and bodies were being pulled out of the local drainage ditches almost faster
than the newspapers could keep track of them. However, Burnett had long
dreamed of turning his back on office work and becoming a full-time writer,
and his new home town was about to provide the inspiration for a novel
which would carve him out a whole new career, and help kick-start the entire
gangster film genre.

Al Capone was exactly the same age as W R Burnett, but he was already
running the city as his personal kingdom, having backed corrupt mayor Big
Bill Thompson's 1926 re-election campaign to the tune of $260,000, and with
the money flowing in from bootlegging, vice, extortion, gambling and any
other shakedown racket you could name, he had such a stranglehold on Chicago

that it had come to be known as the most corrupt city in America. As Richard Hammer wrote in 1975, Capone later estimated 'that his payoffs to the police in the Thompson era averaged $30,000,000 a year and that half the force was on his payroll'. In 1951 the city's greatest novelist, Nelson Algren, wrote a book called *Chicago, City on the Make*, in which he handed down the verdict that 'when Big Bill Thompson put in the fix for Capone he tied the town to the rackets for keeps'. The city and its gang killings became so notorious that tommy guns acquired the nickname 'Chicago pianos' or 'Chicago typewriters' (as in 'I'm gonna play you a tune on my Chicago piano'), while gunfire itself was known as 'Chicago lightning'. In a few short years the city's reputation had spread around the world, even to Soviet Russia, so that when the legendary director of *Battleship Potemkin* arrived for a visit, there was only really one thing that he wanted to see, as the *New York Times* of 13 July 1930 reported:

EISENSTEIN IN CHICAGO
While in the Windy City Eisenstein roamed around the gangster districts with a detective. He rather regretted that due to a recent murder all the gunmen appeared to be in hiding.

Capone and his playmates distorted the whole fabric of life in the town, pushing up prices across the board because of their demands for a cut of the profits from even the smallest business. The money that flowed in was recycled in the form of payoffs and bribes, and the mob would routinely back politicians of every stripe to ensure that they would have influence wherever it was needed. As one witness later testified before Senator Estes Kefauver's Crime Committee:

When we asked the witness, Philip D'Andrea, the ex-Caponeite, whether Al Capone had been a Republican or a Democrat, D'Andrea replied, 'He was a Republican when I fitted his clothes, I guess, and a Democrat otherwise.' I asked him: 'You mean the whole group played both sides of the street?' 'That is right,' the witness answered.

This was apparently standard Mafia practice, as John Follain wrote in his study of the Cosa Nostra: 'It is not uncommon for the organisation to back candidates from different parties at the same time in a single election, given that its aim is simply to profit from pacts with successful candidates.' Capone himself, though, was always keen to stress that he had been born in Brooklyn, and was American, rather than Sicilian. New York may have been his original home, but while he lived there, he had been nothing more than a small-time thug and enforcer. It was only when he moved to Chicago in 1919 to work for mobster Johnny Torrio as a bouncer at a club/brothel called the Four Deuces that he finally found a location worthy of his unique talents. Perhaps it was the healthy fresh air blowing in from Lake Erie that attracted him, or maybe it was just the chance to leave New York, where he was wanted in connection with a small matter involving a disagreement he'd had with another gentleman who was currently residing in hospital on the critical list. Whatever the reason, Capone accepted Johnny Torrio's offer, and found gainful employment changing the sheets at the Deuces, one of a string of whorehouses owned and run by the Big Jim Colosimo gang. In May 1920, Torrio's boss Colosimo, having steadfastly refused to sanction a move into the burgeoning bootleg liquor racket, found himself with a bullet in the back of the head – allegedly courtesy of Al Capone – leaving Torrio in charge of the gang. From time to time during the next five years, in between sleeping with a fair percentage of the hookers on the payroll (and contracting the syphilis which was eventually to kill him), Capone shot it out with the police and rival gangs and eventually became Johnny Torrio's right-hand man. When his boss decided to move to Italy in 1925 (after being gunned down in an assassination attempt in retaliation for the killing of mob boss Dion O'Banion), the man they sometimes called Al Brown or 'Scarface' wound up running the whole gang.

For all the negative effects on the city that Al undoubtedly had during the 1920s, some residents of Chicago had cause to remember him in a slightly more positive light. As the Depression kicked in during the aftermath of the 1929 Wall Street crash, Capone provided soup kitchens out in the streets for those in need of a meal, while jazz musicians in search of employment found it most often in one of Al's clubs. Milt Hinton – then a struggling teenage violinist – told Studs Terkel:

> It was 1929 and Al Jolson's *Jazz Singer* was the first sound movie with music. That ended live music at the movies, the piano and the violin. All the guys I knew, the best of them, Stuff Smith and Eddie South, were out of work.
>
> Along comes Al Capone, opening the Cotton Club in Cicero: black musicians for white customers. Most of the kids in my class at Wendell Phillips, sixteen, seventeen years old, got a job at Al's place.

Whatever anyone thought of Capone, if you lived in Chicago it was impossible to ignore him. The local papers and newsreels were full of mob stories, and, because of prohibition, if you went out in the evening to anywhere that alcohol was available, then it would certainly be to one of the joints owned or protected and supplied by the hoods. W R Burnett, arriving in the big bad city as a would-be writer with five unpublished novels to his credit, found that the experience hit him like an express train: 'The city of Chicago appalled me . . . why, you could be run over by a bus in Chicago and nobody would even look at you.' Mob-related bombings were a commonplace event, either as a result of people throwing 'pineapples' (hand grenades) or planting 'soup' (dynamite, nitro-glycerine etc.), while the sound of gunfire could be heard in all sorts of places, as Burnett later recalled:

> I 'heard' one killing over the radio. It happened in a café while a dance band broadcast was in progress. Two shots came over distinctly, the music slurred to an abrupt stop, then the air went dead.

Burnett himself, of mixed Welsh and Irish ancestry, had hardly grown up surrounded by shady Sicilian characters and neighbourhood extortionists from the local Black Hand gang, but their world was now all around him, and its influence was impossible to ignore. As he later said: 'I didn't know anything about gangsters, but I read the newspapers.' Soon he became friendly with a low-ranking Italian mobster who went by the name of Barber, and in him he found a first-rate source of information about the world of the gangs and the motivations of their members. Barber held the frequent gangland killings to be no more immoral than those carried out by soldiers in a war, and routinely justified them for purely business reasons. Burnett's new friend was not a member of the Capone gang, but worked for a rival mob – that of Bugs Moran. Barber was the pay-off man on Chicago's North Side for Moran's second-in-command Terry Druggan, and as such he was well placed to advise the aspiring writer on the authenticity of his new chosen subject. Membership of Moran's gang was something of a risky occupation, as several gang members discovered in 1929 when Capone's boys lined them up against a garage wall in North Clark Street and cut them down with machine guns in the St Valentine's Day Massacre. (In fact Burnett, together with a writer from the *Chicago Tribune*, went along to the scene of the crime, but 'I couldn't go inside. I saw it, I just saw it. It was a slaughterhouse – blood all over the wall and guys lying around on the floor. I got one look at it and I said, 'Uh, uh.' I didn't want any of that.')

Although the exploits of Scarface Al are widely held to have been the catalyst for *Little Caesar*, Burnett himself pinpointed a much less well-known Chicago gang as the initial inspiration for his book. Admittedly, it would probably have been impossible to write a gangster story while living in the Chicago of the late 1920s and not to have been influenced by many of the widely-publicised details of Capone's career, yet it was the life and death of the leader of one of the city's Black Hand gangs of the previous decade which first caught Burnett's attention:

> By chance, I discovered a volume put out by the Chicago University Press, dealing with gangsterism in Chicago. In this coldly factual survey, I came across an account of the rise and fall of the Sam Cardinelli gang. This account served as the nucleus for the novel that was originally called *The Furies*, and later, by a tremendous stroke of luck, *Little Caesar*.

The book in question was a groundbreaking sociological study by Frederick M Thrasher entitled *The Gang – A Study of 1,313 Gangs in Chicago*, fortuitously published in 1927, the year of Burnett's arrival in the city. Although mostly concerned with school-age gangs whose members were generally younger than Capone and his followers, it contained a brief two-page description of some of the Sam Cardinelli gang's robberies and killings, several details of which were to show up almost unchanged in the novel *Little Caesar*. Cardinelli had been particularly active around 1915, running one of Chicago's Black Hand extortion gangs, in which the victims would be sent a short note, signed with a picture of a black hand, to the effect that they should pay protection money or face having their business or their home blown to pieces, usually with themselves and their families inside. Operating chiefly in Little Italy (the area bounded by Oak and Taylor Streets and Grand and Wentworth Avenues), the gang reduced many buildings to rubble, and also carried out numerous robberies. By the time Thrasher was writing his book, Cardinelli and his main lieutenants were dead and buried, but he felt that they represented a good example of what he termed the 'ordinary garden variety of criminal gang', whose activities he described as follows:

> Their usual 'racket' is 'stickups' and the ordinary types of robberies and burglaries. Yet their depredations have been so bold and so

36

numerous in recent years that even bootleggers and the gamblers are afraid of them. The Sam Cardinelli gang, which was successful for a considerable time, appears to have been of this type. Although the leader and two of its members were hanged and a fourth was sent to prison for life, the surviving members of the group are still said to be working together as a Black Hand gang.

Cardinelli himself had been in his late thirties, but the rest of his mob were much younger. He would plan their bombing raids and robberies, and often leave it to his henchmen to go and carry them out. In Burnett's novel, Cardinelli provides the basis for the character of gang boss Sam Vettori, whose outfit is gradually taken over by Rico 'Little Caesar' Bandello, his ambitious lieutenant. Bandello's real-life equivalent in the Cardinelli gang appears to have been the second-in-command, teenager Nicholas Viana, known as 'the choirboy', who shot and wounded two policemen while being searched on the street, and also killed a saloon owner and one of his customers during a raid. The latter event, as described in Thrasher's book, was combined by Burnett with elements from a further account given by the sociologist of the Cardinelli gang's robbery of a poolroom:

> On one occasion, Errico, one of the members, planned the holdup of a South Side poolroom. He entered the place and at his signal Nicholas Viana, Frank Campione, and Tony Sansone entered with revolvers and robbed fifteen customers, Errico among the rest. During the holdup one of the customers put his hand in his pocket and was immediately shot through the heart by Campione. He died instantaneously. After the trio had fled, Errico remained only long enough to avert suspicion.

The real-life poolroom holdup and Viana's murder of a saloon owner provide the basis for *Little Caesar's* pivotal incident – the robbery at the Casa Alvarado where Rico guns down the policeman. Other incidental details given in Thrasher's book find echoes in Burnett's novel, such as the fondness for opulent clothes and possessions displayed by the real-life Valley Gang, who 'boasted that they have worn silk shirts and have ridden in Rolls Royce automobiles since the war'. Nevertheless, the Cardinellis and their type were always going to be a mere footnote in mob history, and the brief description given by Thrasher only served to provide a springboard for the ideas which

Burnett had been formulating. His other great inspiration involved throwing most of what he had learned about conventional written English in the bin, and attempting to tell his story in the language of the streets:

> Suddenly one night it came to me. The novel should be a picture of the world as seen through the eyes of a gangster. All conventional feelings, desires, and hopes should be rigidly excluded. Further, the book should be written in a style that suited the subject matter – that is, in the illiterate jargon of the Chicago gangster.

In this respect, Burnett certainly succeeded, so that when the book was published in 1929, his friend Barber from the Bugs Moran outfit, having first praised it as an accurate representation of mob life, was then moved to enquire how it was that a college graduate such as Burnett could write 'such lousy grammar'. The novel is full of slang terms which would not at that time have been commonly found in most of the fiction cluttering up the *New York Times* bestsellers list: safecracking is 'tapping a box', guns are 'gats' or 'rods', policemen are 'bulls', an automobile is a 'can' and a hanging is a 'necktie party'. Burnett himself later said of the novel: 'It has been translated into twelve languages, including English, as a witty friend of mine says.'

Rico as a character has no use for alcohol and little use for women ('Me, buy a diamond ring for a skirt?'). All that really counts with him is his own appearance, and his appetite for power:

> Rico was standing in front of his mirror, combing his hair with a little ivory pocket comb. Rico was vain of his hair. It was black and lustrous, combed straight back from his low forehead and arranged in three symmetrical waves.
>
> Rico was a simple man. He loved but three things: himself, his hair and his gun. He took excellent care of all three.

From the very first page of the book, when the reader is introduced to the Sam Vettori gang, it's clear that the boss himself is getting old and lazy, while his lieutenant, Rico, is sharper and hungry for more. Vettori is 'a big man, fat as a hog', and is evidently used to having things his own way. Yet this initial description of Rico gives notice that he is one to be watched:

Rico sat with his hat tilted over his eyes, his pale thin face slightly drawn, his fingers tapping. Rico always played to win.

The gang's base of operations is a joint whose name leaves no doubt as to the Sicilian origins of most of its members, and which is always written on the printed page just as it would have appeared on its neon sign:

CLUB
P
A
L
E
R
M
O
DANCING

Vettori has planned the robbery of a nightspot called the Casa Alvarado, which has a safe that 'a baby could crack' and a cashier's office that is 'lousy with jack'. One of the gang members, Joe Massara, is to pose as a customer apparently being held up with all the others, having tipped off the robbers that the coast is clear. Rico finds Massara untrustworthy because he works as a dancer ('What's all this dancing? A man don't dance for money'), and is convinced that he will eventually 'turn yellow'. During the robbery, Rico shoots a customer named Courtney, who happens to be a policeman and had been reaching in his pocket for a gun – all of which recalls the poolroom shooting described in Thrasher's book, during which the gang member called Errico worked as the 'inside man' like Massara, and Frank Campione shot a man who put a hand inside his coat. In the novel, the gang's getaway driver, Tony Passa, panics after the robbery while trying to dispose of the car, and is later gunned down by Rico, having shown distinct signs that he would soon confess all to a local priest. As noted earlier, this is also reminiscent of the other Cardinelli killing described in Thrasher's book:

> Five members of the gang, including Nicholas Viana, the 'choir-boy', entered a saloon and in the course of a holdup killed the proprietor and one customer. The gang escaped in an automobile driven by Santo Orlando and later found at his home. Ten days

later Orlando was found in the drainage canal with several bullets in his body. The police believe that the gang, fearing the arrest of Orlando and that he might confess, murdered him in cold blood.

The city's drainage canal was a popular spot for the disposal of unwanted corpses, but, for the purposes of his novel, Burnett has Tony shot down outside St Dominick's Cathedral, recalling the killing of Capone's arch-rival Hymie Weiss outside Chicago's Holy Name Cathedral on 11 October 1926:

> Rico fired. A long spurt of flame shot out in the darkness. Rico emptied his gun. Tony fell without a sound.

Throughout the novel, Rico is obsessed with his own growing public reputation, spending time clipping out news reports of his crimes from the papers, and eagerly agreeing to be photographed by the press at the banquet which is held in his honour, attended by mobsters and corrupt city officials. This 'all publicity is good publicity' attitude was shared by many real-life criminals – the most famous example being Bonnie Parker and Clyde Barrow, who not only photographed themselves constantly but also composed poems about their own exploits and made sure that they fell into the hands of the newspapers. J Robert Nash writes of a Chicago Black Hand bomber called George Matrisciano, active in the decade preceding Capone's rule, who 'always walked about with dynamite in his pockets', and who was so impressed by his own notoriety that he 'could be seen approaching total strangers in Little Italy and proudly showing them a newspaper clipping which described him as 'a terrorist''. Rico's self-obsession is also reflected in his increasingly flashy clothes, by which his rise to power can be charted. His first venture into the world of high fashion finds him modelling a new coat, hat and gloves, 'fawn-coloured spats drawn over pointed patent-leather shoes', a 'diamond horseshoe pin' and 'a red, green and white striped necktie'. Eight pages later he has evidently decided that outfit doesn't quite befit a man of his station, and has once again raided the department stores, apparently in search of clothing that will match the neon sign outside his club:

> Rico was wearing a loud striped suit and a purple tie. He still had on his gloves, yellow kid, of which he was very proud, and his diamond horseshoe pin had been replaced by a big ruby surrounded by little diamonds.

Aiding Rico in his relentless rise to the heights of power and stylishness is his relationship with a man known only as the Big Boy. (This character appears to be very much inspired by Chicago's own Mayor-for-hire, William Hale 'Big Bill' Thompson, during whose four-year term in office the city's finances plummeted from a $3,000,000 surplus to a $4,500,000 deficit.) After gaining control of Vettori's gang, Rico is taken under the Big Boy's wing, and the future looks bright indeed until the police bring gang member Joe Massara in for questioning about the Courtney killing. Massara has been recognised as one of the murder team, while dancing at a nightclub, by a woman who witnessed the shooting. Worn down in jail by the questioning of Flaherty the cop, Joe eventually sells out Rico as the one who pulled the trigger, giving rise to the following newspaper headline:

GENTLEMAN JOE WILTS
GANG CHIEF NAMED AS SLAYER

From this point forward, the heat is on. Stray gang members are rounded up, and Rico quits town with the help of friendly fence Ma Magdalena, setting himself up in a small town called Hammond, under an assumed name, yet finding it hard to adjust to his loss of status:

> He went over in his mind the robbery of the Casa Alvarado and
> all the steps which had led to his own rise and fall. 'It made me
> and it broke me,' he said.

Eventually, Rico begins to build up a new gang in his small-town hideout, but can't resist the temptation to tell several people his real name, and his end comes when he is tracked down by some old Chicago rivals, whose assassination attempts bring him into a final showdown with the police. Rico is gunned down by a man in a derby hat, who is never identified – he may well be a policeman, but he might also be one of the Chicago hitmen who have been on his trail. Whoever pulls the trigger, the novel ends with the mobster dying in a back alley: 'Mother of God,' he said, 'is this the end of Rico?' (This line was originally used at the end of the film, but fear of protests from religious groups led to it being altered to 'Mother of Mercy'.)

Little Caesar was published in June 1929 by the Dial Press, but even before publication it had apparently come to the notice of 28-year-old Hollywood film director Meryvn LeRoy, who was determined that this would not be the end of Rico, and managed to convince producer Darryl F Zanuck that the book was worthy of screen adaptation. However, the story was very nearly not published at all. When the manuscript was rejected by legendary New York book editor Maxwell Perkins at Scribner's, Burnett became discouraged, threw it in a drawer and got a job as a night clerk in a Chicago hotel. Having put aside his dreams of being an internationally-acclaimed novelist, it's perhaps understandable that his new occupation failed to satisfy him, and suicide began to seem like a more appealing alternative: 'Rather than spend my life working in a hotel – or a business office – I'll walk into Lake Michigan till my hat floats.' Luckily, a few weeks later he had a change of heart, dug out his manuscript and sent it to the Dial Press, who decided that Rico Bandera was a character the world needed to meet. Within months Hollywood was knocking at the door.

For the purposes of making a huge impact on the film-going public, the novel of *Little Caesar* could not have been published at a more fortunate time. Although there had already been many gangsters marching across the screens of the nation, together with numerous stage plays and magazine stories – to say nothing of the genuine mobsters taking up space in the newsreels, on the radio and in the papers – the book's publication coincided with the time when cinemas across America were switching over to the showing of sound films. Still regarded in some industry quarters as a novelty, the talkies were nevertheless proving a big hit with the public, and the film version of *Little Caesar* was to be the first gangster picture in which sounds of all the chattering tommy guns and screeching car tyres were to really make an impact. Josef von Sternberg had made the Oscar-winning *Underworld* in 1927 (a Chicago-set gang story in which the mobster's flower shop is reminiscent of that which had been owned by deceased gang boss Dion O'Banion), but this had been a silent film. The first all-talking gangster picture is generally said to be Bryan Foy's *The Lights of New York* (1928), although the audio quality was primitive. While Roland West's *Alibi* (1929) was much more adventurous in its use of sound effects, and even Edward G Robinson had appeared in a pre-Rico film role as a gangster in Robert Florey's *The Hole in the Wall* (1929), in many ways the field was still wide open when Mervyn LeRoy began shooting *Little Caesar* in 1930.

The fact that Burnett's book had come to the attention of a Hollywood figure such as regular Warner Brothers director Mervyn LeRoy was fortunate indeed. LeRoy's short biography in Clarence Winchester's *World Film Encyclopedia* (1933) happily listed Mervyn's height (5 ft 7 in), his weight (9 st 4 lb), and the fact that he had spent 'eight years on the vaudeville stage' and was married to one Edna Murphy, but failed to mention that he was the cousin of powerful Tinseltown mogul Jesse Lasky, and was in the process of leaving Edna for a 1934 marriage to a woman named Doris, daughter of another Hollywood kingpin, Harry Warner of Warner Brothers. In short, he had a lot of clout, but, that aside, he was a very fine and prolific director who could bring in a picture quickly and within budget, enabling him to deliver an average of seven movies a year at that time. LeRoy already had some experience of depicting the guys with the tommy guns and fedoras onscreen, having made a film in 1929 called *Broadway Babies*, in which a chorus girl hangs around with gangsters, and winds up involved in a full-scale gang war during the finale. He also directed a prison drama entitled *Numbered Men* in 1930, shortly before beginning work on *Little Caesar*, so he was hardly coming to the story of Rico fresh from a background of drawing-room comedies.

A writer named Robert N Lee was busy on a script based on Burnett's novel, but the key question for LeRoy and his producer, Hal Wallis, was the matter of which actor should be cast in the role of Rico. LeRoy initially had great hopes for a young unknown he had spotted, but his boss Darryl F Zanuck took one look at the resulting screen test and accused him of wasting $500 on a no-hoper whose ears stuck out at right-angles, at which point Mervyn had to abandon thoughts of employing Clark Gable and look elsewhere. Happily for all concerned, they then tested a New York theatre actor called Edward G Robinson for the lesser part of Rico's sidekick Otero. As Burnett later said of the casting of Robinson:

> He had made two pictures that bombed. He was ready to go back to New York when they called him in to test for the George Stone part [of Otero]. He said, 'What are you testing me for this part for, what's the matter with Rico?' He had confidence in himself. They began to think it over and said, 'Why not? The guy is little, he looks right . . . '

Robinson himself, interviewed by *Film Review* at the age of 79 on the set of his last picture, *Soylent Green* (1973), remembered it this way:

> One of my Broadway plays was *The Racket*, a gangster melodrama. We were supposed to go to Chicago with it, but with Al Capone grabbing all the headlines Chicago wouldn't let us in. So we took

it to Los Angeles, where Hollywood moguls first saw me and cast me as an Al Capone-type killer in *Little Caesar*, the movie that really put me on the map.

The theatre also provided the film's leading lady, Glenda Farrell (in the part of Olga Strassof, Joe Massara's girlfriend), who was brought to LeRoy's attention after having been cast as an equally hardboiled dame in a Broadway play – yet another example of how common the depiction of fictional mobsters was becoming in mainstream American entertainment in the years leading up to the making of *Little Caesar*. Like many who appeared in these films, Edward G Robinson included, she would find it hard to escape being typecast in the years that followed:

> I first played a gangster's moll on Broadway in *On the Spot*, which led to *Little Caesar* in Hollywood. And then all those wise-cracking, heart-of-gold blondes. I played so many bad girls that when I arrived in London in 1937, the headline read, 'Tough Baby Arrives'.

Burnett himself, although delighted with Edward G Robinson's portrayal of Rico, was less than thrilled with much of the casting, pointing out that his story of Italian gangsters with surnames like Vettori and Massara was being played by decidedly non-Sicilian actors such as Stanley Fields and Douglas Fairbanks Jr. (On the other hand, it might be argued that since one of Hollywood's biggest successes to date, *The Jazz Singer* (1927), had featured a white Al Jolson painted up to look 'black' while singing songs which were anything but jazz, authenticity was never likely to be particularly high on their list of priorities.) However, the studio was keen to retain some of the novel's toughness, and since the dialogue in the Robert N Lee's original script was reportedly too highbrow for the lowlife characters in question, and not sufficiently similar to the style of speech used in Burnett's book, Francis Edwards Faragoh was brought in for a rewrite. As with most Hollywood scriptwriting stories, the business of establishing exactly who wrote what is very difficult, particularly in the case of any film that went on to become a worldwide hit, and it's said that Robert Lord and Darryl F Zanuck also had a hand in the writing. Nevertheless, the final screen credit read 'Continuity by Robert N Lee, Screen Version and Dialogue by Francis Edwards Faragoh,' and when the screenplay was later published, it was Faragoh's name alone which appeared as author. Almost inevitably, even what was contained in Faragoh's script was quite substantially changed during shooting, with many scenes omitted and much dialogue either altered or curtailed. What LeRoy appears to have done is tighten up the whole narrative, dropping any extraneous dialogue, and often letting the pictures tell the story, which is hardly surprising, given that these were still the very early days of film sound recording, and that he, like all his crew, had learned their trade in the silent days, and were more used to images that spoke for themselves. One of the key lines in Burnett's book, which also becomes (in slightly modified form) a key line in the movie, appears not as dialogue but as a silent-film-style title card which is placed between two scenes and reads:

> Rico continued to take care of himself, his hair and his gun
> - with excellent results

In general, although much survived from the original novel, and some lines of dialogue such as Rico's banquet speech to his own gang are lifted almost verbatim, the overall effect was to take a reasonably hardboiled story and soften it up a little for public consumption. This was almost inevitable, given the censorship restrictions at the time, and the prevailing wisdom that gangsters should not be glorified onscreen. The character of Rico, tough as he is, has eventually to be depicted as a whining egomaniac, living in a cheap fleabag hotel and desperately phoning up the police in order to complain about his depiction in the press; too stupid to realize that the cops will be tracing the call. This kind of behaviour is nowhere apparent in the novel, and Burnett was particularly dismissive of the change, telling Ken Mate and Patrick McGilligan in *Film Comment*:

> I was disappointed in the film because they conventionalized it. That stuff about Rico in a flophouse – try to imagine Rico in a flophouse! It's the last place he'd ever be. And in the movie version, the fence, the old woman, she turns against Rico and tells him off. Hell, he would have killed her. Amazing!

Whereas in the book Joe Massara is pulled in by the cops and breaks down in jail, getting life imprisonment after naming Rico as the one who killed Courtney, in the film version it is Joe's girlfriend Olga who phones the law and spills the beans, leaving Douglas Fairbanks Jr's Joe character free from the guilt of having ratted out a friend and able to go onto fame and fortune in his dancing career. (In a sentimental ironic twist, Rico is gunned down at the close of the picture while hiding behind a giant billboard advertising 'The Laughing Singing Dancing Success Joe Massara and Olga Stassoff in *Tipsy Topsy Turvy* at the Grand Theatre'.)

Over the years much has been made of the supposedly gay subtext to the relationship in the film version between Rico and Joe Massara, and Burnett is supposed to have complained to producer Hal Wallis about Douglas Fairbanks Jr's handling of the latter role in this respect. Certainly, in the book Rico is the first to criticise Joe to gang boss Vettori ('Joe's no good,' he tells him, and swears he'll 'turn yellow' one day, which is in fact what happens), whereas in the film Rico consistently defends Joe, saying, 'Joe is all right. He's the best front man in the world.' Later, when Joe spends most of his time dancing, Rico is seen to be upset that he doesn't come around any more and seems to have no interest in the gang. When told that it was Joe who phoned in a tip to the mob to try to warn Rico that some gunmen were out to shoot him, Rico is pleased – 'I didn't think he cared enough.' Once Rico is living in an expensive new apartment, he invites Joe for a visit, and tells him again that dancing is no way for a mobster to be earning a living:

> I kinda took a pride in you Joe, brought you into the gang, pushed
> you ahead. But now you're gettin' to be a sissy.

When Joe's girlfriend Olga finally picks up the phone and sells out the gang to the police, it seems as if she's doing it almost out of jealousy, to loosen the hold which Rico has on her man – 'We'll never have any peace until Rico is gone.' Learning that the cops are now on his trail, Rico's response is, 'This is what I get for liking a guy too much.' In the book, it is more the character of Otero who is given to declarations of love, following Rico around like a faithful dog:

> Only Rico; he is my friend. He is a great man like Pancho Villa
> and I love him with a great love. I would not shoot Rico if he shot
> me first.

Regardless of what the film-makers had in mind in their depiction of these relationships, the other characters, like the plot itself, are all dwarfed by Edward

G Robinson's star-making portrayal of Rico. However stagey and primitive the film may appear to modern sensibilities, the force of his characterisation in the title role still shines through over seventy years later. It's possible to imagine the impact that he made in January 1931 when the film opened in New York at the Strand Theatre on Broadway, and the police had to be called in order to cope with the crowds which lined up outside. Demand was such that they ran eleven shows a day from 9.00 am to 4.30 am the following morning. If *Little Caesar* made Edward G Robinson, Edward G Robinson certainly made *Little Caesar,* as the critics were quick to recognise. The film opened some months ahead of Jimmy Cagney's equally career-defining appearance in *The Public Enemy*, and before the end of the year Robinson was already talking warily to the press about the dangers of becoming typecast in such roles, telling the *New York Times* on 20 September 1931 'that if he never fired another revolver, or talked out of the corner of his mouth again, he would be happy as well as satisfied'. The article noted that 'his previous career on the stage had also meant typecasting – he was usually seen playing 'nice old gentlemen with whiskers . . . '

Trade paper *Variety* gave the film an excellent review in their 14 January 1931 edition, noting that the film had to be good just in order to stand out from all the previous gangster tales which had been flooding the market, and singling out Robinson for particular praise – 'one tough mugg, in the title part, who is tough all the way from the start, when he's a bum with ambition, to the finish, when he's a bum again, but a dead one.' Admitting that the story itself contained nothing much that was new to the screen, the reviewer nevertheless praised both the direction and the actors, and observed that 'there are enough killings herein to fill the quota for an old time cowboy-Indian thriller'. Still, the main focus of the review was Robinson:

> For a performance as 'Little Caesar' no director could ask for more than E G Robinson's contribution. Here, no matter what he has to say, he's entirely convincing, because of the lines he speaks and the way he speaks them.

Time magazine's reviewer, writing the following week, agreed that the subject matter was nothing new – 'undoubtedly the most familiar of current screen figures is the fearless, ambitious gangster who becomes rich on the fruits of evil and dies in the last reel in a heroic manner' – but attributed the picture's ability to rise above the usual B feature clichés to the strength of Robinson's performance, backed up by LeRoy's sure hand in the direction.

> With less adroit handling *Little Caesar* might easily have been no
> more than a fair program picture and its central character merely
> a reflection of his many forerunners. Instead, actor Edward G
> Robinson has made his role the supreme embodiment of a type.

The review went on to credit the screen Rico with far more complexity than his counterpart in the novel, calling him 'a gangster of Greek tragedy, destroyed by the fates within him', but complained that Fairbanks was miscast in his role as a 'tough Italian thug'.

Internationally, the verdict was generally favourable, although one British reviewer was slightly concerned about his readers' ability to make sense of the dialogue, calling it 'quite exciting entertainment for those who can understand the middle western accent'. At $700,000, the film was hardly low-budget for its day, and Warner Brothers' publicity department worked overtime, billing *Little Caesar* as 'The Picture Gangland defied Hollywood to make!' and claiming that real machine gun bullets had been fired on set during some of the action sequences.

The film was a massive hit with the public. It received an Academy Award nomination for Francis Edwards Faragoh and Robert N Lee's script, and made a worldwide star of Edward G Robinson. Mervyn LeRoy went on to direct such classics as *I Am a Fugitive From a Chain Gang* (1932), *Gold Diggers of 1933* (1933) and *The Bad Seed* (1956), to say nothing of producing *The Wizard of Oz* (1939). In later life he also helped John Wayne direct *The Green Berets* (1968), his flag-waving hymn of praise to the joys of the Vietnam war. *Little Caesar* itself became one of the archetypal gangster pictures, influencing much of what was to come, and even leaving its mark on other film genres such as juvenile delinquent movies – *High School Caesar* (1960, 'Mob rule in a high school! He had more rackets than Al Capone!') and blaxploitation – *Black Caesar* (1973, 'The cat with the .45 calibre claws!'). Even real-life gangsters apparently knew a good thing when they saw it, in particular one Chicago mobster named Joseph Vincent Di Varco, who was aged nineteen when the film appeared. Di Varco, a man with strong ties to Las Vegas, was known to the police in relation to various suspected gang murders, as well as loansharking, vice and gambling, but more commonly known to his associates by the name of Little Caesar.

Edward G Robinson went on to play various Rico-like characters in films down through the years – most notably gangster Johnny Rocco in John Huston's *Key Largo* (1948) – but right up until his death he was still most closely associated with the character of Rico, and when Charles Higham interviewed him for the *New York Times* six months before his death, they headlined the article 'Little Caesar is Still Punching'.

> The voice is still Little Caesar's: harsh, stabbing, authoritative. The eyes still have a fierce intensity, the wide frog mouth as tight with determination as ever behind the grizzled Hemingway beard.

As for W R Burnett, he not only went on to write a string of million-selling novels before his death in 1982, including *High Sierra* (1940) and *The Asphalt Jungle* (1949), but he also wrote or co-wrote scripts for numerous Hollywood films, such as Howard Hawks's *Scarface* (1932), *This Gun For Hire* (1932), *I Died a Thousand Times* (1956) and even *The Great Escape* (1963). Yet he never downplayed the importance of *Little Caesar*, his first published novel, which he had begun with a quote from Machiavelli:

> The first law of every being is to preserve itself and live. You sow hemlock, and expect to see ears of corn ripen.

The film-makers, fearful that this kind of quote might go way over the heads of their audience, substituted a quote from the Bible ('For they that take the sword shall perish with the sword'), but that wasn't exactly the message which Burnett was trying to put across:

> I was reaching for a gutter Macbeth – a composite figure that would indicate how men could rise to prominence or money under the most hazardous conditions, but not much more hazardous than the men of the Renaissance. Nobody understood what I meant by the quotation from Machiavelli at the front of *Little Caesar* . . . It meant, if you have this type of society, it will produce such men.

The Big Sleep

Bogy'n Baby paired off for a hot time – and the big thrill in cold, cold crime!

Film: The Big Sleep
Director: Howard Hawks
Leading players: Humphrey Bogart, Lauren Bacall, John Ridgely,
Martha Vickers
Year of release: 1946

Book: The Big Sleep
Author: Raymond Chandler
Year of publication: 1939

If Raymond Chandler had never written another novel apart from *The Big Sleep*, and if Humphrey Bogart had only made one appearance in a film – as Philip Marlowe in the screen adaptation of Chandler's book – it would have been enough. Both novel and film were reasonably well praised at the time of their first appearance, but with hindsight those early reviews don't seem to do justice to the reputations which they were later to acquire. This is hardly surprising. As Chandler himself wrote in the introduction to his story collection *The Simple Art of Murder* (1950), 'The average critic never recognizes an achievement when it happens. He explains it after it has become respectable.'

Down through the years Chandler has been chewed over, talked-up, slapped down, canonised and psychoanalysed, depending on the prevailing fashion, but he and his fictional creation Philip Marlowe remain just about the most famous thing there is in American detective writing. Hammett got there first, Jim Thompson was usually much tougher, and Paul Cain was way out there in the uncharted swamps (as Chandler himself acknowledged, calling *Fast One* (1936) 'some kind of a high point in the ultra hard-boiled manner'), but the 51-year-old ex-English public schoolboy turned washed-up oil executive who published a novel called *The Big Sleep* in 1939 left his mark in the public consciousness in a way quite unlike any other crime writer.

Born in 1888 in Chicago to an Anglo-Irish mother and an American father, Raymond Chandler was moved to London in 1895 after said father did a runner. An education at Dulwich College, some time as a schoolteacher, active service with the Army and the RAF during World War One and even a brief time spent writing for the *Daily Express* failed to completely break his spirits, and in 1919 he moved permanently to California, where he was to live for the rest of his life. He spent much of the 1920s as the world's least-motivated businessman, working for the Dabney Oil Syndicate in Los Angeles. However, along came the Depression, and he was given the traditional reward handed down by big business when times are tough – the sack (although some reports suggest that it was his fondness for going into what he later termed 'executive session' with the occasional bottle of whiskey that had more to do with this event than the state of the economy). Whatever the reason, he found himself, aged forty-three, attempting to carve out a new career for himself as a writer of mystery fiction for the pulp market: 'I concentrated on the detective story because it was a popular form,' he said later in a letter, 'and I thought the right and lucky man might finally make it into literature.' As it turned out, he did, but it took him most of the 1930s to even begin making some sort of a living wage, during which time he wrote and rewrote his stories before submitting them to *Black Mask* magazine and *Dime Detective* with a care and attention to language which was very uncommon in a field where some writers were routinely turning out several thousand words a day. Chandler later recalled that he had taught himself the art of writing a detective story by taking a novella of Erle Stanley Gardner's, deconstructing the plot, and then repeatedly writing a story based upon those events until he had something of his own. The end result, he told Gardner, was finally good enough that he thought it a shame that he couldn't in all conscience send it off to anyone for publication.

In December 1933 when Chandler's first story, 'Blackmailers Don't Shoot', appeared in *Black Mask* magazine, Dashiell Hammett was still the giant figure in hardboiled detective writing, although his era of active writing had already drawn to a close. Chandler often had harsh words for other writers in the mystery field, such as Mickey Spillane and James M Cain, but he always admired the author of *The Maltese Falcon*, and acknowledged him as an influence: 'Hammett is all right. I give him everything. There were a lot of things he could not do, but what he did he did superbly.'

The 18,000 words of 'Blackmailers Don't Shoot' had taken a sizeable chunk of Chandler's year to write, and netted him the hardly princely sum of $180 – a fraction of what he had been earning during his business career. The private-eye hero of his story was a character called Mallory, who was to reappear in Chandler's next story 'Smart-Aleck Kill' (*Black Mask*, July 1934). In 'Finger Man' (*Black Mask*, October 1934) and 'Killer in the Rain' (*Black Mask*, January 1935) he experimented with un-named private detectives, but by the following year's 'The Man Who Liked Dogs' (*Black Mask*, March 1936), his protagonist had acquired the name Carmady, which he was to retain for three further stories. When Chandler switched to *Dime Detective* magazine in November 1937, he took the opportunity to rename his private eye once again, calling him Johnny Dalmas, in which guise he remained up to 1939, when he finally became Philip Marlowe, who was to be the central character in all of Chandler's fiction from this point forward, barring a brief excursion under the name John Evans in the September 1941 *Detective Story* magazine piece, 'No Crime in the Mountains'. (Just to make the situation slightly more confusing, when these stories were later reprinted in the collections *The Simple Art of Murder* (1950) and *Trouble is My Business* (1950), the private eyes were all renamed Philip Marlowe, apparently at the instigation of the publisher.) The name may have been subject to change during his career in the pulp magazines, but the essentials of his character were already present in embryo form as far back as 1933. In his later years, Chandler discussed the character of Marlowe with several correspondents who had written to him asking for clarifications, by which time of course his hero had already been picked over by critics for more than a decade. In a long letter about Marlowe to Mr D J Ibberson on 19 April 1951, Chandler wrote:

> He is slightly over six feet tall and weighs about thirteen stone. He has dark brown hair, brown eyes, and the expression 'passably good looking' would not satisfy him in the least. I don't think he looks tough. He can be tough. If I ever had the opportunity of selecting the movie actor who could best represent him to my mind, I think it would have been Cary Grant.

Given that Chandler's creation, along with Hammett's Sam Spade, helped establish the image of the private eye which was then taken up and repeated time and again in books and films, it's interesting to note that the same letter stresses that Marlowe does not have, and never has had, a secretary, and has never bothered to subscribe to a telephone answering service, both usually considered essential in the genre. Whereas Hammett brought to his stories the knowledge gained during many years of experience working for the Pinkerton Detective Agency, Chandler had no such background, and although happy to discuss the attributes, likes and dislikes of his most famous creation, he was also careful to explain that he was writing fiction, not fact. In October 1951 he wrote to a Mr Inglis:

> . . . you must remember that Marlowe is not a real person. He is a creature of fantasy. He is in a false position because I put him there. In real life a man of his type would no more be a private detective than he would be a university don. Your private detective in real life is usually an ex-policeman with a lot of hard practical experience and the brains of a turtle or else a shabby little hack who runs around trying to find out where people have moved to.

Although hardly prolific, Raymond Chandler was a regular and much-admired contributor to the pulp magazines of the 1930s, but the money he was making was barely enough to survive. The next logical step was to venture into the field of novel writing, and in 1938 he began work on the book which was to become *The Big Sleep*, at which point all his hard work for *Black Mask* and *Dime Detective* paid off in a very direct way, since he was to construct the novel using elements combined from several of his previously-published magazine stories. This process, which he called 'cannibalizing', was something he was to employ in the writing of several of his novels. A little over a decade later, he recalled the book's origins as follows:

> *The Big Sleep* was written in the spring of 1938 and was based on two novelettes called 'Killer in the Rain', published January 1935, and 'The Curtain', published September 1936. Included in this book also was a fairly long sequence from a novelette called 'The Man Who Liked Dogs', published in March 1936.

In fact, the situation was slightly more complex, as explained by Philip Durham in his 1964 introduction to the volume of stories entitled 'Killer in the Rain', which was issued after Chandler's death in response to demand for a reprinting of that part of the author's pulp work which had later been reworked for the novels:

> In *The Big Sleep*, the author drew from 'The Curtain' for Chapters 1-3, 20, 27-32 and from 'Killer in the Rain' for Chapters 4, 6-10, 12-16. With the exception of small bits borrowed from 'Mandarin's Jade' and 'Finger Man', Chapters 5, 11, 17-19, 21-26 were added . . . The twenty-one borrowed chapters, however, were expanded considerably beyond their original state in the short stories.

This set a pattern which Chandler continued in the novel *Farewell, My Lovely* (1940), which drew upon the stories 'The Man Who Liked Dogs' (*Black Mask*, March 1936), 'Try The Girl' (*Black Mask,* January 1937) and 'Mandarin's Jade' (*Dime Detective*, November 1937), and the novel *The Lady in the Lake* (1943), which contained elements of 'Bay City Blues' (*Dime Detective*, June 1938), 'The Lady in the Lake' (*Dime Detective*, January 1939) and 'No Crime in the Mountains' (*Detective Story*, September 1941). In this way, most of the results of Chandler's poorly-paid 1930s writing career were put to good use in the production of the novels which would go on to sell millions during the 1940s, and which, by the end of the war, would help to make him not only world famous but also comparatively rich.

Chandler famously said that he wanted to take the murder 'away from the upper classes, the weekend house party and the vicar's rose-garden, and back to the people who are really good at it', and certainly the subject matter of *The Big Sleep* was very far removed from the usual accepted topics of conversation in what passed for 'polite' society: smutty photographs, dope addicts, nymphomaniacs and live-in rent boys mingle informally with the usual crowd of tooled-up hardmen, blackmailers, two-bit grifters and bookie's runners. The book may be set in Hollywood, but the likes of Shirley Temple and her toothy, wholesome chums are nowhere to be seen. In short, almost everyone is some kind of a scumbag except for Marlowe himself, and he's disappointed, but hardly surprised, to find himself in such a world. The Los Angeles which Chandler arguably did more than anyone else to enshrine in fiction had mushroomed during its last two decades from a rural town into a huge, sprawling metropolis which by 1938 contained, as Roy Meador pointed out, six hundred brothels, three hundred gambling houses and one thousand eight hundred bookies. Under the circumstances, it's not entirely surprising that Chandler found his attention being drawn to subjects other than questions of whatever might be lurking in 'the vicar's rose garden'. In a later profile of the now-successful author written by Irving Wallace ('He Makes Murder Pay,' *Pageant Magazine*, July 1946), it was claimed that one of the central strands of the plot of *The Big Sleep* was drawn from real life:

> 'I learn something too hot for the papers to publish,' he [Chandler] says, 'and it starts me thinking and then my imagination takes over.' It is said that his first novel, revolving about a fat homosexual who ran a rental library of pornography, had its basis in unprintable fact.

If Chandler's choice of subject was earthy and mostly from the wrong side of the tracks, then so was his language. Having learnt to write 'proper' English at an Edwardian public school, he then enthusiastically dispensed with most of the formalities in favour of a slangy, cynical American vernacular which has since been much imitated but rarely, if ever equalled. He was looking for the same vitality and descriptiveness of language which he found in the English of Shakespeare's time – a world away from the hidebound stuffiness of the Victorian era into which he was born. He may have grown up in their world, but it's impossible to imagine Mrs Gaskell or Anthony Trollope cutting loose with the following:

> 'Eddie's a handful of mush,' I snarled. 'Canino would take him with a teaspoon. He'll take him the way the cat took the canary. A handful of mush. The only time a girl like you goes for a wrong gee is when he's a handful of mush.'

The average conversation between most of these people, even the ones that aren't trying to shoot each other, is characterised by a protective layer of irony and sarcasm, such as, 'I don't mind if you don't like my manners. They're pretty bad. I grieve over them during the long winter evenings,' or 'You leak information like a radio announcer.' Even the people whose speech and manner is that of a more formal bygone age, such as the dying General Sternwood, still express themselves with a directness which sets the novel apart from anything found in the pages of contemporary mysteries by Agatha Christie or Dorothy L Sayers. Attempting to hire Marlowe to investigate a blackmail attempt which has been made in connection with his daughters, General Sternwood is more than able to put his cards on the table with regard to his family's reputation and habits:

> I think they go their separate and slightly divergent roads to perdition. Vivian is spoiled, exacting, smart and quite ruthless. Carmen is a child who likes to pull wings off flies. Neither of them has any more moral sense than a cat. Neither have I. No Sternwood ever had.

During the course of the novel, Marlowe fends off advances from both Sternwood girls (one of whom actually tries to entice him with the immortal line 'Hold me close, you beast.'), gets to the bottom of Geiger's blackmail demand, solves a couple of murders, talks tough to the local mobsters, reluctantly kills a bad guy who deserves it and manages to avoid being gunned down by several interested parties. The individual scenes, rather than the plot itself, were always the most important thing to Chandler, and he keeps the pace up unremittingly, probably mindful of his own advice: 'When in doubt have a man come through the door with a gun in his hand.' Finding out exactly who-done-it is not the main entertainment he offers his readers – it's the way in which the tale is told and the sparks which the characters strike off each other which set the novel apart. As for the title, Chandler kept his audience waiting until almost the very last page of the book for an explanation:

> What did it matter where you lay once you were dead? In a dirty sump or in a marble tower on top of a high hill? You were dead, you were sleeping the big sleep, you were not bothered by things like that. Oil and water were the same as wind and air to you. You just slept the big sleep, not caring about the nastiness of how you died or where you fell.

Naming a book after a slang term for death worked very well for Chandler, so much so that he used the device again in 1953 when he published a novel called *The Long Goodbye*. As for having the corpse of the mysterious Rusty Regan finally show up buried in a sump, well, like the man says, who cares where they put you, and wasn't Chandler in oil himself for most of the 1920s?

The Big Sleep was published in America in a first printing of 5,000 copies on 6 February 1939 by Alfred A Knopf of New York, which was about the amount which any successful mystery hardback was reckoned to be able to sell at the time. In the event, Chandler quickly doubled these sales, and was immediately singled out as a cut above the average in what was already an overcrowded market. His short biography on the dust jacket of the first edition began with the words: 'Raymond Chandler has had that type of career which is commonly referred to as "checkered"', as indeed he had, but from this point onwards, even though the reviews were encouraging rather than wildly enthusiastic, his days of struggling and financial insecurity were over.

Review copies of the novel were sent out in a special cover which carried the following confident endorsement from the publisher, using a message which was repeated in trade adverts in the press: 'In 1929 we gave you HAMMETT, in 1934 we gave you CAIN, in 1939 we give you RAYMOND CHANDLER. We predict that THE BIG SLEEP will duplicate the success of

The Thin Man and *The Postman Always Rings Twice*, and will promote it and advertise it accordingly. Read this copy now for your own pleasure.' When the British edition was published the following month by Hamish Hamilton, the promotional campaign adopted a similar argument, saying, 'We recommend this novel with enthusiasm. In our opinion it will repeat the success of *The Postman Always Rings Twice*', and many early reviews compared Chandler to Dashiell Hammett, James M Cain or both. Later on, once his success was an established fact, he complained about this in a letter, arguing that he admired Hammett, 'But James Cain – faugh! Everything he touches smells like a billygoat. He is every kind of writer I detest, a faux naif, a Proust in greasy overalls, a dirty little boy with a piece of chalk and a board fence and nobody looking. Such people are the offal of literature, not because they write about dirty things but because they do it in a dirty way.' (That was written in October 1942. By March 1944 Chandler had been involved in co-scripting the film adaptation of Cain's *Double Indemnity*, and wrote to the greasy Proust in question: 'Dear Jim, it was very kind of you to send me an inscribed copy of your book and I'm very grateful to you.')

In addition to making comparisons with two of the leading exponents of the hardboiled school, initial reviews were also keen to stress the sordid nature of the novel's subject matter: *The New Yorker* (11 February 1939) called it a 'pretty terrifying story of degeneracy in southern California by an author who makes Dashiell Hammett seem as innocuous as Winnie-the-Pooh,' while Will Cuppy, writing in the *New York Herald Tribune* on 5 February, praised the novel's 'admirable hardboiled manner', but went on to complain that 'Mr Chandler has almost spoiled it with a top-heavy cargo of lurid underworld incident, and he should therefore be stood in a corner and lectured upon the nature and suitable use of his talents.' Isaac Anderson in the *New York Times* wrote, 'The language used in this book is often vile – at times so filthy that the publishers have been compelled to resort to the dash,' but allowed that 'as a study in depravity, the story is excellent, with Marlowe standing out as almost the only fundamentally decent person in it'. This latter review depressed Chandler thoroughly, as he noted in a letter to his publisher, Alfred A Knopf, on 19 February 1939, but he also commented, 'however, there's a very good notice in today's *Los Angeles Times* and I don't feel quite such a connoisseur of moral decay as I did yesterday. They have Humphrey Bogart playing the lead, which I am in favour of also. It only remains to convince Warner Brothers.' This is particularly interesting given the fact that Bogart in 1939 was still chiefly known as a screen heavy, without the romantic, leading-man aura his tough-guy persona would later acquire after the success of films such as *The Maltese Falcon* (1941), *Casablanca* (1943) and *To Have and Have Not* (1944).

In the UK, the reviewer from *The Times* (8 March 1939) ventured the opinion: 'It is not Sunday-school literature,' just in case anyone was thinking of buying a copy for the moral instruction of their children, while Nicholas Blake in the 31 March edition of *The Spectator* found it 'very American and very, very tough after the *Thin Man* fashion. Almost everyone in the book, except the detective, is either a crook or wonderfully decadent, and the author spares us no blushes to point out just how decadent they are.' All in all, the reception was friendly, and Chandler himself received $2,000 for the initial sale of 10,000 hardbacks. Having done above-average business on its first appearance, the novel went on to do very well indeed in 1942 when it was made available in a paperback edition, published by Avon Books, with a quote on the cover from the Los Angeles News which read: 'James Cain, John O'Hara, Dashiell Hammett, move over, you've got a new pal.'

Raymond Chandler's literary success in the crime field inevitably brought him to the attention of Hollywood, who at first attempted to chip off stray chunks of his work and shoehorn them into any plot in need of assistance. *Farewell, My Lovely* was reworked and emerged, kicking and screaming, in May 1942 under the title *The Falcon Takes Over*, the third in RKO's series of films based on the character created by Michael Arlen and starring George Sanders. Marlowe's fictional exploits were also plundered later that year in the service of another long-running series detective, Brett Halliday's Mike Shayne, when Twentieth Century Fox used significant amounts of Chandler's novel *The High Window* as the basis for the film *Time to Kill*, released in December 1942. However, the following year, Hollywood finally wised up and hired Chandler himself to work upon a script, although even then, it was a screen adaptation of someone else's novel – *Double Indemnity*, by James M Cain, the man he'd been calling 'the offal of literature' only twelve months previously. The resulting classic film noir, released in 1944, was a huge popular success which helped open the door for Hollywood's mid-1940s hardboiled crime renaissance, proving to the studios that the Hays Office could be successfully subverted or defied, and that many subjects previously considered too daring or immoral for the screen could now be addressed. *Double Indemnity* also received a brace of Oscar nominations, including one for Chandler and Billy Wilder as co-scriptwriters. Chandler had initially been offered the job because Wilder had been impressed with one of his novels – *The Big Sleep*.

By the following year, it had become clear that the film studios had latched on to the crime boom and were throwing their full weight behind it. Several of the key pictures of this time were either adapted from Chandler's books or scripted by him, a fact acknowledged by the *New York Times* on 8 August 1945 when they published an article by Lloyd Shearer entitled 'Crime Certainly Pays on the Screen – The growing crop of homicidal films poses questions for psychologists and producers', which quotes two expert witnesses, James M Cain and Chandler himself: 'My own opinion,' Chandler says, 'is that the studios have gone in for these pictures because the Hays Office is becoming more liberal.' The article described how *Double Indemnity* had proved such a success, and then went on to describe the effect which this had had upon the Hollywood studios:

> Forever watchful of audience reaction the rest of the industry almost immediately began searching its story files for properties like *Double Indemnity*. RKO suddenly discovered it had bought Chandler's novel, *Farewell, My Lovely*, on July 3rd 1941. If *Double Indemnity* was so successful, why not make *Farewell, My Lovely*? And make it RKO did, under the title *Murder, My Sweet*. Twentieth Century Fox followed with *Laura*. Warners began working on Chandler's *The Big Sleep* for Humphrey Bogart and Lauren Bacall. MGM excavated from its vaults an all-but-forgotten copy of James Cain's *The Postman Always Rings Twice*. The trickle swelled into a torrent and a trend was born.

At this point, the film version of *The Big Sleep* was well-known enough to be mentioned in such a discussion in the national media, and yet it was still nearly a year away from its general release. How it came to be made, and then delayed, for quite so long, is almost as complicated a story as that of the novel from which it was taken.

Regardless of the developing trend for tough-minded crime pictures, in July 1944 Warner Brothers Pictures and director Howard Hawks had something more particular on their minds – the enormously enthusiastic response of preview audiences to the sight of their top screen star Humphrey Bogart and his new leading lady, Lauren Bacall, in a *Casablanca*-style thriller entitled *To Have and Have Not*. Convinced they'd have a major hit on their hands, studio boss Jack Warner turned to the film's director, Howard Hawks, and asked him if he had another story suitable for the couple. As Hawks later told Peter Bogdanovitch: 'The next day I bought the rights to *The Big Sleep* and the next time I saw Jack Warner I showed him the picture.'

Bogart and Bacall had become romantically involved during the making of *To Have and Have Not*, a situation complicated by the fact that he was still married to his alcoholic third wife Mayo Methot, and Bacall was the jealously-guarded protégé of director Hawks. Still, in recent years Bogart had become one of the biggest stars in the world, 'Hollywood's number one pistol-packer,' as Jerry Asher wrote in the January 1944 edition of *Photoplay*, 'the merchant of menace,' and was well on the way to becoming a sex symbol:

> Since *The Maltese Falcon* and *Casablanca*, scriptwriters have been instructed to toss him an occasional romantic bone. Now, whenever a producer has a new picture to discuss, Bogie opens the conversation by saying: 'What is it this time – kiss or kill?' . . . He thinks movie villains should form a union and demand a more active sex life – in pictures, of course, for screen 'heavies'.

If an adaptation of Chandler's *The Big Sleep* was to be the first pairing of Bogart and Bacall after *To Have and Have Not*, the main difficulty facing the scriptwriters – apart from the labyrinthine plot – was the fact that there is no great romantic coupling at all in the book, and Marlowe ends up alone. Both Sternwood daugthers throw themselves at him during the course of the narrative, but one is a mentally unstable, drug addicted killer who poses for nude photos in her spare time and the other a hard-drinking, mobster-linked gambler who has already been married three times, most recently to an ex-bootlegger and IRA man called Rusty Regan, whose murder she's helped to cover up. Not exactly dream casting for Hollywood's brightest new screen goddess. Nonetheless, Hawks later said that he told the scriptwriters, 'Don't monkey with the book – just make a script out of it. The writing is too good,' and in many ways, by Tinseltown standards, this is exactly what they did, while greatly expanding the Bacall part (Vivian, the elder and more stable of the two Sternwood daughters), airbrushing away most of her sordid past, and writing in new scenes not derived from the novel in which she and Bogart could exchange bright, sparkling repartee and elegantly smutty double entendres.

The initial script was written by novelist William Faulkner (who had also worked on *To Have and Have Not*) and Leigh Brackett during August and September of 1944, and principal photography began on 10 October. Two major factors then came into play, which were to have a profound effect on the course of shooting. Firstly, *To Have and Have Not* was finally released in October, and Lauren Bacall was almost transformed overnight from just another 20-year-old starlet into one of the biggest new screen sensations in years. Secondly, Bogart's highly combustible marriage to Mayo Methot began to finally unravel under the added strain of his new attachment to Bacall, and, as his home life came more and more to resemble a war zone, Bogart ran for cover, checking into the Beverly Hills Hotel, causing the press to descend in search of a divorce story. A few weeks later, he moved back in with his wife, and told Bacall – with whom he was working virtually every day on the film set – that they'd have to stop seeing each other. Just to add to the disruption, the poor November weather in Los Angeles brought a spate of lost days due to illness among the cast and crew: Hawks and the actor playing Eddie Mars (John Ridgely) came down with the flu, while Bacall contracted laryngitis. Meanwhile the normally ultra-professional Bogart, who was to appear in every scene of the picture, began drinking even more heavily than usual and showing up late for shooting, and the production began to slip badly behind schedule.

Meanwhile the script was being rewritten as filming progressed, with minor additions from Hawks himself and, according to Bruce F Kawan, there were also contributions made by 'an uncredited, six-foot-two chorus girl whom Hawks called Stuttering Sam'. Eventually, Faulkner bowed out, and another of the *To Have and Have Not* team – writer Jules Furthman – was brought in for rewrites. Bacall made the cover of *Life* magazine, and was being given the full star treatment in most other papers during shooting, including a memorable build-up from powerful columnist Walter Winchell, under the headline 'Bacall of the Wild', while *The Big Sleep* was being spoken of as part of the new trend in crime pictures: 'Hollywood, according to present indications, will depend on so-called 'red meat' stories of illicit romance and crime for a major share of its immediate non-war dramatic productions,' said the 19 November edition of the *New York Times*, which went on to comment on MGM's recent announcement that they were to adapt *The Postman Always Rings Twice* – a novel long held to be 'unfilmable' due to censorship problems. 'The screen version of Raymond Chandler's *The Big Sleep*, in production at Warners, is said to be another example of ingenuity in treating psychopathic and psychological matters.'

As Christmas 1944 approached the film slipped even further behind schedule. Bogart's home life had descended into utter chaos, and on 23 December he suffered an alcohol-related crisis necessitating sedation from the studio doctor and was unable to work for most of the next week. Faced with the impossibility of trying to shoot material around an actor who dominated every scene, Hawks reluctantly shut down production for several days, and he and Jules Furthman worked hard at trying to shorten the remaining script and come up with a new ending which would tie things together and allow them to wrap up shooting in January. Howard Hawks was the producer, as well as the director on this film, and, as he explained later, the more money he saved during shooting, the more he would make for himself. Warners, too, were becoming restless about the prospect of throwing limitless amounts of cash at this troubled production.

Nevertheless, the scenes which were being captured on film had a remarkably confident, untroubled air about them, and, as Lauren Bacall later wrote, 'In spite of my personal anguish, the movie was great fun. A marvellous cast, and we all liked each other.' Bogart had returned to work on 28 December, and by 12 January 1945 he had completed primary shooting. Then, on 29 January, he spoke (under the influence of several adult beverages) to George Frazier of *Life* magazine in New York, saying he was in love with Lauren Bacall, whom he referred to as 'Baby'. This nickname and the story were splashed all over the press in the next few days, sounding the death-knell for Bogart's marriage and giving the still-unseen film version of *The Big Sleep* yet more pre-publicity. Even without two of the most famous stars in the world appearing in the lead roles, the high profile of Raymond Chandler at that time would have created a great deal of anticipation – as the author noted in a letter to Charles Morton on 15 January, by that stage *The Big Sleep* and *Farewell, My Lovely* had 'between them, in some form or other, sold almost three quarters of a million copies'. In the face of all this, it seems incredible that studio boss Jack Warner would then choose to shelve the film version of the novel for almost a year and a half, but this is exactly what he did.

Warner's decision was based primarily on a desire to launch his hot new star, Lauren Bacall, in a 'serious' drama – namely *Confidential Agent*, an adaptation of a Graham Greene novel – which she began shooting after her principal photography on *The Big Sleep* was completed. Thus, although a version of the latter was shown to a certain number of US combat troops out in the Pacific islands during the last stages of the war that summer, its planned domestic release was shelved by the studio and *Confidential Agent* took its place in the schedules, opening to reviews which almost uniformly panned Bacall's performance and hinted that *To Have and Have Not* had been an unrepeatable fluke. 'Confidentially, it stinks,' said the *Hollywood Review*, while other journalists called its leading lady 'extraordinarily inept'. Moving swiftly to protect their investment, Warners approached Howard Hawks in the autumn of 1945 with a view to having new scenes written for *The Big Sleep*, filled with wisecracking, sexy dialogue between their two recently married co-stars, in a bid to recapture the elusive chemistry which the public had so enjoyed in *To Have and Have Not*. Thus, Chandler's book was to be turned into even more of a love story, perhaps at the expense of plot comprehensibility, but the end result was that some new scenes were added, others were reshot, and still more footage was cut, allegedly including much featuring Martha Vickers in the role of the younger Sternwood daughter, Carmen, whose performance some felt was overshadowing that of Bacall. This was certainly the story which had reached Raymond Chandler, as he wrote to his English publisher, Hamish Hamilton, on 30 May 1946, before he'd seen the finished cut of the movie:

> The girl who played the nymphy sister (Martha Vickers) was so good she shattered Miss Bacall completely. So they cut the picture in such a way that all her best scenes were left out except one. The result made nonsense and Howard Hawks threatened to sue to restrain Warners from releasing the picture. After long argument, as I hear it, he went back and did a lot of reshooting.

It's certain that Hawks was lured back to do the reshoots with an offer of $10,000, and the main result of the six days' work in January 1946 was a memorable scene in which Bogart and Bacall meet up in a restaurant, speaking lines which were about as suggestive as you could possibly be in a film of that time without getting closed down by the censors:

Bacall: Speaking of horses, I like to play them myself, but I like to see them work out a little first. See if they're front runners or come from behind . . . I'd say you don't like to be rated, you like to get out in front. Open up a lead. Take a little breather in the back straight and then come home free.

Bogart: I can't tell till I've seen you over a distance of ground. You've got a touch of class, but I don't know how far you can go.

> Bacall: A lot depends on who's in the saddle.

Howard Hawks later implied that this speech was basically his idea, while Lauren Bacall said in her autobiography that Jules Furthman wrote it, and still other sources mention the writer Philip Epstein. Asked by Joseph McBride how he was able to get such smutty remarks past the censorship board, Hawks replied: 'They said they were gonna object to it, and then they thought it over and decided they liked it so much that they were gonna let it go.' In fact, the days of the iron rule of the censors were already coming to an end, and Warner Brothers itself had formally resigned from the Hays Office at the end of May 1945, with United Artists going the same way – an unthinkable occurrence at the time when Chandler had first published his novel.

These, then, were just some of the twists and turns that Howard Hawks' production *The Big Sleep* had been through in the two years between August 1944 when work on the script began and 31 August 1946 when the film was finally given an American release. What had been written and shot as a wartime film, still containing dialogue references to the petrol rationing system ('Hello Bernie. It's Marlowe. How are you fixed for Red Points?'), now emerged into a very different post-war world, in which hardboiled detective pictures were a dime a dozen. Its plot was reckoned by the cast and crew to be so confusing that even Bogart, Hawks and Chandler hadn't a clue who was supposed to have killed Owen Taylor, the Sternwoods' chauffeur, although when the director cabled the book's author to question him about this, studio boss Jack Warner merely complained that he was wasting seventy-five cents on the price of the telegram over such trivialities. In the event, none of this mattered, and even some less-than-rapturous reviews couldn't stop the public lining up in their thousands to make it one of the smash hits of the year.

Variety, reviewing the picture on 14 August, saw 'plenty of box office potential', and praised pretty much all of the cast, including Bacall: 'Bogart matches wits with dealers in sex literature, blackmail, gambling and murder. Before he closes his case he has dodged sudden death, been unmercifully beaten, threatened, fought off mad advances of one of the Sternwood females, and fallen in love with another.' Manny Farber, writing in the *New Republic* (23 October), called it an 'unsentimental, surrealist excitement', with 'the feeling of an opium smoker's fantasy'. He laid into Bogart and Bacall, claiming that the former's 'detective is a limited, dull person' and that the latter 'creates a large empty space in the movie'. However, there was praise for Howard Hawks and his skill in 'graphically suggesting voyeurism and other forms of sexuality', while 'the chief impression you get of their world is that the pay is rotten, the people – especially the women – are uninhibited and no one lives to middle age'. Other reviewers, when not being sarcastic, were merely confused, such as Philip T Hartung, writing in *The Commonweal* on 6 September 1946:

> The main trouble with this picture, outside of its trying too hard, is that the story is too cryptic. It gathers up a good cast portraying a lot of unpleasant people, works up a series of very exciting episodes, but never adds up as a whole . . . In any case, even the title is without meaning, and you're never sure just what's up . .
> .

Evidently, Hartung had failed either to read or understand Chandler's novel (one of the major crime bestsellers of recent years), or he wouldn't have felt the title to be 'without meaning', but then, even though the author was well-known for the care he took in naming his books, it still seemed to cause confusion several decades later, when Peter Bogdanovitch interviewed Howard Hawks about the film:

> Bogdanovitch: What do you think the title refers to?
>
> Hawks: I don't know, probably death – it just sounds good.

Chandler himself was generally very happy with the picture, and with Bogart's portrayal of Marlowe. Hawks, he felt, had 'the gift of atmosphere and the requisite touch of hidden sadism', and as for Bogart, he thought him 'so much better than any other tough-guy actor':

> As we say here, Bogart can be tough without a gun. Also he has a sense of humour that contains that grating undertone of contempt. Ladd is hard, bitter and occasionally charming, but he is after all a small boy's idea of a tough guy. Bogart is the genuine article. Like Edward G Robinson, all he has to do to dominate a scene is to enter it.

Certainly the film had made changes to Chandler's novel. Vivian Sternwood was renamed Mrs Rutledge, signifying some previous but less sordid past than that which Chandler had given her. Younger sister Carmen, although still apparently a drug addict (a fact implied by references to her being 'high as a kite', and Bogart sniffing her glass at Geiger's death scene as if it contained something stranger than alcohol) is no longer a murderous lunatic, and the film's hasty resolution implies that she can be sent away not to an asylum, but for a drying-out cure at a drug rehab clinic. Carmen's two nude scenes – one at Geiger's and one in Marlowe's bed, become nothing more shocking than the wearing of a Chinese robe and an attempt to bite Bogart's hand, while Eddie Mars – admittedly not the novel's most sympathetic character – becomes the all-purpose fall-guy for the evils in the film, leaving the Sternwood family free to come up smelling of roses. Geiger's porn racket itself is merely hinted at, and his homosexuality is mostly signalled through his supposedly decadent taste in home furnishings. Teenage killer Carol Lundgren's compulsive swearing, rendered in the novel as 'go _ yourself,' is toned down to one solitary 'take a jump', but his live-in gay relationship with Geiger has pretty much disappeared altogether. (This, however, didn't discourage critic Michael Walker, in his 1992 essay 'The Big Sleep: Howard Hawks and Film Noir', who saw in Marlowe's pursuit of the killer Lundgren 'a middle-aged man cruising to pick up a young man', and his kicking and tying up of said murderer to be examples of 'gay bashing' and 'bondage'. Walker sees Marlowe as a repressed bisexual, and also finds a gay subtext in the exchange between him and Eddie Mars – 'I've got two boys outside.' 'Oh, it's like that is it?' As critics of Freudian analysis have often remarked, sometimes a candlestick is just a candlestick.)

The scriptwriters brought to the story many witty, hardboiled lines which weren't contained in the original novel; most of them apparently courtesy of Leigh Brackett, who shared the final screenwriting credit with Furthman and Faulkner. Apart from the aforementioned equine erotica scene, there were other enjoyable inventions such as the scene with Bogart and Bacall in Marlowe's office (where she calls up the police, and they hand the receiver back and forth with comments like, 'wait a minute, you'd better talk to my mother'), and other moments where they're simply making fun of each other:

Bacall: My, you're a mess aren't you?

Bogart: I'm not very tall, either. Next time I'll come on stilts, wear a white tie and carry a tennis racket.

Bacall: I doubt if even that would help.

For the newly-married Bacall, making films and hanging out with Bogart (including dinners with good friends such as Peter Lorre and passing Tinseltown figures such as Mr Las Vegas, Bugsy Siegel), this was the happiest time of her life. Humphrey Bogart, in the year of *The Big Sleep's* release, was now the highest paid actor in the world, pulling in a then-massive annual salary of $467,361, according to his biographers A M Sperber and Eric Lax. He still had many films ahead of him, but his appearance as Marlowe, together with his earlier portrayal of Sam Spade in *The Maltese Falcon*, nailed down an archetype of the screen private detective which is very unlikely ever to be surpassed. 1946 was also just about the high-water mark for Raymond Chandler's time in Hollywood; a year in which the July issue of *Pageant Magazine* estimated that his 'annual income from murder on the screen and between covers is around $100,000'. Not bad for someone who'd spent five months of 1933 writing a story which netted him just $180.

Philip Marlowe has since shown up every so often in film adaptations, on radio and on television, but it's been hard for anyone to escape the long shadow of 1940s Los Angeles and the figure of Humphrey Bogart. Of the various attempts which have been made, probably the most ill-advised would be Michael Winner's disastrous 1978 'remake' of *The Big Sleep*, which shot itself in the foot from the very beginning by setting the film in England. Despite having such a magnificent actor as Robert Mitchum in the role of Marlowe, the director of *Won Ton Ton: The Dog Who Saved Hollywood* (1976) proves conclusively over the course of 100 minutes that he isn't Howard Hawks. Interviewed at the time in the July–August 1978 issue of *American Film*, Michael Winner commented 'It's only a small coterie of film buffs who care for the original *Big Sleep*.' As they used to say back in Chandler's day: tell that to a mule and he'll kick your head off.

In a Lonely Place

Look Deep into These Eyes! Is it Love, Hate or Murder?

Film: In a Lonely Place
Director: Nicholas Ray
Leading players: Humphrey Bogart, Gloria Grahame, Frank Lovejoy,
Robert Warwick
Year of release: 1950

Book: In a Lonely Place
Author: Dorothy B Hughes
Year of publication: 1947

In a Lonely Place is one hell of a film, and one hell of a book, but apart from the title and the names of several characters they have virtually nothing in common with each other. It's tempting to wonder, when *Variety's* reviewer in May 1950 called Nicholas Ray's film 'a faithful adaptation of Dorothy B Hughes' story', whether he'd read even the first paragraph of her novel. Nevertheless, while the two stories take wildly different routes down the hardboiled highway, by some strange process they share a common atmosphere and an unforgettable sense of post-war Los Angeles at night, where people are no better than they ought to be, and fog-bound Tinseltown is going a little rusty around the edges. Great films often come from mediocre books, and Hollywood has certainly ruined its fair share of fine novels, but in this case both versions emerge as classics of their kind. For Humphrey Bogart, whose own production company Santana made the picture, it was a role which took him away from the tough-talking private eyes of *The Maltese Falcon* (1941) and *The Big Sleep* (1946), or the romantic hero of *Casablanca* (1943). Similarly, when compared with earlier Dorothy Hughes books, such as her 1941 wartime mystery *The Bamboo Blonde*, *In a Lonely Place* is an altogether darker and more serious proposition. Book and film stand as singular achievements, a little apart from the other works of their instigators.

That Hollywood chose to do a screen adaptation of Dorothy B Hughes's 1947 novel *In a Lonely Place* was hardly surprising. Of her previous books, *The Fallen Sparrow* (1942) had been filmed in 1943 with John Garfield in the lead role, while *Ride the Pink Horse* (1946) was brought to the screen as a Robert

Montgomery vehicle in 1947. In addition to producing roughly one thriller a year throughout the 1940s, she was also well known as a reviewer of mystery stories for newspapers such as the *New York Herald Tribune* and the *Los Angeles News*, and was given an Edgar award for her work as a critic in 1950, the year that *In a Lonely Place* was released.

Born in Kansas City, Missouri in 1904, Dorothy Belle Hughes had been a journalist and a published poet before turning to novel writing in 1940. 'I always intended to write books from when I was six years old and learned to write words,' she recalled. 'I wrote poetry, then short stories, before writing novels. It is true indeed that one learns to write by writing, and it takes time to learn to handle your material.' To be a female author of hardboiled fiction in those days was unusual enough, but to write a first-person narrative from the viewpoint of a male serial killer was breaking new ground by anybody's standards. Nevertheless, in 1947, decades before the avalanche of books concerning real or fictional multiple-murderers such as Ted Bundy or Hannibal Lecter, that's precisely what Dorothy Hughes set out to do.

> It's in a lonesome place you do have to be talking to someone,
> and looking for someone, in the evening of the day.

With this introductory quote from the Irish dramatist and poet John Millington Synge, Hughes both makes reference to her novel's title and at the same time hints at the impulse to seek out company which will eventually lead to the downfall of its protagonist, Dixon Steele. A young man, recently demobbed after war service, is living in a 'borrowed' apartment belonging to an old acquaintance called Mel Terriss, who has allegedly gone to Rio, conveniently leaving Dix the use of his flat, his clothes, his car and even his charge accounts in various shops around town. Steele claims to be writing a detective novel, but on the rare occasions he approaches a typewriter it is only ever for the purpose of writing letters to his rich uncle back East, begging for an increase in the monthly allowance which appears to be his sole means of support. Dix shuns contact with his neighbours, making sure to leave the apartment at times when there is unlikely to be anyone else around, and he deliberately garages his car some distance away, so that no one can check up on his movements.

From the very first pages of the novel, as the reader is drawn into the mindset of Steele by the first-person narration, there is no doubt that he is a disturbed individual who derives pleasure and a sense of power from following lone women on foggy nights:

He knew she heard him for her heel struck an extra beat, as if she had half stumbled, and her steps went faster. He didn't walk faster, he continued to saunter but he lengthened his stride, smiling slightly. She was afraid.

Although the woman reaches the safety of home before Dix can close in, his intentions are obvious to the reader. Having missed out on one potential victim, he decides on a whim to look up his old army buddy, Brub Nicolai, but their friendship can never be the same as in the old days, since Brub is now a married man. Worse than that, he has joined the police force and is in fact part of the team investigating the string of unsolved killings which Dix has been committing. To himself, Steele is just an average guy with 'a good-looking face but nothing to remember, nothing to set it apart from the usual' – the kind that blends in to the crowd. Interestingly enough, when the British police at long last caught up with Peter Sutcliffe, the vicious 1970s serial killer that the media had dubbed the Yorkshire Ripper – who in fact looked more like a tame, if somewhat sleazy wine waiter from a downmarket Spanish restaurant than some fearsome personification of evil – he had the same kind of self-image as Dix Steele. He thought he was the everyday man that nobody would notice, who could commit murder after murder without ever being found out. 'It got to the stage where I thought I was invisible,' Sutcliffe told the police, 'because I never got caught.'

Thirty pages into the novel, as Dix's solitary life becomes more entangled with Brub and his wife Sylvia, it becomes clear to the reader that he has raped and strangled a girl, and that this is in fact the sixth murder he has committed in the last half year:

> Her name was Mildred Atkinson and she had led a very stupid life . . . She was twenty-six years old and she was a good girl, her parents sobbed . . . The only exciting thing that ever happened to her was to be raped and murdered. Even then she'd only been subbing for someone else.

The 'someone else' referred to here is a girl called Betsy Banning, a local heiress who closely resembles a girl called Brucie whom Dix and Brub had known over in England during their wartime service. Everybody in their platoon had been attracted to her, Brub tells his wife, but 'no one had a chance with old lady-killer Steele present'.

Having formed a link with the Nicolais, Dix is further drawn out of his isolation by a chance encounter with one of his neighbours at the apartment complex. Her name is Laurel Gray, and he becomes fascinated by her: 'She was greedy and callous and a bitch, but she was fire and a man needed fire.' While at first their affair seems idyllic, she gradually becomes frightened by the glimpses of violence beneath Dix's seemingly normal exterior.

Regularly scanning the papers to see how they are reporting his killings, Dix is unable to restrain himself from visiting Brub at police headquarters for a lunch date, where they discuss the character of the killer. ' . . . I honestly don't think he ever does escape,' says Brub. 'He has to live with himself. He's caught there in that lonely place.' Through Brub, Dix meets Captain Jack Lochner, the head of the Homicide division, and even drives out with them to visit the desolate spot where Mildred Atkinson was murdered. As the first-person narration says, 'It would be lonely up here at night.'

Gradually the police, Laurel and the Nicolais become more and more suspicious of Dix, but through it all he feels that his hands are steady, his alibis strong and his public mask absolutely faultless. Running absurd risks, such as returning to the coffee shop where he'd previously taken one of his victims, he seems completely unable to see himself as he must appear to others. Laurel disappears from his life, yet he continually hopes that she will be back in a day or so and that they will resume their affair. In fact, Laurel has become so scared that she has finally gone to the police with her fears. The end for Dix, when it comes, is a surprise to no one but him. He has murdered the Banning girl, just as he had murdered her lookalike Brucie in England several years before, which seems to have been the original killing which sparked off this whole string of murders. Mel Terriss, whose apartment, car and possessions Dix had been using, turns out to have been the victim of yet another of these homicides, although this one was for purely practical purposes. The others, Hughes shows, were an integral part of what makes Steele tick. He's a killer, and so he kills, just as an artist must paint or an actor must act, and when he had first encountered the happy home-life that the recently-married Brub and Sylvia have found for themselves, his first response had been to shrink away from it: 'To hell with happiness. More important was excitement and power and the hot stir of lust.'

Given the state of motion picture censorship laws in 1949 when Humphrey Bogart's Santana production company first acquired *In a Lonely Place* with a view to adapting it for the movies, a woman-hating psycho whose 'hot stir of lust' has the coroner's boys dragging inert victims out of the bushes every couple of weeks wouldn't at first sight appear to be obvious leading-man material. Add to that the fact that the deranged rapist-killer in question also happens to be an ex-member of Uncle Sam's finest, recently returned from making the world safe for democracy, and the choice seems even stranger. After all, William Bendix's Navy-veteran-with-head-problems character in *The Blue Dahlia* (1946) had been originally intended by scriptwriter Raymond Chandler as the killer in that film, but this was changed as it was felt to be a slur on the good name of the armed forces. Nevertheless, Dorothy B Hughes's novels had already provided good roles for two of Bogart's contemporaries in the tough-guy field – John Garfield and Robert Montgomery. Bogart, however, was arguably still the biggest star in the world at that time, and there was a limit as to how far away from his well-established matinee-idol-with-a-pistol image he could afford to move. In the event, the film version manages to tread a careful path around these obstacles, telling a story which on the face of it has nothing to do with a serial killer. However, the role of Dix Steele does represent a serious shift away from Bogart's more usual characters, and the undercurrent of barely-controlled violence he displays could easily be those shown by the killer in the novel. Dix, in the film, stops just short of murder, several times. A few seconds more, in each case, and he would be the killer of the book. As with all film noir of the classic era, the chance to wallpaper the screen with piles of corpses was simply not available due to the prevailing restrictions of the time, but what is remarkable is the power of the stories that were able to be told in spite of this.

1949 was turning out to be a fine year for fear, paranoia and long, dark shadows. Just after the war, a series of articles had appeared in the *Chicago Tribune* claiming that communists had infiltrated all levels of Hollywood intending to corrupt the youth of the nation with Stalinist propaganda. Undaunted by the stupidity of these claims, the House Un-American Activities Committee, featuring shy, retiring self-publicist Congressman Richard Nixon, had descended upon Tinseltown in 1947, ready to cleanse the dream factory of anyone vaguely more left-of-centre than J Edgar Hoover. Alarmed by this turn of events, liberal Hollywood figures such as John Huston banded together to form the Committee for the First Amendment, aimed at protecting various rights to free expression enshrined in the Constitution. Early members of the CFA included Humphrey Bogart, whose extensive FBI file dated back to 1936, listing him as a suspected communist – a completely false accusation. He had already been forced to appear before an earlier HUAC committee in 1940, when it was chaired by Congressman Martin Dies. This situation arose because of the testimony of a man called John L Leech, who named Bogart and others as communists. The fact that the appropriately named Leech was lying on a grand scale didn't seem to concern Dies, and much inflammatory material was leaked to the press before the total discrediting of Leech's testimony. In October 1947 Bogart and Bacall were at the head of a delegation of the CFA that flew to Washington to protest that their civil rights were being violated by the HUAC investigation, but the hearing turned into a well-publicised shouting match between the committee chairman J Parnell Thomas and scriptwriter Jack Lawson. Press and public turned against the protesters, largely because the committee witnesses' refusal to testify was interpreted as a sign that they had something to hide. The fallout from this was swift and damaging to the careers of all concerned. Out of it came the Hollywood blacklist, and by 3 December Bogart was forced by studio head Jack Warner into publicly denying to the press that he was a communist and saying that the Washington trip had been 'ill-advised, even foolish'.

In a Lonely Place's director Nicholas Ray had himself been appearing in FBI files since 1941, when he was suspected of writing 'communist propaganda'. Then in November 1943 he was named by Senator Fred A Busley of Illinois in a list of people working for the Office of War Information who were held to be communist sympathisers. A far more likely target for the red witch-hunt than Bogart, Ray later gave credit to RKO Pictures owner Howard Hughes for using his political influence to save the young director from being blacklisted. Given the paranoid atmosphere of the previous years, it's hardly surprising that the film version of *In a Lonely Place* presents Hollywood as a less-than-glamorous town where a scriptwriter like Dix Steele has to write all kinds of melodramatic tripe in order to keep his job, and is at the mercy of ignorant studio executives, such as the loutish character at a restaurant who has 'set the son-in-law business back fifty years'. Naturally, Bogart socks him on the nose.

In 1949, Nicholas Ray was still in the early stages of his career, and had been chosen to direct *In a Lonely Place* as part of a two-picture deal with Bogart's Santana company after the actor had seen a private screening of Ray's début feature, *They Live By Night*. This film had been made two years previously, but had been shelved by the studio, although many Hollywood insiders like Bogart had already seen it and liked it. Eventually, after a favourable response to the picture's UK release – 'If the director had taken the trouble to be French,' said the *Spectator*, 'we would be licking his boots in ecstasy' – *They Live By Night* finally emerged in Ray's home country. By this time he had already directed several other pictures, including *Knock on Any Door* (1949), a Bogart vehicle for

Santana. The production company had recently bought the film rights for Dorothy Hughes' novel, and so *In a Lonely Place* became the second part of Ray's deal with Santana.

'Nick was a tall, well-built man,' wrote Bernard Gordon, a blacklisted scriptwriter who worked with Ray some years later, with 'a curiously hesitant manner of speech. A friend of his said, 'If you telephone Nick Ray and no one answers, that's Nick.' Nevertheless, by 1949, in addition to directing films, Nicholas Ray had also found the time to marry actress Gloria Grahame – a relationship that quickly turned sour. They first met when she played a character called Estrellita in his second film, *A Woman's Secret* (1948). Aged twenty-two, she had already been married once before: 'The film was a disastrous experience,' said Ray later, 'among other things because I met her . . . I was infatuated with her but I didn't like her very much.' Despite the fact that their personal life was coming apart at the seams, or possibly even because of that fact, Ray actively campaigned to secure the part of Laurel in *In a Lonely Place* for Gloria, rejecting studio suggestions that it would be a good role for Ginger Rogers. Originally, Bogart had wanted his wife Lauren Bacall for the part, but Warners refused to lend her out to Santana for this production. In casting his own wife in the role, Ray had to make assurances to the studio that their personal relationship would not affect the picture, and he undertook to move out of their home and sleep in a converted dressing-room on set during shooting. The situation becomes even more curious in the light of the fact that the studio-built set for Dix's apartment was based on the ground-plan and decor of Ray's first apartment in Hollywood, the Villa Primavera at 1304 North Harper, where he had lived in 1944.

Aware of the difficulty of filming such a story under existing censorship restrictions, producer Robert Lord began by sending Hughes's novel to the Production Code Administration, saying, 'We intend to have the protagonist kill only one person within the framework of the story. He has killed another person before the story begins.' At this stage it seems clear that Bogart's character was intended to be a murderer, and there is evidence to suggest that many scenes of the film were in fact shot with this in mind, which also explains the temporary shooting title given to the project – *Behind the Mask*. During preliminary discussions with head censor Joseph I Breen, Robert Lord told him: 'I wish Mr Bogart were Shirley Temple so that we could do stories of sweetness and light with him. But since he is not, we will have to push the steam roller uphill to make stories of this type with him.'

Evidence that Bogart was unlikely to start sporting ringlets and singing *On the Good Ship Lollipop* was spread all over the tabloids after a brawl at swank New York nightspot El Morocco on the night of 23 September 1949, involving a couple of stuffed toy pandas, a skinful of booze and an attention-seeking starlet. Given that Andrew Solt had been working since August turning Bogart's role of Dix Steele into that of a Hollywood scriptwriter who drinks with both hands and picks fights in restaurants, it all seemed pretty close to life imitating art – a view that silent film legend Louise Brooks later endorsed in her memoir, *Lulu in Hollywood*: '[*In a Lonely Place*] gave him a role that he could play with complexity, because the film character's pride in his art, his selfishness, drunkenness, lack of energy stabbed with lightning strokes of violence were shared by the real Bogart.' As the man himself famously remarked, 'The trouble with the world is that everybody in it is about three drinks behind.'

Exactly how those involved in the script and the making of the film managed to remodel the character of Dix Steele so that the character was transformed from a self-deluding, obsessive rapist and killer into a bad-tempered but ultimately romantic flawed semi-hero is hard to say. In the opening titles, Andrew Solt is credited with the screenplay and Edmund R North is listed as having adapted the story from Dorothy B Hughes's novel. Solt, in later years, gave the impression that the script was his, and that Nicholas Ray shot the whole thing entirely as written, unable to change a word because Bogart had apparently said, 'It's okay. We'll make it as it is.' Solt said of Ray: 'He was the director and I would write the scenes and we would discuss it, that's all. He gathered what I had in mind, otherwise he couldn't have made it so well.' However, far from being set in stone, it seems that there were numerous script changes, and according to Ray's biographer Bernard Eisenschitz, out of 140 pages of script 'only four made it to shooting without revisions'. Columbia Pictures went so far as to issue a story synopsis shortly after filming had commenced which suggests that Dix kills Laurel, which tends to support the theory that there was a gradual change of emphasis during revisions to the story. Ray himself said many years later that he just couldn't face having Dix kill Laurel: 'I thought, Shit! I can't do it, I just can't do it. Romances don't have to end that way. Marriages don't have to end that way, they don't have to end in violence for Christ's sake, you know.'

In the end, what emerged was a script filled with first-class, wisecracking dialogue, and a film which wasn't afraid to disappoint the more sentimental expectations of its audience. Most of the laconic asides found here are not drawn from the dialogue used in the novel:

| Mildred: | Before I started to go to work at Paul's I used to think that actors made up their own lines. |
| Dix: | When they get to be big stars, they usually do. |

Even when being interrogated by the police as a murder suspect, Bogart is given lines which help him to retain echoes of his sardonic, Philip Marlowe persona:

| Captain Lochner: | Why didn't you call for a cab? Isn't that what a gentleman does? |
| Dix: | I didn't say I was a gentleman, I said I was tired. |

In a Lonely Place began shooting on 25 October 1949 and was completed by 1 December. Apart from three days' location shooting in LA, including a star turn by the Beverly Hills City Hall on North Crescent Drive in the tricky and demanding role of Beverly Hills City Hall, all other work was done on the sound stages at Columbia Pictures.

The celluloid Dix Steele is instantly established in the first scene as a cynical Hollywood professional who's seen it all and is more than happy to get involved in a fight: 'I make it a point never to see pictures I write,' he tells an actress in the adjoining car at a stop sign, before making somewhat less-than-tactful comments about her choice of husband: 'You shouldn't have done it honey, no matter how much money that pig's got.' Despite all that, he's mostly a lovable character, and after this opening confrontation he immediately shows his better nature at a fashionable Hollywood restaurant called *Paul's* – a thinly-disguised version of Bogart's real-life favourite hangout, *Romanoff's* – defending alcoholic actor Charlie Waterman (Robert Warwick, an old friend who had worked with Bogart on stage and onscreen as far back as 1922). Dix himself is clearly popular with Paul, the restaurant owner (Stephen Geray), and Mel Lippman (Art Smith), his agent, although both are clearly aware of his capacity for losing his temper in a dangerous manner. All these characters clearly see something to admire in Dix's character, in direct contrast to the suspicions of Captain Lochner – 'He's hiding something, and I doubt it's the proverbial heart of gold.' However, it's when Dix meets Laurel, even as they are both entangled in a murder investigation, that his most favourable side is brought out, followed by his dark side.

Despite the fact that her marriage was on the rocks and that she was, at best, only the third choice for the role of Laurel, it's hard to imagine anyone playing it better than Gloria Grahame. In the novel, when Dix first meets Laurel, he observes, 'She wasn't beautiful, her face was too narrow for beauty, but she was dynamite,' and in her first dialogue scenes at the police station, Grahame, totally in command of the situation, effortlessly brings this description to life. After her relationship with Nick Ray fell apart, she eventually went on to marry his son, which may account for the director's less-than-charitable comments about her over the years. During her Hollywood career she also took some serious flack from the press at times, not least a sarcastic article in the June 1956 edition of *Photoplay*, which seriously undermines the tired theory that all publicity is good publicity:

> Let's not be beastly to Gloria Grahame. Let's be charitable – and forget the lisp that irritates so many people. Let's overlook the fact that she wears no make-up so that her skin shines (as one critic put it) 'as though she's greased for a Channel swim' . . . Now it is true that Gloria Grahame is not renowned for her wit and sparkling conversation off the set. She can be very difficult indeed . . . Moody, unpredictable, she is also something of a snob . . .

Nearly half a century after the anonymous writer of this particular piece of hack journalism put the boot in, Grahame's work in the role of Laurel, like her unforgettable performance in *The Big Heat* (1953), still stands to put her in the very first rank of noir heroines – tough, funny and very much her own woman:

Dix: Go ahead and get some sleep and we'll have dinner together tonight.

Laurel: We'll have dinner tonight, but not together.

While the novel tells the story of a twisted killer brought down by his own actions, the film becomes less of a murder hunt and more the story of a failed love affair, fatally wounded by misunderstandings and by Dix's inability to control his dangerous temper. Initially, *In a Lonely Place* is dominated by the killing of Mildred Atkinson – 'Strangled by the vice-like grip of an arm,' in Captain Lochner's melodramatic words – but by the end of the film, when her true killer is revealed to be her boyfriend, Henry Kessler, it's almost an irrelevance. This is partly due to the fact that Kessler is a character who has barely appeared in the film at all, but mostly because *In a Lonely Place* is not the story of a murderer, but that of a man on the brink of violence, and how this affects the people around him. Laurel is warned about this from the first days of the relationship both by her lesbian masseuse, Martha, who delights in telling Laurel how Dix broke his last girlfriend's nose, and also by the more well-intentioned figure of Mel the agent:

Laurel: There is something strange about Dix, isn't there? Dix doesn't act like a normal person. I'm not even sure he didn't kill Mildred Atkinson.

Mel: You knew he was dynamite. He has to explode sometimes.

Laurel has been brought to this point of doubt by incidents such as their car crash on the way home from a beach picnic at the Nicolais', caused in the first place by Dix's reckless driving. When the young owner of the other car calls him a 'blind, knuckle-headed squirrel', Dix beats him senseless and is only narrowly restrained from smashing his head in with a rock. All this is consistent with the information held in the police files about Steele's past arrests: 'Fractured producer's jaw. Fired. No charges preferred.' Given that it's also implied that he has a history of beating up women, it's hard to imagine a Hollywood star of Bogart's magnitude playing such a double-sided, morally ambiguous character these days, but then, in an age once again plagued by textbook happy endings, plastic surgery and perfect white teeth, it's hard to imagine a modern Hollywood star remotely like Bogart at all.

In the final scene, having been cleared of murder at the same time as almost killing the leading lady, Dix Steele walks off into what passes for a sunset in smog-bound Los Angeles, and, as Nick Ray said later, 'You do not know whether the man is going to go out, get drunk, have an accident in his car, or whether he is going to go to a psychiatrist for help.' Clearly, anyone looking for a *Forrest Gump*-style, heartwarming slushy message at this point would probably have emerged from the cinema speechless with rage. As it stands, it's precisely because the film fails to deliver the standard, sanitised Hollywood ending that the film has such power. 'Yesterday this would have meant so much to us,' says Laurel, on being told that Dix has been cleared of suspicion of murder. 'Now it doesn't matter. It doesn't matter at all.'

The filming of *In a Lonely Place* was completed on 1 December 1949, and the US release was on 17 May 1950. Seemingly unsure how to market a film where the hero is a borderline psychopath, the distributors plastered their one-sheet posters with the remarkably boring advertising slogan, 'The Bogart Suspense Picture With the Surprise Finish.' Luckily, the same publicity campaign's insert posters featured the much more appropriate line, 'Look Deep into These Eyes! Is it Love, Hate or Murder?' Trade paper *Variety* wrote, 'Humphrey Bogart as a temperamental, fistic-loving screenwriter, generates *In a Lonely Place* into a box office winner,' but expressed reservations about the lack of 'an audience-pleasing ending'. *Newsweek*, in a very positive review in their 5 June edition, said, 'Nicholas Ray has keyed his baleful theme to the tension one might expect watching a child play with a cobra.' Regarding the character of Dix Steele – 'a war veteran and movie scriptwriter suffering from a touch of battle-rattle' – they were full of praise, but one suspects they had inside information about the story changes which were made during shooting: 'In one of his most subtle and demanding roles Bogart proves conclusively he can give his comic-strip tough-guy roles a vigorous third dimension when the script demands. In this particular film one gets the impression that the disturbingly malevolent character he created had to be whitewashed in the last reel for the benefit of more squeamish moviegoers.'

Reviewers in general found much to praise in the film, but it failed to set the box office alight. Nevertheless, although Bogart may have won an Oscar the following year for *The African Queen*, and Grahame did the same a year later for *The Bad and the Beautiful*, it is *In a Lonely Place* which has grown in stature and reputation as the years have passed (although Lauren Bacall, in her 1979 autobiography, *By Myself*, strangely doesn't mention the film at all). As early as 1955, in a *Films & Filming* Bogart retrospective called *Gunman No. 1*, Peter Barnes wrote: 'One feels that his best performance in the romantic style was *In a Lonely Place* in which he played an unstable Hollywood scriptwriter involved in a murder case. His love scenes with Gloria Grahame had a depth and passion rare in the American cinema.' In 1961, when Nicholas Ray was interviewed by *Sight & Sound*, they reported the directors' own verdict on his career so far:

> His best film, he feels, is *Rebel Without a Cause* (most of us would probably agree), he has a solid affection for *The Lusty Men*, a story about rodeo people, starring Robert Mitchum and Susan

Hayward, which has hardly been revived since its first appearance in 1952, and a reminiscent interest, slightly tinged with scepticism, about *In a Lonely Place*, his Hollywood murder story.

Calling the film a Hollywood murder story is a little like calling *Psycho* a film about the theft of some money, but that probably just goes to show how the picture resists pigeonholing. It's certainly a love story, albeit a strange one, and its most famous lines – 'I was born when she kissed me, I died when she left me, I lived a few weeks while she loved me' – wouldn't necessarily look out of place in a Barbara Cartland novel. Yet here they are spoken by Dix as part of a script he is writing, just a few minutes after he has nearly beaten an innocent motorist to death, and it's difficult to imagine any romantic novelist having their hero's face light up with excitement while saying 'You get to a lonely place in the road, and you begin to squeeze . . . Squeeze harder! It's wonderful to feel her throat crush under your arm.' A complex role, riddled with contradictions, it's arguably the finest performance of Bogart's career, and while *In a Lonely Place* may have been one of Nicholas Ray's earliest films, it's unquestionably one of his best.

All things considered, the director may not have taken the trouble to be French, but on the strength of this film alone, maybe people *should* have been licking his boots in ecstasy.

Kiss Me, Deadly

I Don't Care What You Do To Me, Mike – Just Do It Fast!

Film: Kiss Me, Deadly
Director: Robert Aldrich
Leading players: Ralph Meeker, Albert Dekker, Cloris Leachman,
Paul Stewart
Year of release: 1955

Book: Kiss Me, Deadly
Author: Mickey Spillane
Year of publication: 1952

'They killed a dame and tried to frame me for it. They wrecked my heap and put me in the hospital. They're figuring us all for suckers and don't give a hang who gets hurt. The slobs, the miserable slobs.' I rammed my fist against my palm until it stung. 'I'm going to find out what the score is, kid. Then a lot of heads are going to roll.'

Mike Hammer in *Kiss Me, Deadly*

Some people have called Micky Spillane's Mike Hammer a sadomasochistic, misogynistic fascist, while other people really didn't like him at all . . . Nasty, brutish and short-tempered, a kind of Genghis Khan in a suit and tie, with a simplistic set of morals and a hair-trigger fuse, he first emerged in the 1947 novel *I, the Jury*, and, in a string of books over the next five years, over-ran the *New York Times* bestseller lists like a barbarian horde. Critics absolutely despised Spillane and his creation, but with hindsight it seems clear that at the time of the McCarthy witch-hunts, an All-American, gun-toting, Commie-hating, one-man attack force like Mike Hammer, who makes John Wayne look like a pinko hairdresser, was tailor-made to sell books by the millions.

Certainly, by 1952 when Mickey Spillane published his seventh novel, *Kiss Me, Deadly*, it's hard to imagine the author crying himself to sleep each night worrying about his reviews: the character he'd invented back in 1946 in order to raise $1,000 to help build a new house had already brought him wealth beyond most people's wildest dreams. 'I call myself the chewing gum of American literature,' he's been quoted as saying, but there was a time when the top-ten list of all-time bestsellers from any source included seven books written by Spillane.

Frank Morrison Spillane, nicknamed Mickey by his father, was born in Brooklyn on 9 March 1918. He kicked off his writing career while still in high school, achieving his first publication shortly after graduation, and went on to do a lot of work for pulp magazines, chiefly as a story-writer for comic books. During World War Two, Spillane served in the Air Force as a fighter pilot instructor. Then, when peace broke out, he worked up a comic book private eye hero called Mike Danger, but was unable to place it with a publisher. Undaunted, he renamed the character Mike Hammer, and used him as the lynchpin of a novel called *I, the Jury*, allegedly written in only nine days. The rest, as they say, is hysteria. Cynical, post-war America went Hammer-crazy, so that by 1951, his new novel *The Big Kill* was published with an initial print run of 2.5 million copies. The critics, meanwhile, threw up their hands in horror, and Spillane himself was giving out conflicting messages; at one point telling reporters that 'a couple of my best friends are prostitutes', while simultaneously attracting enormous press coverage for having become a Jehovah's Witness.

Kiss Me, Deadly, the novel which appeared the following year, does not, at first glance, appear to be the work of a newly-enthused religious convert, and the book's romantic interludes would probably have caused a certain amount of discomfort at the average vicarage tea party:

> Her hands were soft on my face and her mouth a hot, hungry thing that tried to drink me down. Even through the covers I could feel the firm pressure of her breasts, live things that caressed me of their own accord.

Meanwhile, Old Testament concepts of vengeance are also somewhat enthusiastically adhered to:

> I wasn't after talk, Carl. I wanted to see your face. I wanted to know it so I'd never forget it. Some day I'm going to watch it turn blue or maybe bleed to death. Your eyes'll get all wide and sticky and your tongue will hang out and I won't be making any mistake about it being the wrong joe.

Certainly, Mike Hammer belongs to a class of lone-wolf detective who would sooner gun down the bad guys than haul them up before a judge, a trait Spillane's biographers Max Allan Collins and James L Traylor described as the 'private eye-for-an-eye' school of behaviour. Indeed, Mickey's hard-as-nails approach was so recognisable (and influential) in the early 1950s that hardboiled writer Evan Hunter was moved to parody it in a 1954 short story called 'Kiss Me, Dudley' – an action-packed yarn in which hero Dudley Sledge kills virtually every other character involved, most of them innocent bystanders:

> 'They're outside,' I said, 'all of them. And they're all after me. The whole stinking, dirty, rotten, crawling, filthy, obscene, disgusting mass of them. Me, Dudley Sledge. They've all got guns in their maggoty fists, and murder in their grimy eyes.'

The above description could easily fit the objects of Hammer's rage in *Kiss Me, Deadly*: 'The Mafia. The stinking, slimy Mafia. An oversize mob of ignorant, lunkheaded jerks.' In a complex story where characters often seem to drop off the face of the earth (usually after they've been seen speaking to Mike Hammer), the initial cause of all the trouble is a two million dollar shipment of drugs, belonging to the Mafia, which has gone missing. As the novel opens, a woman named Berga Torn flags down Hammer late at night in his car on a lonely road, having recently escaped from a mental hospital. He picks her up, talks his way through a police roadblock, and then they are waylaid by a team of mobsters, who beat Hammer senseless, torture Berga to death, load them back into their car and then drive them both off the nearest cliff. Waking up some days later in hospital with the police breathing down his neck, Hammer is understandably annoyed, and decides to take on the Mafia, single-handed:

> They tried to kill me and they wrecked my car. That last part I especially didn't like. That car was hand built and could do over a hundred. And for all of that a lot of those top dogs are paying through the kiester, starting now.

From this moment, bodies start piling up wherever he goes, and pain is the name of the game: ' . . . he screamed the same time the muzzle rocketed a bullet into his eyeball and in the second he died the other eye that was still there glared at me balefully before it filmed over . . . ', 'The gun was there in his fist coming up and around as I brought my foot up and the things that were in Charlie's face splashed all over the floor . . . ', 'I put everything I could find into the swing that caught the side of his neck and mashed his vertebrae into his spinal cord and he was dead before I eased him to the floor . . . '. Tracking down Mafia boss Carl Evello to his home, Hammer delivers some straight talking: 'No crap. You play games with somebody else, but not me' – while also managing to chat up the hood's half-sister, Michael Friday. A little later, once Evello has joined the ever-increasing list of candidates for the coroner's meat-wagon, Friday gives Hammer some vital information, but pays the price for snitching on the mob. She is just one of several women in the novel who find Mike irresistible – 'The fire and the cushiony softness and the vibrancy made a living bed of her mouth' – including Lily Carver, who shoots Hammer in the final showdown, and then murmurs 'Deadly . . . deadly . . . kiss me . . . ' Although by the last page Mike has rescued Velda, killed the Mafia's sinister Mr Big (Dr Soberin), and recovered the stash of drugs from a locker at the City Athletic Club – to say nothing of leaving assorted mob gunsels draped over traffic signs or discovering the joys of rigor mortis in choice locations around town – he himself is wounded, and the novel's payoff line deliberately leaves his fate unclear.

When *Kiss Me, Deadly* first appeared in 1952, it hit the ground running and registered on both the *New York Times* and *Herald-Tribune* bestseller lists; an achievement no crime novel had so far managed. However, from this peak, and after seven books in five years, Spillane then waited nine years before publishing another novel. Nevertheless, he was very far from dropping out of the public eye during that time, and also felt the first tentative signs of Hollywood biting at his ankles, starting with Harry Essex's three-dimensional version of *I, the Jury* (1953), where Hammer appeared in the possibly less-than-convincing guise of little-known actor Biff Elliot. The following year brought the non-Hammer Spillane adaptation, *The Long Wait*, starring Anthony Quinn, together with the sight of Spillane himself appearing in *Ring of Fear*, a tale of dark deeds among circus folk, which took advantage of the author's own skills in this area. During his time away from the typewriter, Mickey liked to get physical on the trampoline, was often shot from a cannon, and did his share of deep-sea diving, fencing and stock-car racing. Meanwhile, actor Larry Haines was starring as Mike Hammer in a radio series called *That Hammer Guy*, and an LP entitled *Mickey Spillane's Mike Hammer Story* was released in 1954 (featuring Mike Hammer's only appearance in a short story, *Tonight, My Love*). Music from this album also showed up in the film *Ring of Fear*. A syndicated comic strip, *From the Files of . . . Mike Hammer*, written by Mickey Spillane, Ed Robbins and Joe Gill, appeared from 1953 to 1954, and included a story called *Half Blonde,* which, interestingly enough, employed the image of Pandora's box, which was not used in Spillane's novel, *Kiss Me, Deadly*, but surfaced the following year in Robert Aldrich's film adaptation.

What was permissible on the printed page in 1955 was often very far from being allowed in the cinemas, but even so, when Robert Aldrich was asked by Victor Saville – who owned the screen rights to Spillane's work – to make a film based on *Kiss Me, Deadly*, the director agreed, 'provided he would let me make the kind of movie I wanted and provided I could produce it'. Although Aldrich was from a rich East Coast family – one of his cousins was Nelson Rockefeller – his natural politics were liberal, left-of-centre, and he'd worked his way up from the ground floor after first going to Hollywood in 1941. Having gained valuable experience under key directors such as William Wellman, Lewis Milestone, Abraham Polonsky, Jean Renoir, Charlie Chaplin and Joseph Losey, he'd had his first shot at the megaphone and the big chair with an Edward G Robinson baseball picture called *The Big Leaguer* in 1953. By 1955 he was moving up in the world, and *Kiss Me, Deadly* would bring him to the attention of all kinds of people, including the Catholic Legion of Decency.

The usual sneering critical opinion of Spillane and all his work has generally presented something of a problem to admirers of the film *Kiss Me, Deadly*; one which they have tended to solve in much the same way as Aldrich himself, by denying that there was anything much in the novel which found its way into the film. 'The book had nothing,' Aldrich told *Sight & Sound* in 1968, 'we just took the title and threw the rest away.' This might make for a snappy press quote, but, when the novel and the film are compared, it's possibly fairer to say that although many things were changed, the film-makers used a great deal of the spirit of Spillane's novel, and, without the book, the film which the writers of *Cahiers du Cinema* and so many others have rightly praised for the last five decades simply wouldn't have existed. The most obvious difference between the film and the book is that the container, which everyone is literally dying in order to find, happens to be full of radioactive nuclear material, rather than drugs, and so it is the fate of the world, rather than two million dollars, which is at stake. Nevertheless, many of the characters, plot twists and action set-pieces are lifted pretty much intact from Spillane's novel. A few examples should suffice: the opening scenes with Christina/Berga's torture and killing and the car being pushed off the cliff; the revoking of Hammer's PI and gun licenses; the hood who is beaten up after following Hammer; the building superintendent and his overbearing wife; the two bombs hidden in the new car which the mob have given Hammer; the nervous truck-driver who was at the wheel when the mob faked an accident by pushing someone out into the road; Carl Evello's sister Friday picking up Hammer outside the mansion; Lily Carver pretending to hide in the basement; the kidnapping of Velda; Evello's stabbing at the hands of his own men; the autopsy which reveals the key in Christina/Berga's stomach; the disputed container being found in a locker at the Athletic Club; Lily Carver going up in flames in the final scene.

There is however a crucial change of emphasis with regard to the character of Mike Hammer, which alters the story markedly, and shifts it away from being a right-wing revenge fantasy. Spillane's first-person narration invites the reader to identify with the private detective and his moral crusade against the bad guys. Aldrich and his co-scriptwriter A I Bezzerides took the Hammer character at face value, but to them he was a symbol of the misuse of brute force, and a metaphor for the ham-fisted tough-guy tactics employed by Senator Joseph McCarthy and his House Un-American Activities Commission's attack upon Hollywood's liberal left. The location of the story is switched from the New York of the book to Los Angeles, both for financial reasons and also in order to reinforce the underlying message about the effect of the blacklist in that city. In the role of Hammer, actor Ralph Meeker deliberately plays the scenes as a cocky, defiantly unlikeable and none-too-bright macho lunkhead – 'All right. You've got me convinced. I'm a real stinker,' – whose cynical grin is at once both slimy and unconvincing. Clearly, Aldrich did not intend that his audience sympathise with his 'hero'. Right from the start, although he picks up the Berga Torn character (here renamed Christina in order to facilitate the plot's use of Christina Rossetti's poetry), Hammer is hardly a knight in shining armour:

Hammer: A thumb isn't good enough for you, you've got to use your whole body.

Christina: Would you have stopped if I used my thumb?

Hammer: No.

The action in the opening scenes is lifted directly from the book, but the dialogue is mostly new. As in the novel, the Christina character has escaped from an institution – 'So, you're a fugitive from the laughing-house?' – and is on the run from a shadowy selection of mobsters because she knows the whereabouts of some valuable merchandise. Following a torture scene that is brutally effective for its day (achieved mostly by dint of oblique camera angles coupled with more screams than an Elvis gig), Hammer and the dead girl take a one-way trip down the side of the canyon without the aid of a safety net and his car's chances of ever winning 'Best of Show' at an auto rally are shot all to hell.

Once Hammer wakes up in hospital to find that it's now three days after the crash, the next few scenes firmly establish how little admiration the film-makers have for their main character. He's questioned first by policeman Pat Murphy (Wesley Addy), who spends the whole film demonstrating a dislike bordering on contempt for Hammer, in marked contrast to the policeman in the book, who's called Pat Chambers, and is an old and trusted friend. However, Murphy's attitude is positively cordial compared to that of the boys of the Interstate Crime Commission, who pull Hammer in for a grilling as soon as he can walk, seemingly just for the pleasure of sneering at him like some sort of a cross between a Shakespearean chorus and a group of playground bullies:

'He calls himself a private detective.'

'His specialty is divorce cases.'

'He's a bedroom dick.'

'He gets information against the wife, then he makes a deal with the wife to get information against the husband.'

'He has a secretary – at least that's what he calls her.'

'She's very attractive. Real woo-bait.'

In the books, Mike Hammer steers clear of divorce cases, and is hardly pimping Velda to trap errant husbands but the film depicts him as a much lower form of life. 'Open a *window*,' says one of the Feds after the private eye has left the room, just in case any viewers are in any doubt about where their sympathies are supposed to lie by this stage. Yet not all of the characters in the film regard Hammer in this light, and he obviously has some friends. Nick the mechanic, for instance, appears to think that the sun shines out of Hammer's twin tail-pipes, and his willingness to help Mike out eventually leads to him getting his suit pressed for free by the mob, only this time with his body still inside it. Although based on the mechanic in the novel (who's named Bob Gellie and is merely hospitalised rather than crushed flat), the character of Nick is much more of a cartoon, with a chirpy manner similar to Manuel in *Fawlty Towers*, and a disconcerting habit of saying 'Va-Va-Voom!' and 'Pretty-Pow!' as if auditioning for a part in the *Batman* TV series. Similarly, the hep-talking bartender at the *Pigalle* club clearly knows Hammer and is concerned for his health:

> Bartender: Hey man, you sure look beat, you look real lean, real wasted. What's got ya, man? It don't look like you're with it?

> Hammer: Give me a double bourbon and leave the bottle . . .

Of course, the women in the film, as in the novel, all seem to want to get up-close and personal with Mike after only the briefest of introductions, but since they're mostly either hookers, alcoholics, gun-toting maniacs or a winning combination of all three, that's probably not intended as much of a character reference. Christina jumps in front of his car wearing nothing but a trench coat and within minutes is psychoanalysing Hammer while name-dropping dead Victorian poets. Velda practices ballet at home and has a neat line in femme-fatale put-downs: 'Do me a favour, will you. Keep away from the window. Somebody might blow you a kiss.' The screen version of Friday appears to have drunk a whole crate-load of booze for breakfast and is extremely anxious for Mike to give her some help in lying down, while Lily Carver is plainly a sure-fire candidate for a straight-jacket right from her opening appearance. Even before Lily's first scene, there's an obvious clue that she might not be a solid, upright citizen, when the building supervisor in charge of the apartment that she used to share with Christina remarks that Lily deliberately let her old flatmate's pet bird die after she went missing.

The violence in the film, while unable to quite match the eye-gouging sadism of the novel, is nonetheless very upfront for 1955, as exemplified by the fate of the anonymous mobster who attempts to follow Hammer down a dimly-lit street. Manfully struggling back into the fray after having had the back of his head repeatedly smashed against a wall, the hood is then punched backwards down a very long and painful set of concrete steps. Similarly, the slimy autopsy doctor who attempts to bargain with Hammer for a cut of the loot winds up with his fingers enthusiastically slammed in a desk drawer in a fashion which would certainly raise doubts about his future piano-playing abilities. However, at the same time, the film's two chief muscle-boys, Charlie Max and Sugar, are some of the most politely-spoken, even lyrical, enforcers you're ever likely to encounter, and it's hard to picture Lucky Luciano's footsoldiers coming up with philosophical lines like 'We're here on this world such a brief span.' The doomed Christina is also of a somewhat literary frame of mind: despite the fact that a team of mob goons with pliers are on her trail, and that Hammer is clearly not the poetry-reading type, she decides to leave a clue for him in the form of a two-word note referring to a Rossetti sonnet. 'Remember Me,' says the note which she posts to him from the gas station, and from this, and the Rossetti book which he finds later at her apartment, he begins mulling over some lines from the poem, *Remember*, which say:

> For if the darkness and corruption leave
> A vestige of the thoughts that once I had,
> Better by far you should forget and smile
> Than that you should remember and be sad.

Strange to say, this exposure to romantic literature strikes a chord with the private eye – a seemingly unsentimental type whose first comment upon leaving hospital was to exclaim 'Mmmm, look at all the goodies!' at two passing young women – and he rightly deduces that Christina is telling him that he'll be able to find the solution to the riddle inside her dead body. This is a slightly less convincing riddle than the one which Spillane uses in the novel, where Berga Torn sends a note to Hammer reading 'The way to a man's heart . . . ,' thereby suggesting the stomach in a more direct fashion. Still, with its poetry, classical music, ballet and references to Lot's wife and Pandora – none of which are found in the novel – the film was deliberately raising the story to the level of a fable, where the unleashing of nuclear power can stand as a metaphor for the damage done to civil liberties and democracy by the crudely-wielded power of McCarthy and HUAC, and to have told the story in any more of a straightforward manner at that time would have meant running serious risks by all concerned. It wasn't until twenty years later, with Martin Ritt's *The Front*, starring Woody Allen, that Hollywood finally made a film that tackled the blacklist head-on.

Kiss Me, Deadly was filmed on a budget of $425,000 in a tight shooting schedule of twenty-one days during December 1954, wrapping up two days before Christmas. Location work was done at Malibu Beach, and in LA's Bunker Hill area, while studio shooting took place at the old Famous Players-Lasky studio at 201 North Occidental Boulevard (then known as John Sutherland Productions), which Aldrich himself later bought in 1968.

Robert Aldrich's previous film, *Vera Cruz* (1953), had been criticised for its depiction of violence, and he was clearly anticipating problems in this regard with *Kiss Me, Deadly*, and so in the 20 February edition of the *New York Herald-Tribune,* the director published an article entitled 'You Can't Hang Up the Meat Hook', explaining, in advance of the film's release, his handling of the Christina torture scene. At the same time, Aldrich was having to plead his case to the censorship board, who had rejected the film after an initial preview, on the grounds that it was not permissible for a character like Hammer to be seen taking the law into his own hands in such a way. After much discussion, Aldrich was finally able to get approval for the film, telling the board that he was combining 'the commercial values of the Spillane properties with a morality that states justice is not to be found in a self-anointed, one-man vigilante'.

Then, on the eve of the film's release on 18 May 1955, the Catholic Legion of Decency put the ecclesiastical boot in, saying that they were going to give the film a 'Condemned' rating, at which point Aldrich complained to the censor, saying that 'the Legion has even failed to recognise any voice of moral righteousness'. In the end, after cuts were made, they relented to the extent of classifying it as a 'B' – meaning 'morally objectionable in part for all'.

Variety's reviewer, clearly not overly alarmed by the prospect of the morally objectionable, called the film a 'hardboiled private eye meller from the Mickey Spillane pen, featuring blood, action and sex for exploitable b.o.', even complaining that Ralph Meeker's Hammer appears to 'go soft in a few sequences'. Reservations were also expressed about the comprehensibility of the many plot twists: 'the trail leads to a series of amorous dames, murder-minded plug-uglies and dangerous adventures that offer excitement but have little clarity to let the viewer know what's going on'. Meanwhile *Newsweek's* 25 April 1955 edition told its readers that the new Spillane adaptation was 'a good cut above its predecessors'. In a review which concluded with the verdict 'Out of this world', they expressed the opinion that 'Hammer isn't much of a role for any actor who isn't in need of a punching-bag or a psychoanalyst. Meeker handles it all right, however, by not trying to be either particularly likeable or sinister.' Aldrich was praised for having 'assembled a number of nubile nitwits – Cloris Leachman, Marian Carr, Maxine Cooper, and Gaby Rodgers – but Mike keeps backing away from their caresses'. *Newsweek's* reviewer also had no trouble identifying the film-makers' distance from their central character, commenting that 'Aldrich and screenwriter A I Bezzerides arrange to have right-thinking people, including Wesley Addy as an FBI man, look down on Hammer as a postgraduate of *Blackboard Jungle*.'

For all the film's deeper psychological and metaphorical intentions, there were certainly a few people in the publicity department determined to market it as an all-action shoot-em-up: 'Blood Red Kisses – White Hot Thrills' screamed the posters, 'Mickey Spillane's Latest H-Bomb.' The theatrical trailer certainly played down the Victorian poetry angle, opting instead for babes in swimsuits, Hammer banging someone's head against a wall, women screaming and a dramatic voice-over intoning:

'Girls fleeing in terror from things beyond description!'

'He was out to get men who tortured women, and killed with the ferocity of wild beasts! This was their jungle!'

'This woman's lips, cold as steel, lethal as a gun, gave him the terrifying clue he sought!'

Interestingly, given the later controversy which arose, the trailer ends with a shot of Hammer and Velda together in the surf, watching the nuclear explosion at the beach house. Some prints of the feature fail to show this scene, and finish with the words 'The End' appearing over a shot of the explosion. It's been said in some quarters that only the British prints of the film have the scene in which Hammer and Velda are shown in the water, but the print which *Variety's* reviewer watched clearly included this scene, since they wrote: 'everything goes up in flames except Hammer and his warm brunette secretary, who manage to escape . . . ' Aldrich himself, in a letter written shortly before he died to his biographers, Edward T Arnold and Eugene L Miller, said:

I have never seen a print without, repeat, without Hammer and Velda stumbling in the surf. That's the way it was shot, that's the way it was released; the idea being that Mike was left alive long enough to see what havoc he had caused, though certainly both he and Velda were both seriously contaminated.

The film did respectable business at the US box office, but nothing spectacular, and Aldrich moved on to other projects, unaware that *Kiss Me, Deadly* was shortly to have a far-reaching effect on young film journalists in France, many of whom went on to become key film directors in the decades to come. *Cahiers du Cinema*, in particular, championed the film as an important example of the genre that they were in the process of defining as *film noir*, while Claude Chabrol loved it, saying that Aldrich had made something great out of 'the worst material he was able to find'. Initially somewhat confused by this reception, Aldrich told François Truffaut in a *Cahiers du Cinema* interview in November 1956: 'I regret having accepted the job of making *Kiss Me, Deadly*. Two horrible films had already been made of the Spillane series, and I should have refused.' In an article written by Aldrich for *Films & Filming* in June 1958, entitled *The High Price of Independence*, the director discusses his career at some length, but his only comment about *Kiss Me, Deadly* is that it 'did not do too well' – indeed, it's interesting to see, through the pages of this magazine, how attitudes towards this film changed over the years. In 1960, *Kiss Me, Deadly* was still very far from being hailed as a masterpiece in England, to judge from this news item in *Films & Filming's* August edition:

> The National Film Theatre is presenting a season called *Beat, Square and Cool* . . . in the programme will be found Kubrick's *Killer's Kiss*, Aldrich's *Kiss Me, Deadly* and Lerner's *Murder by Contract*. The titles are enough to suggest an obsession among young American film-makers with the sordid and the vicious, an ugly, repellent neurosis.

Nevertheless, when 1961 rolled around, some critics were evidently developing a taste for ugly, repellent neurosis. Raymond Durgnat felt compelled to write, in an article entitled *Cupid v. the Legions of Decency*, 'As usual, the answer to Mickey Spillane is not to ban Mickey Spillane but to put *Sons and Lovers* in paperback form . . . Mickey Spillane's novel *Kiss Me, Deadly* may be 'bad' but Robert Aldrich's film based on that novel is arguably a minor classic.' Needless to say, by the following year, the film was almost being held up as an example of the good old days, and in this November 1962 review of *Dr No*, *Kiss Me, Deadly* was being used as a stick to beat the new horror of James Bond films:

> What *Dr No* lacks is a sense of style, that bold formalised handling Aldrich gave *Kiss Me, Deadly* . . . Just as Mike Hammer was the softening up for James Bond, so Bond is the softening up for . . . what? A fascist cinema uncorrupted by moral scruples? The riot of a completely anarchist cinema?

By 1968, of course, the words 'a fascist cinema uncorrupted by moral scruples' plastered all over a movie poster would probably have brought the crowds in by the millions, but by then *Films & Filming* were calling *Kiss Me, Deadly* 'one of the most remarkable works of the Fifties,' and even Aldrich wasn't being nearly so harsh in his assessment of the picture: 'I was very proud of the film,' he told Joel Greenberg in the Winter 1968/69 issue of *Sight & Sound*, 'I think what irritates some people – and I've been mis-quoted about this so many times – is that they think I have disowned the importance of the film. I haven't. What I have said is that it has an importance juxtaposed against a particular political background, an importance that's not justified if it's juxtaposed against another one that by accident happens to fit. It did have a basic significance in *our* political framework that we thought rather important in those McCarthy times: that the end did not justify the means.'

However, in the 1 October 1970 issue of *Rolling Stone*, confused flower children too stoned to even spell the words 'McCarthy witch-hunt' in the dirt with a stick were being offered the following comforting advice:

> If things are getting too heavy for you this film is really up your alley – you'll either jump off a bridge or flash that it isn't so bad after all . . . the film reverberates in retrospect long after you've seen it. *Kiss Me, Deadly* is a funky jewel.

By August 1973 Aldrich was telling John Calendo in *Andy Warhol's Interview* magazine: 'I had a career due to the European reaction to *Kiss Me, Deadly*,' and went on to say: 'Spillane, you know, never understood that this was the greatest Spillane put-down in a long time. He just thought it was a marvellous picture.'

Spillane was right. It is.

Hell is a City

From dark till dawn . . . From dives to dames . . . From cops to killers . . .

Film: Hell is a City
Director: Val Guest
Leading players: Stanley Baker, John Crawford, Donald Pleasence,
Maxine Audley
Year of release: 1960

Book: Hell is a City (US title: Murder Somewhere in This City)
Author: Maurice Procter
Year of publication: 1954

In 1959, England's Hammer Films were at the crest of a wave, having broken through into the international market with classy, full-colour Gothic horrors such as *The Curse of Frankenstein* (1957) and *Dracula* (1958), which made world-wide stars of Peter Cushing and Christopher Lee. According to the rule book, a small company operating out of an old house on the banks of the Thames near Windsor wasn't supposed to have smash hit films that provoked queues up and down Times Square and Hollywood Boulevard, but, for a while, their combination of strict budgets, imaginative direction, world-class production design and killer marketing put them right at the top of the heap.

Although their name quickly became associated with the horror genre, Hammer's first major international success had been with science-fiction, in the shape of Val Guest's 1955 big-screen adaptation of Nigel Kneale's hit TV series, *The Quatermass Experiment*. Filmed in a deadpan, monochrome style seemingly straight from the newsreels, it had a hard-edged core of credibility running through it, despite its far-fetched storyline. Guest's paranoid, noir-tinged follow-up, *Quatermass II* (1957), was even better, and in the last months of 1959 he brought this same fast-moving, documentary style to Hammer's film version of a Maurice Procter crime novel called *Hell is a City*. Making very effective use of location shooting in and around Manchester (at a time when most British features routinely faked everything from the Swiss Alps to the African bush without ever leaving the confines of the Greater London postal district), the film helped launch Stanley Baker as a leading actor and paved the way for a whole division of down-to-earth television coppers. Shot right at the end of the last great decade of film noir, *Hell is a City* is one of the only authentic British contributions to the genre, and, like *Get Carter*, which was also neglected for many years after its release, is simply one of the best crime films to have emerged from the UK since the war.

Although it may be hard to believe, there was once a time when cinema and TV screens weren't crawling with fictional police officers, and the concept of basing a story around the day-to-day workings of a crime squad was actually a new idea. Whole generations have grown up on the likes of *Columbo*, *NYPD Blue* or England's *The Bill*, and the genre is now so familiar that scriptwriters are tempted to throw in all manner of unconvincing quirks just to be different. These days a hard-bitten, no-nonsense crime-solving police official called *Kommissar Rex* holds down an expensive hour of prime-time TV each week in Germany, undaunted by the fact that he is, in fact, a dog, but back in 1954 when Maurice Procter's novel *Hell is a City* first appeared, the branch of crime writing now termed the police procedural was all but unknown. Procter himself had served nineteen years in the constabulary in the north of England, a fact which his publishers were keen to emphasise: 'The idea of being a novelist had been with him since boyhood,' said the publicity material. 'He ate, slept, worked his beat, wrote and rewrote until he found a publisher. His first book was something new: a story about *real* policemen and police work.'

Maurice Procter was born in Nelson, Lancashire in 1906, and had already served in the Army as well as the police before setting out in 1947 to write novels full-time. He explored police work as a theme in his first six books, but it was the seventh – *Hell is a City*, published in 1954 – which introduced the character Chief Inspector Harry Martineau, who was to feature in a further thirteen novels between then and Procter's death in 1973. 'He couldn't have been as good a bobby as he is a novelist,' wrote Gerald Bowman in the *Evening News,* 'or he'd have finished up as Chief Commissioner.'

Hell is a City is set in a fictional metropolis called Granchester, a very thinly-disguised version of the Manchester which Procter knew so well from his days in the force, but it takes its title from a poem by Shelley called *Peter Bell the Third*, written in 1819 about another city entirely:

> Hell is a city much like London –
> A populous and a smoky city;
> There are all sorts of people undone,
> And there is little or no fun done;
> Small justice shown, and still less pity . . .

95

Chief Inspector Martineau quotes the first two lines of this stanza towards the end of the novel, while high on a roof looking down on Granchester, shortly before his final confrontation with the main villain, Don Starling. The two have known each other since childhood, both having grown up in poverty, the one opting for a life of armed robbery and violence, the other winding up as 'the hardest hitter in the Granchester police'. Both are tough, no-nonsense characters, but the main difference between them is Martineau's basic belief in the law – clearly echoing that of the author – and that villains should be punished for their crimes. 'The two young men were enemies as naturally as wolf and wolf-hound.'

Given that Procter's book has been out of print for many years, and its story differs in some respects from the film adaptation, it's worth outlining the main events and characters. The novel tells the story of a robbery carried out by Don Starling's gang, who hijack a bag containing thousands of pounds belonging to local bookmaker Gus Hawkins. Since the bag in question is chained to the wrist of Gus's assistant Cicely, they bundle her into their getaway car, but Starling accidentally kills her with a badly-aimed blow from a cosh. At this time, Starling is already a fugitive, having just escaped from a prison where he was serving fourteen years for an earlier jewel heist in which he had shot and wounded a policeman. Now, having killed the girl, he has nothing else to lose, because in 1950s Britain, murder is a hanging offence. The others in the getaway car are also liable to the same punishment, as accessories.

> The same fear was upon them all. They were reminded of a man
> they all knew by sight. He kept a pub in Hollinwood. The name
> of the pub was *Help the Poor Struggler*. The man's name was Albert
> Pierrepoint. He was the public hangman.

The shadow of the death penalty hangs over the entire book, and it seems clear that Procter, like Martineau, believed in it as sentence for certain crimes. Albert Pierrepoint was the most famous British hangman of the twentieth century, having executed many war criminals after the Nuremberg trials, as well as people such as Ruth Ellis, John Christie and Derek Bentley. A jovial landlord who liked to entertain his customers by performing conjuring tricks and singing *Danny Boy* at closing time, he had moved by the time of the novel's publication to a new pub, the *Rose & Crown* at Hoole, near Preston, where he was annoyed by false newspaper reports that he was displaying a sign reading

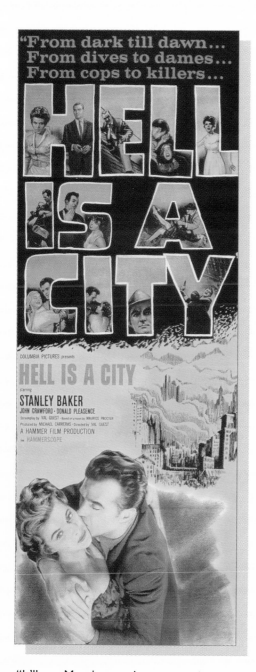

"He couldn't have been as good a bobby as he is a novelist, or he'd have finished up as Chief Commissioner."

"It'll put Manchester down as a grimy, dirty city,' say the local councillors..."

Mario Puzo: "So I told my editors OK, I'll write a book about the Mafia, just give me some money to get started."

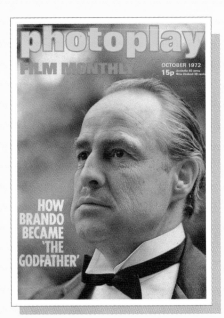

Francis Ford Coppola: "I was getting 'fired' every other week. The things they were going to fire me over were, one: wanting to cast Brando. Two: wanting to cast Pacino. Wanting to shoot in Sicily; wanting to make it in period. The very things that made the film different from any other film."

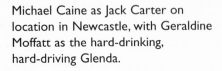

Michael Caine as Jack Carter on location in Newcastle, with Geraldine Moffatt as the hard-drinking, hard-driving Glenda.

Michael Caine: "I didn't want to play the cliché heavy, the hardcase with a soft centre. Actors have been doing that since Paul Muni's *Scarface*. I wanted, very simply, the truth now."

Warren Oates as Dillinger: "You're being robbed by the John Dillinger Gang, that's the best there is. These few dollars you lose here today, they're gonna buy you stories to tell your children and great grand-children. This could be one of the great moments in your life. Don't make it your last."

A collection of some of Chandlers' 1930s pulp stories, including *Finger Man* (*Black Mask*, October 1934), whose casino gambling sequence was reworked for the novel *The Big Sleep* (1939).

Josh Logan: "Not since Attila the Hun swept across Europe leaving five hundred years of total blackness has there been a man like Lee Marvin..."

Senator Estes Kefauver: "Behind the local mobs which make up the national crime syndicate is a shadowy, international criminal organisation known as the Mafia, so fantastic that most Americans find it hard to believe it really exists."

Jean-Luc Godard: "We can make the film anywhere. We can make it in Tokyo."

W.R. Burnett: "It has been translated into twelve languages, including English, as a witty friend of mine says."

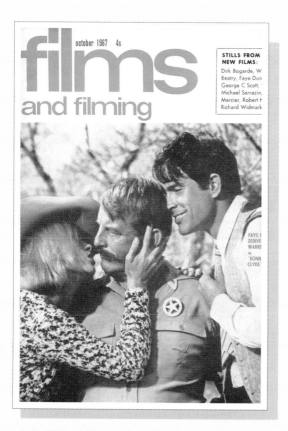

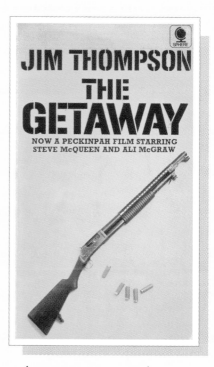

Anonymous crew member:
"To work with Steve McQueen
[was] to work with a complete
and thorough child."

John Toland: "a couple of 'punks' who 'were in
the flesh about as loveable as Ilse Koch and
Martin Bormann.'"

Machine-guns, rifles, automatic pistols and bullet-proof vests found at the scene of the
January 1935 final showdown between the Feds and Ma Baker & her boys.

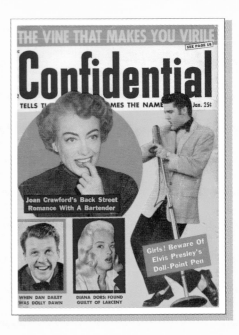

Robert Bloch: "I had a notion that a person is never more defenceless than when taking a shower... a sudden intrusion is a very shocking thing."

"A grandstand view up the collective unterhosen of Tinseltown's finest."

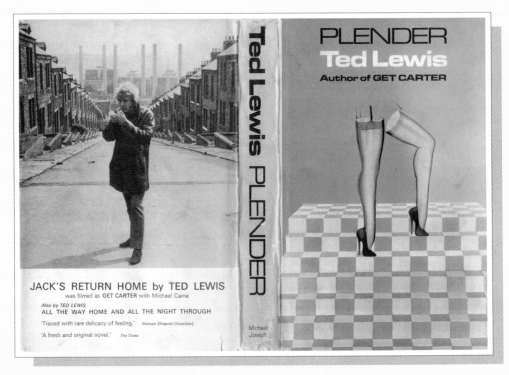

Ted Lewis on location in Newcastle during the filming of *Get Carter*, pictured on the rear cover of his follow-up novel, *Plender* (1971)

Robert Bloch, still in the shadow of Norman Bates, wrote the script for this 1966 feature, which was billed as "A New Peak in Shriek."

Shelley Winters: "*Bloody Mama* isn't a violent picture. It's against violence!" A young Robert De Niro can be seen on the right in the lower cover photo, as Ma's glue-sniffing son Lloyd.

James M. Cain's "unfilmable" 1934 novel, *The Postman Always Rings Twice*, finally makes it to London's cinemas in 1946.

James Ellroy: "To this day, the cases in there continue to drive me. Here it is, forty one years later, I remain driven, morally and psychically, by what I got out of that book. It's fucking astonishing."

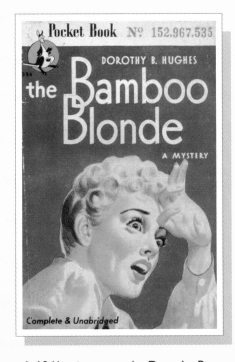

A 1941 crime story by Dorothy B. Hughes, whose writing was to take a much darker turn with the 1947 serial killer novel *In a Lonely Place*.

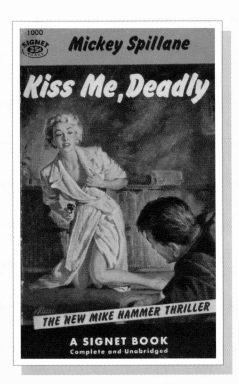

Robert Aldrich: "The book had nothing, we just took the title and threw the rest away."

'No hanging about this bar'. Pierrepoint was old friends with the Manchester CID, and Procter would presumably have known him from his days on the force.

Inspector Harry Martineau is shown to be an unhappily-married man who'd rather stay out in a pub after a full day of police work than go home to his bored, unsympathetic wife. When at last he does return, they argue incessantly. 'I try to keep this place nice, and you treat it like a doss house,' she tells him, while he says things would be all right 'if you justified your existence by having a baby or two'. Away from home, he is tempted more than once by barmaid Lucky Lusk, who also happens to be an old girlfriend of Don Starling. By contrast Martineau's assistant, Detective Constable Devery, can't wait to get away from work so that he can see his fiancée, Sylvia 'Silver' Steele, the deaf mute daughter of a furniture dealer. (Procter evidently had a fondness for giving his female heroines exotic names beginning with the letter 'S' – his 1960 Martineau novel, *Devil's Due*, features a romance between a junior member of the constabulary and a dazzling blonde by the name of Sable Spurr.)

Don Starling has broken out of prison and returned to Granchester in order to retrieve the stolen jewels from his last robbery from their hiding place in the wine cellars of the Royal Lancaster Hotel. On the run and short of ready cash, he quickly plans the attempt on Gus Hawkins's bank delivery, but things go wrong. Not only is the girl, Cicely, killed accidentally, but the money has been dusted with a substance called Malachite Green, which stains the fingers of all who handle it. Wanted for murder, Starling seeks shelter with various old acquaintances, including Chloe, a somewhat less-than-reformed good-time girl now married to Gus Hawkins. After a night spent hiding in Hawkins's attic, Starling is almost discovered by Gus, but coshes him over the head before he is recognised.

Meanwhile, Starling's accomplices Lolly Jakes, Clogger Roach and Laurie Lovett are still at large, flush with money but unknowingly bearing tell-tale green marks on their fingers. At an outdoor illegal gambling meeting, Lolly Jakes is arrested in a police raid, having drawn attention to himself by flashing his robbery money around at a similar game the day before. Laurie Lovett's taxi garage is searched by Martineau, and some of the stolen money is discovered hidden in a car engine. As the gang are rounded up, only Starling remains free.

Martineau receives word from the Royal Lancaster Hotel that someone has broken into their wine cellar, and it's clear that Starling has returned and picked up the hidden jewels. Hiding in the warehouse of Furnisher Steele, Starling is accidentally discovered by Silver, who is shot dead after raising the alarm. Trapped during a rooftop shootout with Martineau, during which they are both wounded, Starling is eventually captured. Sentenced to death, he goes to the scaffold in a chapter entitled *The Hangman's Mercy*, which, until Albert Pierrepoint published his autobiography in 1974, was probably one of the most accurate descriptions of the British process of judicial execution available:

> Then Starling saw the strap, and his courage ebbed. A new rope for every murderer, but not a new strap . . . The hangman's assistant moved behind him with the strap, and at a signal pinioned his shaking hands with one adroit jerk. The remaining length of leather was put over his shoulder, and the extra buckle dangled close to his chest.

Martineau recovers from his wounds and on the day of Starling's execution, having once again argued with his wife, he goes out and gets very drunk. Meeting up with the barmaid Lucky Lusk, he very nearly goes off to sleep with her, and later attempts to pick up a whore in the street, but the deal falls through when she recognises him as a policeman. Returning home still drunk to find that his wife has sold his beloved piano, he threatens to rape her in order to have some children, at which point she suddenly decides that kids are a good idea after all. This strange, supposedly 'happy' ending sits very uncomfortably at the close of an otherwise very fast-moving and unsentimental book, and it's hard not to wish that Procter had finished the story with Starling's execution. However, *Hell is a City*, like the best of his novels, has a down-to-earth realism in which police, villains and members of the public all have their bad and good sides, while the violence is squalid and convincing, rather than glamorous. Procter had obviously seen enough in his days on the force to expect too much from anybody. It would be interesting to know what the boys in blue made of a story in which the supposed hero is a borderline alcoholic who chases whores and threatens to rape his own wife. Any way you look at it, this was a long way from *Dixon of Dock Green*. A good deal more downbeat than much of the cosy British crime fiction of its day, the novel was nevertheless successful enough both in the UK and America for Procter to follow it with a new Martineau title virtually every year.

Hell is a City first came to the notice of Michael Carreras at Hammer Films, who had developed the habit of reading a great many novels in search of new material for the studio to adapt into films. (By the late 1950s Hammer were making an average of eight features a year.) Although the company had by this stage moved into an area of film-making in which villains were more likely to suffer a stake driven through the heart than a visit from the boys in blue, Hammer's post-war roster of features had also included *Crime Reporter* (1947), *A Case For PC 49* (1950) and *The Last Page* (1952), so stories of non-supernatural bad behaviour were hardly a novelty for them. As company boss Jimmy Carreras – the father of Michael – famously commented after the success of *The Curse of Frankenstein*, if the public were to switch their tastes from horror to Strauss waltzes, then he'd happily give them Strauss waltzes. (In 1959, the year in which *Hell is a City* went into production, Hammer's output consisted of two war films, three comedies, two horror titles, one detective thriller and a documentary featurette about the origins of the solar system.)

When Val Guest was approached by producer Michael Carreras to direct and write an adaptation of Procter's novel, he had already made eleven films for Hammer, the first being the 1954 comedy *Life With the Lyons*, and the most recent, a hard-hitting drama of the war in the Far East called *Yesterday's Enemy* (1959), starring Stanley Baker. Guest, born in 1911, had gained his first real foothold in the film world back in the 1930s, working on a string of Will Hay comedies such as *Oh, Mr Porter* (1937), but this break came only after a varied apprenticeship: 'I've been a journalist, an actor, I was under contract to Warner Bros for many years,' he recalled. 'I was also a writer. I wrote music. I wrote lyrics . . . '

Guest drew great inspiration from the documentary realism of films such as Jules Dassin's 1948 noir classic *The Naked City*, and he gained a reputation as a director who worked quickly and was very thoroughly prepared – an attribute which greatly appealed to Hammer, whose budgets were tight and who normally favoured a six week shooting schedule. As Guest remarked, 'any director that went into Hammer and started to come on set in the morning not having done his homework the night before would not be there again.' Assistant director Hugh Harlow, who worked on various films for the company at this time, including *Hell is a City*, said later of Val: 'He had a blackboard and easel. He'd be the first one on the set, wherever we were. He'd mark it up with all of his shots for the day. The entire crew could measure their day's progress by what was marked on the board.' Since Val was a director who usually also wrote his own scripts, it's perhaps not surprising that he exercised quite a lot of control and had a pretty good idea of what he was looking for in a film. For one thing, he knew that he certainly wanted Stanley Baker for the role of Martineau. Both actor and director had enjoyed working with each other on the film *Yesterday's Enemy*, and, although it wasn't until *Zulu* (1963) that Baker really became a top-rank bankable name, it was clear in 1959 that he was going places: 'I always believed Stanley had talent,' Guest told *Photoplay*'s Raymond Hyams during filming, 'and think he is enormous star material. At last he is getting the acknowledgement and praise he deserves. But his success has brought me one big worry. How long am I going to be able to afford him?'

Baker, a tough 31-year-old from the Welsh valleys who spent his spare time boxing with his friend, British heavyweight champion Henry Cooper, convincingly matched Procter's written descriptions of Martineau: 'He was a big, strong man, one of the most formidable of a thousand big men in the Granchester police' with 'hair so blond that the grey in it could hardly be discerned even in daylight.' 'I took the role of Martineau,' said Stanley at the time, 'because it's a damned interesting part to play. This cop is not a thug; nor is he a namby-pamby. He's just an ordinary policeman doing his job the best way he can, and worrying a bit about his private life which isn't going so well.' Baker was in fact so suited to the role that Michael Carreras admitted to the press that it was hard to pick an equally tough actor to play the role of Don Starling, saying, 'We had great difficulty in finding anyone else after casting him.' Luckily, help was at hand in the shape of Canadian actor John Crawford, who brought a genuine sense of menace to the part. Crawford later worked extensively in TV, clocking up appearances in *Mission: Impossible, Star Trek*, *Charlie's Angels* and the *Dukes of Hazzard*. He regularly played a Gestapo captain in the TV series *Hogan's Heroes*, but possibly far more terrifying is the nine years he spent as Sheriff Ep Bridges in *The Waltons*.

Donald Pleasence, a relative newcomer to films, was a natural for the role of Gus Hawkins, although he'd been seen most recently digging up or manufacturing corpses as part of that well-known Edinburgh double-act Burke and Hare, in John Gilling's *The Flesh & the Fiends* (1959). Oddly enough, Billie Whitelaw, who met a gruesome end in the latter film, was then chosen by Hammer to play opposite Pleasence as Gus Hawkins's promiscuous wife Chloe. Taking the part of Martineau's tempting 'young, childless divorcee', the barmaid Lucky Lusk, was actress Vanda Godsell, who comes across as more mature and worldly wise than the character as written in Procter's book, and, aged forty, was actually somewhat older than the woman playing Martineau's supposedly less-than-glamorous wife, Maxine Audley. Coincidentally, the two actresses had just spent the summer together appearing in a play called *All In the Family* at the Strand Theatre in London. The other key female role – that of Furnisher Steele's deaf mute daughter Silver, was taken by former model Sarah Branch, who also played Maid Marion to Peter Cushing's evil Sheriff of Nottingham in Hammer's *Sword of Sherwood Forest*, released the same year as *Hell is a City*. Unable to talk in the film, she had no such problems doing publicity: 'I don't like men who are so in love with me that they behave like insects,' she told *Picture Show & TV Mirror*. 'It makes me want to tread on them. I like them to be in love with me – but to be MEN about it!'

With the cast in place, Val Guest, in his customary dual role of scriptwriter and director, began adapting Procter's novel for the screen. Since the fictional city of Granchester is so obviously based on Manchester, the decision was taken to use its real name in the film, and to travel north for extensive location work in and around the city itself before returning to the Associated British Studios at Elstree for the interiors. Immediately prior to this, Guest had experienced difficulties when shooting in the streets of Soho for the film *Expresso Bongo* (1959), as he recalled in an interview while filming interiors for *Hell* at Elstree:

> Whenever a film company goes on location in London they are regarded more or less by the authorities as a nuisance and a major hindrance. It isn't like this in other parts of the country. I've just come back from Manchester and up there I had some simply marvellous co-operation in connection with scenes for *Hell is a City*.

This is reflected in the opening titles of the film, which begin with a credit acknowledging the 'full co-operation of the Chief Constable and the members of the Manchester City Police Force'. Hammer's publicity department issued a photo of Guest deep in consultation with Detective Sergeant Harold Newton apparently going over the finer points of the script at the film's pub location, *The Lacy Arms*, although the page at which they're both pointing contains a scene which was shot on a different set entirely. Genuine policemen were also brought in as film extras, and when shooting outdoors in the city centre, Val and his crew were allowed to temporarily stop the traffic, and succeeded in turning back time at one point, as *ABC Film Review* reported in an item headed *Clock Shock* in their January 1960 issue:

> For a sequence of a fight between Stanley Baker and John Crawford in sight of the huge clock towering above the Refuge Assurance Building, permission was sought and obtained to put the clock back four hours to coincide with film time. This caused some consternation, and people anxiously phoned the Refuge,

the police and the newspapers. But the sequence was filmed in half-an-hour and Manchester got back its Greenwich time.

However, all the advance publicity that the film received during shooting wasn't quite as favourable: Tom Hutchinson ran a short story in the 17 October issue of *Picturegoer* which claimed that 'Manchester wasn't too happy about Associated British's location trip to that city for the making of *Hell is a City* starring Stanley Baker . . . 'It'll put Manchester down as a grimy, dirty city,' say the local councillors . . . ' The film's publicists didn't necessarily help matters in this respect, as the opening paragraph of *Hell's* synopsis sheet put it:

> Manchester. The teeming, constantly moving capital of England's industrial north. Full of the harshness, dirt and smoke of a bustling, prosperous city, a city that never sleeps. A city full of people: some gay, some sad. And some . . . crooked.

Adapting any book into a screenplay always involves changes and simplifications, but in general it's remarkable how faithful Val Guest's script remained to Procter's source novel, and the casting was so effective that it's hard now to read the book and imagine most of the characters looking much different to their screen counterparts. The changes that occurred were generally minor, aimed at streamlining the narrative, or were made in deference to the censorship laws and the moral climate of the time. Whereas the book had the space in which to tell the story of Starling's earlier jewel heist and his shooting of a policeman two years before, none of this is really dealt with in the script. It's merely stated that he was in prison for armed robbery, and has now escaped, having 'slugged a warder getting out'. The injured man is said to be in a critical state – 'If he dies, it's murder'– whereas in the novel, Starling just quietly climbs over the prison wall, and is not even seen escaping. The two main pubs mentioned in Procter's book, *The Prodigal Son* and *The Lacy Arms,* are combined into one for the film, and given the name of the latter (although in reality the name of the bar where the scenes were shot was *The Fatted Calf*). Martineau's piano playing – his second-favourite method of relaxation, next to drinking, in the novel – disappears, as do various relatively unimportant characters such as Peter Purchas, a clerk in Gus Hawkins's office who signals from the window and tips off the robbers.

Slightly more significant were the changes relating to Furnisher Steele and his granddaughter. In the film, Steele's attic rather than the Royal Lancaster Hotel becomes the hiding place for Starling's stolen jewels, and Devery has never met Steele or Silver until he goes along to make routine murder enquires, whereas in the novel they have all known each other for a long time, and the policeman and the girl are due to be married shortly. Silver's death at the end of the book is one of several instances where, in the Britain of the late 1950s, the written word could afford to be more downbeat and less sentimental than a film. Although Silver is also wounded by Starling in the cinema version, when Martineau meets Devery during the closing scenes and asks after her, he's told: 'Oh, she's fine. They say she'll be sitting up before the end of the month.' Likewise, whereas a whole chapter of the novel is devoted to a blow-by-blow account of Starling's hanging, the film contents itself with a couple of shots of the exterior of the prison and the clock (echoing the way that such events were usually depicted in real-life newsreel footage), followed by a close up of Martineau's face.

In terms of sex, the film was pretty liberal for its time, in particular the scene in which Starling partially tears off Chloe's nightdress, as Val Guest remarked to the press during shooting: 'We have a new censor today. The Board have at last realised that if British films hope to stand a chance in the international market they must grow up. The new censor has really been a life saver.' Even so, unlike in the novel, Chloe and Starling are interrupted before they have the chance to sleep together, while at the film's end there is no hint of Martineau trying to pick up the whore who accosts him, nor in this version does he try to go off to sleep with Lucky Lusk. Crucially, she says she loves kids and wants lots of them: in the novel, Lucky's statement that she would never want kids is one of the main reasons why Martineau sobers up a little and goes home to his wife.

Filming had begun on 21 September 1959 and ended 5 November, and there was a considerable amount of publicity generated in the newspapers during that time and in the months leading up to the picture's UK release on 1 May 1960. Val Guest and Stanley Baker both gave the press a fair amount of access, and stories appeared which played up the latter's tough-guy image, such as an article in the 2 January 1960 issue of *Picturegoer*, entitled 'They All Want To Slug Baker', in which the actor explained how people would try to pick fights with him in public: 'It's getting so bad that I can seldom go into a pub and enjoy a pint. I don't know why it is, but usually when I go into a bar there's a character three sheets to the wind who's seen me on the screen.' The cover of that same issue of *Picturegoer* featured the previously unknown actress from *Hell is a City* who played the streetwalker in the closing scene of the film: 'Delyse Humphreys does NOT want to be a film star,' the magazine reassured its readers. 'She says that her ambition is either to be a television hostess or an advertising model.'

The film was given a trade show on 11 March 1960, and then on 7 April, in between listings for *Hell Bent For Leather* and *Heller in Pink Tights, Kine Weekly* announced the forthcoming release of *Hell is a City,* summing up its 'Box Office Angle' as 'Manhunt. British box office red meat'. On 10 April the film had a special northern charity premiere (enlivened by the Manchester Police Band) at the Apollo, Ardwick, where it went on to break the house records for receipts. The London premiere was held at the Warner Theatre, Leicester Square, and celebrities such as Diane Cilento, Millicent Martin, and *Brides of Dracula's* Yvonne Monlaur were duly photographed by *Kine Weekly*, mingling with Val Guest, Michael Carreras, the film's composer Stanley Black and cast members Vanda Godsell, Maxine Audley, Joby Blanshard and Geoffrey Frederick.

For Hammer, a company whose massive public success had generally been accompanied by some of the most mean-spirited, pompous and downright snotty reviews of their era, the critical response to *Hell is a City* must have come as a welcome surprise. *What's On in London* called the film 'a very well made, fast-moving and always gripping British crime thriller, directed with style by Val Guest', while *Variety* judged it to be a 'great police yarn with authentic backgrounds, taut screenplay and first class performances', but commented that 'local dialect may fall a bit strangely on the ears of foreigners', and that 'two or three of the more salty bits of dialog in Guest's fast-moving screenplay have been trimmed for US consumption'. Even the normally scathing *Films & Filming*, while reassuring their readership that 'Hammer Films have not sullied their record by producing a work of art,' were unusually complimentary about the script, the direction and the 'bold and vivid exterior photography' which 'result in a work, derivative though it may be, that is undeniably tense and exciting'. Several pages later, however, in a review of the same company's *Never Take Sweets From a Stranger*, they returned to form, accusing Hammer's 'assembly line' of churning out films 'dealing only in the lurid and the loathsome' and claiming that 'only an exceptionally sick society could possibly want and tolerate such films'.

By June 1960 the picture was doing very healthy business across the UK, and also fared well in November when released in the US, although it's probably safe to assume that whichever poster artist was responsible for the classic New York-style skyscrapers adorning the American publicity material had most likely never actually seen a photograph of Manchester. Arrow Books reissued Procter's novel in a movie edition, complete with a shot of Stanley Baker on the back cover.

Despite an announcement in the trade journal *Today's Cinema* that Val Guest had signed a new four-picture deal with Hammer, *Hell is a City* turned out to be almost the end of his association with the company. However, working for another studio the following year, he took the documentary newsreel technique which he had perfected in *Hell* and delivered the equally impressive sci-fi thriller, *The Day the Earth Caught Fire*. In his autobiography, *So You Want to Be in Pictures?*, published in 2001, Val Guest writes that *Hell is a City* has 'always been in my top four', but unfortunately says almost nothing else about the film. Back in 1978, when asked by *Little Shoppe of Horrors* magazine to name his favourites among his own films, he replied, 'I have three; one is *Yesterday's Enemy*, the other is *Expresso Bongo* and *The Day the Earth Caught Fire*,' which would seem to place *Hell* in fourth position. Certainly, during a fascinating career that has stretched all the way from 1930s comedies like *Oh, Mr Porter* (1937) via the *Quatermass* films and *Casino Royale* (1966) to 1970s softcore romps such as *Au Pair Girls* (1972) and *Confessions of a Window Cleaner* (1974), Guest has always spoken highly of the picture.

Hammer had plans to bring further adaptations of Procter's Martineau novels to the screen, and *Hell's* début showing on British TV in the mid-1960s also prompted enquiries from various companies interested in developing it into a series for the small screen, with Baker reprising his role as Martineau, but nothing came of these proposals.

With the arrival of video and then DVD, and the general shift in critical attitudes towards Hammer films in the last decade, *Hell is a City* has gained an increasing amount of respect, and even merited a limited theatrical re-release in the UK in 1997. The novel, like the rest of Procter's output, seems to have so far avoided the reissue programmes of modern-day crime book publishers, which is surprising, given the authenticity of their settings and the light which they shed on the criminal subculture of a now vanished post-war England. Both novel and film, although obviously designed as entertainment, display a hard-bitten, matter-of-fact attitude and hold up far better than some of the more escapist products of their era. In bringing the story to the screen, Guest's adaptation benefited greatly from some first-rate acting and Arthur Grant's fluid, understated monochrome photography, while the story is driven relentlessly along by crisp editing and Stanley Black's edgy, jazz-tinged score. If it were an American-made noir of the same era, it would probably already be regarded as a classic of its kind.

'Violent, first rate', said the *London Evening News*. How right they were.

Psycho

A new – and altogether different – screen excitement!!!

Film: Psycho
Director: Alfred Hitchcock
Leading players: Anthony Perkins, Janet Leigh, Vera Miles, John Gavin
Year of release: 1960

Book: Psycho
Author: Robert Bloch
Year of publication: 1959

Real-life criminal: Ed Gein
Active: Late 1940s-1957, Wisconsin, USA

Psycho changed everything. Until then, crime films were usually content to depict violence and sudden death on the cinema screen with a certain discretion. Bullets generally left neat holes, caused limited blood-loss and their capacity for spreading a victim's brains all over the furniture was not something dwelt upon by any film-maker hopeful of getting his finished product past the censors. Even in a classic hardboiled *noir* such as *The Big Heat* (1953), where the sadism and brutality of Lee Marvin's character is very effectively shown by means of the scalding pot of coffee which he throws into Gloria Grahame's face, the full horror of the moment is more implied than seen. By 1967, when Faye Dunaway and Warren Beatty are blasted all over the screen with a case of acute lead poisoning at the end of *Bonnie and Clyde*, it was clear that the boundaries of acceptable cinematic violence had changed dramatically. In between those two films, lay *Psycho*, a low-budget, monochrome robbery-and-murder thriller which rewrote the rulebook to such an extent that even its own director had little clear idea where to go next.

Released in 1960, Hitchcock's charming tale of one boy's love for his mother unleashed a tidal wave of films in its wake which continues right up to the present day. *Scream, The Silence of the Lambs, A Nightmare on Elm Street, Halloween, The Texas Chainsaw Massacre, Repulsion* – these are just some of the better known examples, but none of these or *Psycho* itself would be quite the same were it not for the activities of a shy Wisconsin farmer who died of respiratory failure in a geriatric ward in 1984 aged seventy-eight. His name was Ed Gein. As the contemporary joke went:

Q. What did Ed Gein say to the sheriff who arrested him?
A. Have a heart.

The issue of *Life* magazine for 2 December 1957 carried the usual news from home and abroad: Khrushchev celebrating the 40th anniversary of the Bolshevik revolution, the fashion for wearing the Hawaiian *muumuu* sweeping college campuses and a novelty item about English eccentrics including the nineteenth century philosopher Jeremy Bentham, who had himself embalmed and displayed in the common room of University College London. Burial, he claimed, was a silly, wasteful act. A good corpse 'could be put to sundry uses'. One man who would certainly have agreed with that sentiment occupied eight pages of that same issue of the magazine in a story entitled 'House Of Horror Stuns The Nation'. Ed Gein had such a fondness for corpses that he dug them up late at night from local graveyards and took them home to play. Inspired by pulp magazines such as *Startling Detective* and accounts of cannibalism in the South Seas he would strip off the face and scalp from each skull, taking care to preserve the skin with oils. Padding it out with rolled up newspaper he would hang up the faces on the walls of his home, but he later explained to investigators that some of them were designed to be worn as masks. He made distinctive, flesh-toned leggings from, well, pieces of flayed leg, and wore the entire upper torso of a woman as a kind of apron. Sometimes, at night, he would venture outside the door of his remote farmhouse dressed in the whole ensemble and dance around in the moonlight.

Gein's extreme tastes in the fields of home decorating and leisurewear came to light as police investigated the sudden disappearance of 50-year-old Bernice Worden, who ran the local hardware store in the small town of Plainfield, Wisconsin. Her son Frank had returned from a deer hunting expedition to find evidence of a violent break-in. It being the opening day of the hunting season, most people were out in the woods blasting away at anything that moved, but Frank recalled that Ed Gein had specifically asked Bernice if she would be open that day since he'd be calling in to buy some anti-freeze. Fifty-one-year-old Gein was arrested on suspicion at the house of a neighbour, and two policemen went out to search his decaying old farm buildings. What they found sent them straight back outside, retching uncontrollably.

The headless body of Bernice Worden was discovered in Ed's summer kitchen at the rear of the farmhouse, hung up by the heels and 'dressed out like a deer'. Her head was later discovered in a sack in the corner, her heart in a plastic bag in front of the stove, and a pile of entrails wrapped up in an old suit on the floor. Inside the main house, amidst an incredible litter of decaying food, trashy magazines, collections of used chewing gum and a sink filled with sand were found soup bowls made from the sawn-off tops of skulls, a belt of nipples, a shoebox containing noses and another of genitalia – indeed, so many body parts that it was impossible to tell how many people's remains were there. Much of the furniture had been hand made in imitation of the kind favoured by Ilse Koch, the infamous 'she-wolf' of the SS. Lampshades, a tom-tom, bracelets and a wastebasket were all covered in human skin, as were the seats of four straight-backed chairs. By contrast, the rooms in the house which had belonged to Ed's mother, who had been dead since 1945, were just as she'd left them, since Gein had long ago boarded them shut.

Life magazine merely hinted at these details, but even at that stage they were quoting psychiatrists who speculated that Gein had 'a schizophrenic or split personality'. They pointed to the influence of Ed's mother Augusta, 'a strong-minded woman who believed all other women were sinful'. There were suspicions that the two women Gein had actually confessed to murdering – Bernice Worden and local bar-owner Mary Hogan – had been selected for their supposed physical resemblance to his dead mother. Townspeople told stories to reporters of shy Eddie Gein the local handyman, always willing to help out fixing a fence or doing a spot of babysitting. Older children would sit enthralled as he told them tales of cannibalism, and his house was said to be haunted. Most of their parents just thought he was a couple of cans short of a six-pack but about as harmless as they come. Eventually, in the face of overwhelming evidence, they began to view him as a cunning and devious killer, but the police and psychiatrists questioning him felt that he hadn't really got the slightest idea what all the fuss was about.

The local community, besieged by the national and international media, were further outraged by the news that many of the bodies were not those of murder victims but had been stolen from local graveyards. There were even unsubstantiated rumours that he cooked and ate parts of his victims, but the psychiatrist's report of 13 December stated that 'eating is denied. He also denied having sex relations with the bodies or parts of them as he declares the odour was offensive.' As one Plainfield resident bitterly remarked, 'Halloween came a little late this year.' Several graves were opened and found to be empty, and a forty foot trench was discovered on his property filled with human remains, together with an ash heap where unwanted body parts had been cremated. The true extent of his activities will never be known.

Found clinically insane and unfit to stand trial for murder, Ed was locked up for life in a secure institution. Measured against the popular view of America in the 1950s in which grinning two-car families enjoy all the innocent pleasures that life has to offer and *never* run out of petrol, these events seem barely credible. How could a middle-aged bachelor live for years in the middle of a tiny community in a house piled high with corpses, making odd jokes about embalming to his fellow workers, without anyone noticing? As Max von Sydow's arch-cynic in *Hannah and Her Sisters* (1986) comments after watching yet another documentary about the Nazi death camps, 'The reason they can never answer the question 'How can it possibly happen?' is that it's the wrong question. Given what people are, the question is 'Why doesn't it happen more often?'" In World War Two during the bitter fighting for islands in the South Pacific, US troops would collect the heads of Japanese soldiers as trophies, proudly holding them up for visiting news photographers. As for the good old peace and love vibes of the 1960s, here's a veteran talking to the writer Mark Baker in 1981: 'We had a thing in Nam. We used to cut their ears off. If a guy had a necklace of ears he was a good killer. It was encouraged to cut the ears off, to cut a nose off, to cut a guy's penis off. The officers expected you to do it or something was wrong with you.' These were ordinary 18-year-olds straight out of school, and that was the scariest thing about Ed Gein, his seeming normality.

One man who followed every newspaper article about the Gein case as it unfolded in 1957 was a moderately successful thriller writer called Robert Bloch, who at the time was living some forty miles away in rural Wisconsin. 'There was talk on the radio station about digging up graves,' recalled Bloch. 'I was amazed that Gein could conduct himself without anyone suspecting the truth. I said, 'There's a *story* here.' Writers, for the most part, didn't do gross things in those days. You could zing the reader with one line, then get out.' Few, if any, publishers would have dared print a novel which contained even half of what Ed Gein had actually done, and so Bloch used the basic facts as a springboard for the first draft of a tight little crime thriller called *Psycho* which he produced over a six week stretch in 1958. 'The story basically wrote itself,' he said. 'I came up with his being a motel keeper because of easy access to strangers. I thought, what if he committed these crimes in an amnesiac fugue with another personality taking over? Let's say he has a thing about his mother.

Let's suppose his mother was dead, but he imagined she was still alive – that he *became* his mother while committing the crimes. Then I thought, 'But wouldn't it be nice if she was actually present in some form?' And that is when I came up with the notion that he had actually preserved her body.'

Many of these details have such close parallels with Ed Gein's own life that it's hard to know where the facts finish and Bloch's fiction takes over. There's no evidence that Gein ever disturbed his own mother's grave, or practised taxidermy, but he did preserve body parts. Gein also told psychiatrists that he could not remember any details of the murder of Bernice Worden 'although he admits that he must have been the one who did this'. He claimed to have heard his mother talking to him for about a year after she died, and felt that 'she was good in every way'. In reality she had been a fearsome, bible-quoting tyrant who dominated his every waking hour and warned him to stay away from the women of the town, who were harlots and sinners.

The Norman Bates that Bloch created was a middle-aged, overweight, balding misfit of a man – a far cry from the teen pin-up Anthony Perkins who that year was denting the top twenty with a winsome little number called *Moonlight Swim*. The real master-stroke of the novel however was the early demise of the main female character.

> It occurred to me to do something not generally done in fiction: establish a heroine, give her a problem, make her more or less likeable so that the reader would have some kind of empathy for her, then kill her off about one third of the way through the story. Readers would say, 'My God, *now what?*'.

The method of despatch was Bloch's other trump card: 'I had a notion that a person is never more defenceless than when taking a shower . . . a sudden intrusion is a *very* shocking thing.'

Psycho was published in the summer of 1959 by Simon & Schuster, enjoying healthy sales and reasonably kind reviews, not least from Anthony Boucher in the *New York Times Book Review*. Advance copies had been sent out in February to film companies, but the book was turned down by Paramount's script reader William Pinckard as being 'Too repulsive for films, and rather shocking even to a hardened reader.' However, according to Hitchcock's personal assistant Peggy Robertson, he picked up on the book by himself. 'Every Monday morning Hitch and I used to read the *New York Times Book Review*, and this one Monday, Hitch said, 'Boucher is raving about this book, *Psycho*." The rights were eventually secured in an anonymous bid via MCA for just $9,000. In the words of Bloch's friend Harlan Ellison, 'He got screwed royally.'

At that time in his career Hitchcock was one of the most famous directors in the business, and his recent productions had been glossy Technicolor spectaculars featuring the likes of Cary Grant, Grace Kelly and James Stewart. His characters were either dripping with diamonds or scaling the face of Mount Rushmore, and so the last thing that anyone expected of him was a tightly-shot, monochrome, low-budget crime story about a transvestite, peeping-tom killer who keeps the decomposing corpse of his mother down in the basement and stuffs birds in his spare time. Which is precisely why it appealed to Hitch.

Since October 1955 the director had been presiding over a wildly popular TV series called *Alfred Hitchcock Presents*, a series of black and white thrillers which he would personally introduce, and occasionally direct. The idea of shooting an inexpensive film in a matter of weeks, using most of his regular TV technicians, appealed to him after years of lavish productions. He had noticed that some of the biggest box office successes of the last few years had been relatively inexpensive shockers such as Hammer's *The Curse of Frankenstein*, which had opened in New York one weekend in 1957 during a freak heatwave to packed houses at a time when most other cinemas were deserted. There was also the example of Henri-Georges Clouzot's *Les Diaboliques* (1954), which was based on a novel by Pierre Boileau and Thomas Narcejac that Hitchcock himself had tried to buy. When he failed, he bought another book by the same team which formed the basis for *Vertigo* (1958). Clouzot's film was a psychological thriller that leads the viewer down the garden path to a killer twist ending. 'Hitch talked about being a big fan of *Les Diaboliques*,' said Anthony Perkins. 'It was one of the reasons he wanted to make *Psycho* in black and white.'

As the film rights to Bloch's novel were being snapped up in the spring of 1959, Perkins was six years into his film career as one of the many young leading men who'd been touted as 'the new James Dean'. A series of less than ideal roles, together with the strain of pretending to be straight during years when he'd allegedly spent much of his time in the arms of Tab Hunter meant that he was more than receptive to a friend's advice: 'How about a course of psychotherapy?' For Tony, that was only the beginning of a lifetime of analysis, and indeed, each day when he got up in the morning to play Norman Bates he would visit his therapist for an early morning consultation before going on to the studio. It might be thought that for such a private person, who was firmly in the closet, and well known for romantic leading roles, to take on the role of a transvestite killer in Hollywood in 1959 would be tantamount to career suicide, but Perkins jumped at the chance. He had turned down a part in *Some Like It Hot* (1959) mainly on account of the cross-dressing involved and he wasn't about to make the same mistake twice.

Janet Leigh at that time formed half of one of Hollywood's golden couples, and with her husband Tony Curtis she was seen around town at all the right parties and fundraising shindigs for JFK. The sight of her in the opening shots of *Psycho* in her underwear meeting up with a married man during her lunchbreak was, by the standards of the time, deeply shocking. Carving her up with a butcher knife some twenty minutes later was absolutely unthinkable. 'The thing that appealed to me [about the book] and made me decide to do the picture,' said Hitchcock to François Truffaut, 'was the suddenness of the murder in the shower, coming, as it were, out of the blue. That was about all.' By 1962, when this interview took place, Hitchcock was evidently in no mood to praise Robert Bloch's novel, and played down the sensational aspects of the Gein case, commenting only: 'It was the story of a man who kept his mother's body in his house, somewhere in Wisconsin.'

Joseph Stefano was brought in to adapt Bloch's book for the screen, making Norman a somewhat more sympathetic character and giving more prominence to the Leigh role at the start of the picture, and Bernard Herrmann was contracted to write the groundbreaking score which relied entirely upon strings. Over the years the film itself has been analysed so often that many conflicting stories have emerged, the main area of dispute being the shower scene. Saul Bass, the absolute master of Hollywood title design, is given an extra credit as 'Pictorial Consultant'. No one disputes that he drew out the storyboards for the scene, but in a 1973 interview Bass was quoted claiming that he had directed the entire sequence. This has been emphatically denied by just about every member of the crew, and by Janet Leigh who said, 'I was in that shower for seven days, and Alfred Hitchcock was right next to his camera for every one of those shots.' Assistant Director Hilton Green commented, 'There is not a shot in that movie I didn't roll my camera for, and I can tell you I never rolled the camera for Mr Bass.' Given the number of people worldwide who developed a distrust of showers after viewing the film, it's interesting to note that Janet Leigh has suffered from a similar phobia ever since seeing her first screening. 'If there is no other way to bathe, then I make sure all of the doors and windows in the house are locked, and I leave the bathroom door and the shower curtain open so I have a perfect, clear view. I face the door no matter where the showerhead is. The room, I might add, gets very wet.' Ever since playing that role she has received obscene phonecalls and occasional death threats, which she passes on to the FBI.

Psycho, or Production # 9401 as it was known, was shot between 11 November 1959 and 1 February 1960 for a total cost of $806,947, during which time Hitchcock had enormous fun playing games with the press and teasing them about exactly what was going on behind the virtual news blackout on his closed set, and refusing, at first, even to tell them the title of the film. Soon, a journalist revealed that it was to be called *Psyche*, prompting speculation that Hitch was making a picture based on the myths of Ancient Greece. Once the real title was revealed, it was even rumoured that he had attempted to buy up all available copies of Robert Bloch's book in order to prevent the film's plot-twists from becoming known. Mostly, he contented himself with saying that he was filming the story of a 'young man whose mother is a homicidal maniac'. Once it was known that Anthony Perkins was to play the young man, the director then bandied around names such as Helen Hayes and Judith Anderson as possible candidates for the role of Tony's mother. It then emerged that he would be filming a scene in which a young woman is murdered in a shower, and his response was reported in the 27 December 1959 edition of the *New York Times* as follows:

> Queried about possible censorship problems with this intimate homicide, Mr Hitchcock pouted through petulant lips, 'Men do kill nude women, you know.'

Psycho was released on 16 June 1960 by an unwilling studio to decidedly sniffy reviews from the critics, in part perhaps because Hitchcock had been so 'unco-operative' during production and had antagonized them by refusing to do press screenings and warning them not to reveal the ending. 'A blot on an honourable career,' said Bosley Crowther in the *New York Times*, although he later revised his opinion. 'What a creepie it is,' whined *Picture Show & TV Mirror*. '*Psycho* is really *Sicko*,' while *Esquire* snubbed it as 'merely one of those television shows padded out to two hours by adding pointless subplots and realistic detail'. Cinemagoers, for the first time, were not allowed into the auditorium after the main feature had started, which was thought by many in the trade to be lunacy. In the event, *Psycho* was a colossal hit with the public worldwide, although it failed to win a single Oscar, and Anthony Perkins wasn't even nominated for his portrayal of Norman. Nevertheless, it was the number two moneymaking US film of 1960, pulling in $8,500,000, second only to the remake of *Ben-Hur*, which had cost many times more to produce. Hitchcock complained in interviews that people failed to see the humour in the film, and the money he made from having bankrolled it set him up for life. Tony Perkins went to Europe for five years to work with a string of distinguished directors – including a particularly fine performance as Josef K in Orson Welles's adaptation of Kafka's *The Trial* (1962), shot in Paris in the disused Gare d'Orsay – but was forever haunted by the role of Norman. Speaking to Robin Bean in 1965 about his post-*Psycho* career, he called the role 'one of the greatest gambles I've taken because if that picture hadn't worked, if the public's acceptance of the role hadn't been as complete as it was, it might have been a very disadvantageous thing for an actor to play'. Nevertheless, he was keen to play down the supposedly terrifying effects of the movie:

> Luckily, I think that most of the people who saw the picture enjoyed it in a very good, warm-hearted way. When they were frightened, they were pleased that they were frightened. When I meet people on the street and they talk about *Psycho*, it is always with a smile, with the pleasure of seeing it. Not with the kind of creepy horror that they were scared in a neurotic way by it.

Perkins went on to reprise the role of Norman twice more on film and another time on television before his death in 1992. Shortly before his appearance in *Psycho IV: The Beginning* (1991, scripted by Joseph Stefano), he even appeared as Norman Bates in a TV commercial for breakfast cereal, yelling 'See, Mother? I'm eating my oatmeal!'

Film companies the world over immediately jumped on the bandwagon, in particular Hammer, whose *Taste of Fear* began principal photography in October 1960 and owed an equal debt to *Psycho* and to *Les Diaboliques*. In quick succession the company followed this with *Maniac* (1963), *Paranoiac* (1963), *Nightmare* (1964), *Fanatic* (1965), *Hysteria* (1965) and *Crescendo* (1969), moving *Films & Filming*'s reviewer to remark that 'according to Roget's Thesaurus we can still expect to see *Auto-, Dipso-, Klepto-, Megalo-, Mono-* and *Pyro-maniac* . . . ' Longtime shockmeister William Castle was equally quick off the mark in 1961 with *Homicidal*, which gleefully pillaged large parts of the storyline from *Psycho* and features a decidedly familiar cross-dressing killer. Three years later Castle would employ Robert Bloch himself to script *Strait-Jacket* (1964), in which Joan Crawford has a terrible time with all manner of sharp instruments.

Bloch, like Perkins, never really escaped from the shadow of Norman Bates for the rest of his career, and was justifiably upset at the way all the credit seemed to be given to screenwriter Joseph Stefano or to Hitchcock, 'the inference being that he introduced all the things that seemed to make the film work – killing the heroine early in the story, killing her off in the shower, taxidermy – when, of course, they're all in the book'. Many years later Stefano said:

> We didn't feel we were doing anything outstandingly different, or that it would be a kind of seminal film. And yet all of us were affected by it. The problem that we all had was that it was very difficult to ever top that. It's always difficult when you do a film that is destined someday to become a classic, and is also as phenomenally successful as *Psycho* was; you can't get that kind of smash again. Very few people do. Orson Welles never did. Hitch never had that kind of hit again.

The gradual relaxation of film censorship laws meant that the 70s proved to be the real heyday of the slasher movie, but there's no doubt that Hitchcock with this one film had permanently re-drawn the map of what was permissible. The guardians of taste and decency were predictably outraged at the time, and various horrible slayings were alleged to have taken place after the killers had watched *Psycho*. When questioned about this, Hitchcock merely asked what should be done if it were discovered that before committing murder they had also drunk a glass of milk.

It's not known whether Ed Gein ever saw Hitchcock's film, or knew of its existence. He spent the rest of his life in secure mental institutions, where, although he had an unnerving habit of staring fixedly at any female nurses on the premises, he was generally regarded as a model prisoner. Finally, in 1984, he made one last visit to Plainfield Cemetery, in the middle of the night, when they buried him next to his mother.

Point Blank

There Are Two Kinds of People in His Up-Tight World,
His Victims and His Women. And Sometimes You Can't Tell Them Apart.

Film: Point Blank
Director: John Boorman
Leading players: Lee Marvin, Angie Dickinson, Keenan Wynn,
Carroll O'Connor
Year of release: 1967

Book: The Hunter
Author: Richard Stark (Donald E Westlake)
Year of publication: 1962

1967 was a good year for violence. To judge from the fuss stirred up by the press, cinema screens were becoming ever more awash with gore and brutality as all manner of depravity was flung at the blood-hungry public. Corpses littered the sound-stages, drilled full of lead in glorious Technicolor by hombres with handguns in the slowest of slow-motion, and the audiences couldn't get enough of it. Forget the war in Vietnam (which you could see live and twitching on the TV news every night around dinnertime), or the inner-city rioting in places such as Detroit – these Hollywood homicides were the *real* problem. And which star, according to *Motion Picture Herald's* top ten list of box office heavyweights, loomed over all the others in this year of sadism, explosions and carnage? Lock up your children, bolt the doors and be very, very afraid – it was ol' Mary Poppins herself, Julie Andrews . . .

Actually, the former singing nun may have been at the top of the heap that year, but the other nine heavy-duty stars below her included some pretty macho marquee names: Steve McQueen was at number 10, while Big John Wayne came in at number 8, and even Sean *James Bond* Connery only made number 5. Riding high at number 2, however, just below Julie, was a man who wouldn't have got within a hundred miles of such a list a mere five years before, and whose appearance in a 1967 film during which he doesn't actually kill anyone at all stirred up acres of newsprint about celluloid brutality. The film was *Point Blank*. The man was Lee Marvin, and for a while there, he *was* violence on the screen.

The character played by Marvin in *Point Blank* is such a perfect piece of casting that it could almost have been written with him in mind, and yet, when Pocket Books published a paperback original in 1962 called *The Hunter*, by Richard Stark, the actor was few people's idea of a leading man. Although Lee had a well established career as one of the ultimate screen hard men dating back to his renowned coffee-flinging appearance in *The Big Heat* (1953) and his supremely sleazy turn as the daddy of all bikers in *The Wild One* (1953), it was ironically a comedy role as the permanently-soused gunfighter in *Cat Ballou* (1965) which brought him one of those gold statuettes and the attention of the world. Perfect casting though Marvin may have been, the inspiration for Richard Stark's cold-blooded, relentless anti-hero in his 1962 novel was in fact mostly derived from a simple walk across the George Washington Bridge.

The name Richard Stark concealed the identity of Donald E Westlake, whose first novel, *The Mercenaries,* had appeared in 1960 after nearly a decade of solid work for a variety of pulp magazines such as *Rogue, Manhunt* and *Mystery Digest*. Westlake was born in Brooklyn in 1933 and had done time in the US Air Force, but, ever since he'd read Dashiell Hammett's *The Thin Man* at the age of fourteen, he knew that he just had to become a writer. He told Joe Hartlaub:

> My father wanted me to be an architect. The one thing I learned was that the kitchen and bathroom should be near each other, to simplify the plumbing. Nothing about it interested me. Or about anything else, except making up stories.

In general, Westlake's work for the pulps had been published under his real name, but a few of his short stories, such as 'The Ledge Bit' (*Mystery Digest,* September 1959) and 'The Curious Facts Preceding My Execution' (*Alfred Hitchcock's Mystery Magazine*, September 1960) he had written as Richard Stark. Westlake later explained the origin of this name, in his 1981 introduction to a reprint of *The Hunter*: 'Richard, from Richard Widmark in *Kiss of Death* (1947), and *Stark*, because I wanted a name/word that meant stripped-down, without decoration.' He'd also used other pseudonyms, for instance, on the odd occasions when he wrote softcore novels such as *Campus Doll* (1961), which was signed with the name Edwin West. However, at the time that the idea for *The Hunter* suggested itself to him, Westlake was half way through writing a hardback novel for Random House entitled *361* (1962), 'in which

117

no emotion would ever be stated; only the physical side-effects of emotion would be described.' Feeling that he also had a story outline that would suit a paperback imprint like Gold Medal, and attracted by the notion of having two names and two publishers simultaneously – one for hardbacks, one for paperbacks – he interrupted work on *361* to develop the idea he'd had while walking across the George Washington Bridge:

> I'd been visiting a friend about 30 miles upstate from New York, and had taken a bus back to the city. However, I'd chosen the wrong bus, one that terminated on the New Jersey side of the bridge instead of the New York side (where I could catch my subway). So I walked across the bridge, surprised at how windy it was out there (when barely windy at all anywhere else) and at how much the apparently solid bridge shivered and swung from the wind and the pummelling of the traffic. There was speed in the cars going by, vibration in the bridge under my feet, tension in the whole atmosphere.
>
> Riding downtown in the subway I slowly began to evolve in my mind the character who was *right* for that setting, whose own speed and solidity and tension matched that of the bridge.

The character that emerged, he named Parker, and the emotionless experiments of *361* clearly had something of an effect on his development. 'I saw him as looking something like Jack Palance, and I wondered: Why is he walking across the bridge? Not because he took the wrong bus. Because he's angry. Not hot angry; cold angry.'

Having defined Parker – the professional heist-merchant, always in control of himself, and able to kill with his bare hands if the situation seemed to warrant it – Westlake wrote a tight, stripped-down crime novel around him and pitched it at Gold Medal, who promptly rejected it. At this point, fate stepped in, in the shape of an editor at Pocket Books called Bucklyn Moon, who not only liked the book, but also the character of Parker in particular. Seeing the opportunity for a series, he requested that Westlake rewrite the ending, so that instead of dying in a final shoot-out with the cops, as the first draft had it, Parker would live to re-appear in a succession of sequels. Eventually, Westlake agreed, and fixed things so that his anti-hero could turn the tables right at the last minute, score a bundle of greenbacks and head for the hills, thus paving the way for one of the most highly-regarded series of hardboiled crime novels of them all.

The Hunter opens with the solitary figure of Parker walking across the same New York bridge which inspired his creator, refusing a lift in spite of the filthy weather, spitting occasionally at passing cars and heading towards town with a fixed purpose and vengeance on his mind:

> His hands, swinging curve-fingered at his sides, looked like they were moulded of brown clay by a sculptor who thought big and liked veins. His hair was brown and dry and dead, blowing around his head like a poor toupee about to fly loose. His face was a chipped chunk of concrete, with eyes of flawed onyx. His mouth was a quick stroke, bloodless.

Having been double-crossed, shot and left for dead by his wife and his partners in crime, Parker has killed a guard escaping from prison, and although penniless at the start of the novel, he swiftly cons a bank into giving him access to a complete stranger's account which he then milks dry in an afternoon, thus gaining the funds with which to begin the hunt for his betrayers.

Parker had been part of a team which had travelled to a small island in the South Pacific in order to hijack ninety-three thousand dollars in cash which a group of South American revolutionaries were due to hand over to some arms dealers. The hijack team kill everybody else involved, on both sides of the transaction, but then they turn on each other, at the instigation of gang member Mal Resnick, who wants the whole bundle for himself in order to pay back some mobsters. Having forced Parker's wife Lynn to apparently fill her husband full of lead, Mal escapes from the island, taking her along with him, leaving behind the corpses of other gang members Ryan, Chester and Sill. Parker, however, is not quite as dead as they think he is:

> It was his buckle that saved him. Her first shot had hit the buckle, mashing it into his flesh. The gun had jumped in her hand, the next five shots all going over his falling body and into the wood of the door. But she'd fired six shots at him, and she'd seen him fall, and she couldn't believe that he was anything but dead.

All through the book, Parker has the advantage over people, since they mostly start out from the assumption that he's been dead for over a year. Lynn tells him she's been dreaming about him every night, all about 'how you're dead. And I wish it was me.' Parker, not exactly the soul of forgiveness, simply tells her to 'take too many pills,' which in fact she does, shortly afterwards, but not before she's heard her husband explain the plans he has for his old pal Mal Resnick:

> 'I'm going to drink his blood,' he said. 'I'm going to chew up his heart and spit it into the gutter for dogs to raise a leg at. I'm going to peel the skin off him and rip out his veins and hang him with them.'

The above speech is about as emotional as Parker gets. Mostly he's calm, in control of himself, and merely concerned with doing whatever will best serve his purpose at the time. This includes dragging his dead wife's body out into the park and carving up her face with a knife to avoid her identification by the police, and casually endangering the life of a hooker called Wanda who gives him information about Mal's whereabouts, and who then has to pack and leave town immediately or else the mob would kill her. As for Parker's reaction when the office worker he has bound and gagged accidentally chokes to death during his stakeout observation of the syndicate hotel across the street, he is merely annoyed – 'He didn't like it. It was stupid.' Any way you look at it, this is *not* a nice guy. As Westlake explained, since he had originally intended to kill Parker off at the end of the book: 'I gave him none of the softnesses you're supposed to give a series character, and no band of sidekicks to chat with, because he was going to pound through one book and goodbye.' Nevertheless, the writer found himself with a liking for the character, and the attraction probably lies in the utter certainty he displays in the face of all events. No matter what is thrown at him, Parker survives, often just by using his bare hands, like some kind of modern-day Conan the Barbarian (with shorter hair and a better tailor). While he might not be the most talkative person around, he still has a winning way with words, as when threatening crooked used-car dealer Arthur Stegman, who is part of the chain that leads him from his ex-wife to Mal Resnick:

> She's dead. So is your fat pansy. You can be dead too, if you want.

It may not be poetry, but it seems to get results. In the book, Parker's prime concerns are revenge and the hunt for Mal Resnick. Certainly, he's aware of the share of the heist money that has been taken from him, but this is not originally his main motivation:

> He wanted Mal Resnick – he wanted him between his hands. Not the money back. Not Lynn back. Just Mal, between his hands.

Resnick, a sleazebag of a mobster who likes to call his sidekicks 'Sweetie,' has double-crossed Parker in order to pay back a large debt to the organization. He's a step above the rank-and-file hoods, but, much in the manner of large corporations, there are many levels of bosses above him, and when it becomes clear that Parker is alive, Resnick appeals to these people for help. Sensing that Mal's problems might be bad for business, they throw him to the wolves in a manner that any corporate downsizer might admire: 'We have three possible choices,' says Fred Carter, the highest-level mob boss that Mal has been able to reach. 'Assist you, leave you to your own devices, or eliminate you from the organization. For the moment I think we will pursue number two.'

Soon, Mal is pushing up the daisies, but only after having told Parker that the mob has been given his half-share of the loot – forty-five thousand dollars. Parker strangles Resnick, having learnt where to find the next man in the chain. From this point onwards, he is taking on the whole organization.

'Tell your boss the guy who killed Mal Resnick is here,' he says to the gunman guarding Fred Carter's office. Once inside, he's equally direct: 'You people have forty-five thousand dollars of my money. You'll give it to me.'

In some ways, this behaviour is reminiscent of Mike Hammer's one-man war against the Mafia in Spillane's *Kiss Me, Deadly* (1952), except that there's no hatred involved, and no moral position being taken about good and evil – it's a business debt, pure and simple. (In spirit, though, Parker's character is much closer to that of hitman Johnny Colini in John McParland's 1959 mob novel *The Kingdom of Johnny Cool*, who moves through the book knocking off high-ranking Outfit leaders with cold efficiency.) By killing one person after another, and, more importantly, by threatening the profit margins of this illegal business empire, Parker eventually persuades the mob to come up with the money, even if they do make multiple attempts to assassinate him during the handover. Even the cash itself doesn't seem quite as important as the principle involved. As Parker sees it, the money that Resnick gave them was rightfully his, and so he wants it returned. That he might be up against a powerful force with representatives across the country still seems no reason for him to back down:

> The funnies call it the syndicate. The goons and hustlers call it the Outfit. You call it the Organization. I hope you people have fun with your words. But I don't care if you call yourselves the Red Cross, you owe me forty-five thousand dollars and you'll pay me back whether you like it or not.

The Hunter's first publication in 1962 was quickly followed by such sequels as *The Man With the Getaway Face* (1963) and *The Outfit* (1963), and the figure of Parker established a solid following among the hardboiled fraternity. The film world was a little slower in catching up with him, but then, the censorship situation in the early 1960s would hardly have allowed a remorse-free, habitually successful violent criminal to stalk the cinema screens. A few years down the line, things had changed considerably.

Some sources list a 1964 film adaptation of the Parker novel *The Score* (aka *Killtown*, 1964), yet it fails to show up in reference works, movie databases or even on Westlake's own website. If they've managed to keep it secret from the book's author for nearly four decades, then that's underground film-making with a vengeance.

The first officially-acknowledged Parker appearance on screen came when Jean-Luc Godard took the plunge in 1966 with *Made in USA,* adapted *extremely* loosely from the 1965 Stark novel *The Jugger*. The virtually plotless storyline ditches most of the book, turns Parker into a female reporter named Paula Nelson (Anna Karina) and wheels out Marianne Faithfull to distract attention from the political speeches by singing *As Tears Go By*. Chairman Mao was probably applauding wildly, but it's tempting to imagine that Gerry and Sylvia Anderson's butler from *Thunderbirds* would have been equally appropriate casting for the lead role.

The following year, however, another French director, Alain Cavalier, made *Mise à Sac* (aka *Pillaged*), based on Stark's novel *The Score*. Here the let's-rename-Parker game continues, and he appears in the guise of a character called Georges (Michel Constantin), but although the film was highly regarded in France, it received extremely poor distribution elsewhere. This was not to be the fate of the other Stark adaptation released in 1967, made in

Hollywood by a British director whose only previous film had been *Catch Us If You Can* (1965), a Fab Four-style poptastic romp featuring the Dave Clark Five. Nevertheless, when John Boorman teamed up with the man who was currently leading the Dirty Dozen to a bloody victory night after night across the world's cinema screens, Mr and Mrs Parker's hard-faced boy finally found a home.

> Not since Attila the Hun swept across Europe leaving five hundred years of total blackness has there been a man like Lee Marvin . . .

Although the above character reference would have been perfect for the posters of *Point Blank*, it's actually a quote from Josh Logan, who had the pleasure of directing Lee in the 1969 all-singing, all-mud-splattered, gold-prospecting yarn *Paint Your Wagon*, an experience which evidently left a deep impression. As for Boorman, one story above all else sums up the way he and his gun-toting, two-fisted star bonded over many bottles of the hard stuff during the shooting of the director's first Hollywood picture. Marvin, a 43-year-old ex-US Marine who'd killed people in the Pacific during World War Two, was just going through a divorce and was also becoming, on the back of his current hit, *The Dirty Dozen* (1967), one of the biggest stars in the world. Boorman was a 34-year-old director who'd worked his way up through British television before being given a break in 1965 with the Dave Clark feature. Late one night in Beverly Hills, the police stopped Boorman as he was driving very slowly along the street and, according to Donald Zec's account, the conversation went something like this:

> 'Do you realise you have Lee Marvin on the roof of your car?'
> 'Of course.'
> 'Well, drive carefully.'

The two had first met when Marvin was over in London shooting *The Dirty Dozen*, and, as John Boorman remembered in Peter Biskind's *Easy Riders, Raging Bulls*:

> There was a complete loss of nerve by the American studios at that point. They were so confused and so uncertain as to what to do, they were quite willing to cede power to the directors.

London was this swinging place, and there was this desire to
import British or European directors who would somehow have
the answers.

First things first, Boorman and his scriptwriters, Alexander Jacobs, David
Newhouse and Rafe Newhouse, changed Parker's name to Walker, and the
title of the story from *The Hunter* to *Point Blank*. That accomplished, they
moved the setting of the action from New York to California, so that they
could take extensive advantage of location shooting in Los Angeles and San
Francisco. At a time when many pictures were still chained to the two-
dimensional clapboard buildings littering the studio backlots, Boorman's
film got out into the streets (and even down into the sewers) in such a way
as to give the convoluted story a much-needed grounding in reality. The
other key factor which gives the film its hard edge of believability is the
tough-as-nails performance of Lee Marvin himself. Here was a man whose
Malibu house was wallpapered in guns and who slept with a large axe above
the head of his bed, in case of burglars. Indeed, the scene in *Point Blank*
where Marvin bursts through the door and blasts hell out of his screen-
wife's bed with an automatic so terrified his then girlfriend Michelle that
she asked him what he might do if she ever took a lover. Marvin smiled,
'Why don't you do it baby, and find out?'

Having found an actor capable of personifying Stark's amoral protagonist
with such conviction, Boorman then set about presenting the action of the
story as if it were all part of some kind of hallucination. In 1972 the director
told Gordon Gow:

I always think that watching films is very like dreaming. There's
a mystical quality that's very exciting. So I try to make my films
in a way that will touch the spectator's dream world: to use
areas of uncertainty, touching the twilight of people's thoughts
– because this is where communication takes place . . . If *Point
Blank* was fragmented, that's because the Lee Marvin character
was a fractured man with a distorted view of the world.

The story begins with its central character somehow surviving after having
been gunned down at point blank range, and then apparently swimming
across the treacherous waters between Alcatraz Island and the mainland,
despite the fact that the currents are said to be impossible to overcome.

Small wonder that most other people have given him up for dead. 'The film was pitched to a level that I'd call *possible* fantasy,' said Boorman. 'The film in its entirety might have been a projection in Marvin's mind at the moment of death.' This view is reinforced by Lee Marvin's first line of dialogue after he has been shot: 'How did it happen? A dream . . . a dream . . . ' while the reviewer for *Variety* noted that *Point Blank* has a 'bad-dream atmosphere which appears to be deliberate'. The director later admitted the influence of European arthouse films such as *Last Year in Marienbad* on his treatment of a very American subject – the hardboiled gangster drama – and this in turn had an effect on subsequent Hollywood crime films. 'There are specific influences,' said Boorman. 'The close-up effects date back to Griffith, of course, and the elliptical cutting is from Resnais and especially the time-juggling of *Hiroshima, mon amour*. It is valid, I feel, to draw upon such influences . . . A lot of Hollywood directors and writers have told me that they were influenced by the techniques of *Point Blank*; but they were unfamiliar with the *nouvelle vague* directors, and they didn't know that I had taken the techniques from someone else.'

Perhaps Philip French's review in the Spring 1968 edition of *Sight & Sound* comes closest to summing up the way in which the story had been adapted for the screen, remarking: 'Boorman and his scriptwriters use *The Hunter* as a trampoline.' While many elements of Stark's novel survive the transition – most notably the character of Walker himself, the double-cross pulled by Mal Resnick and the relentless pursuit of progressively higher levels of the Outfit chain of command – these are relocated into another world entirely, which is part high-tech nightmare, part groovy 60s drug-dream and part European arthouse fable. If at times it doesn't make sense, the implication seems to be that only the terminally square or culturally unsophisticated would dare to complain.

Although the character of Walker/Parker remained essentially the same during the transition from novel to screen, his motivation was somewhat altered. In Stark's novel, Parker is working on his own, and revenge, rather than money, is his primary obsession. In the film, Walker is continually being briefed and railroaded by Yost, the shadowy figure played by Keenan Wynn, who also turns out to be the Outfit boss named Fairfax. Boorman and his scriptwriters show Walker almost as a barely-housebroken Rottweiler – very dangerous, but none too bright, who can be let loose on various people whose legs need chewing, and seems only capable of repeating, 'I want my ninety-three grand.' Parker in the novel is made of much smarter stuff, and

Walker onscreen is much closer in spirit to the character of Sailor in Dorothy B Hughes's 1946 hardboiled classic *Ride the Pink Horse*, wading ever-deeper into a dangerous situation, his mind fixed upon nothing but the money which is owed to him by his boss, a corrupt Senator:

> 'What do you want?' he asked.
> Sailor dropped the antics. 'You know what I want,' he said.
> 'What do you want?' the Sen repeated.
> His voice was as tight as the Sen's. 'I want my dough.'

In Boorman's film, the deserted prison island of Alcatraz becomes the scene of the robbery and doublecross, rather than the unnamed island way out in the Pacific that figures in the book. However, as several reviewers pointed out, Alcatraz may be photogenic, but it's hard to believe that organised crime would engage in weekly search-lit nocturnal helicopter touchdowns on such a visible landmark near one of the largest population centres on the West Coast for the purposes of exchanging large quantities of mob money.

Mayhem surrounds Walker, and he is clearly a very dangerous man, yet he himself wanders through the entire film without killing anyone at all, which is in marked contrast to the novel, where any undertaker lucky enough to have followed Parker around for a week or two would have been seriously considering hiring extra help in order to cope with the workload. Nevertheless, for its time, the matter-of-fact killings and brutality in *Point Blank* were certainly regarded as shocking. In a year when the carefully-choreographed slow-motion deaths of Dunaway and Beatty during the final scenes of *Bonnie and Clyde* were regarded as the ultimate in screen violence, the sight of Lee Marvin delivering repeated eye-watering blows to the groin of an already-prone victim or breaking a bottle in another hood's face, certainly raised the stakes in terms of what was permissible, and had precious little to do with 1967's Summer of Love. While there's scant evidence in the film of the thousands of hippies then converging on San Francisco's Golden Gate Park (and Lee Marvin in particular seems more than able to resist the urge to wear flowers in his hair), some echoes of Boorman's 'swinging sixties' Dave Clark Five film occasionally surface. The camerawork is similar in many ways, with its extreme close-ups and almost abstract framing, and *Catch Us If You Can* also featured a sinister and manipulative collection of older men who operate out of high-rise offices in an ultra-modern skyscraper, but they were advertising executives rather than mobsters. The endings of both films take place in a selection of deserted buildings on small offshore islands – in Boorman's début feature the location is an abandoned holiday resort, rather than a disused prison. When the action of *Point Blank* moves to a swinging joint called The Movie House, it turns out to be more of a soul/jazz club catering to a slightly older crowd in suits, than the usual Hollywood approximation of a teenage hangout, such as the Pigeon-Toed Orange Peel, the tie-dyed, body-painting go-go palace which Clint Eastwood's defiantly un-switched-on cop stalks through in *Coogan's Bluff* (1968).

As a young English director making his first US picture, Boorman points his cameras at all the flashy, bright shiny surfaces of the American dream, blending pieces of San Francisco, LA and Santa Monica into one urban landscape filled with high-tech appliances, high-rise bachelor pads and endless freeways choked with chrome-heavy Detroit dream-machines. Walker seems almost like a survivor from a more primitive era, staring uncomprehendingly at a cold-cream advert on TV and blasting a telephone to pieces with high-velocity ammunition when it fails to deliver the correct message. This new world, in which the Outfit are a neatly-groomed corporate nightmare, and wads of greenbacks are fast losing ground to credit cards, seems to be something beyond his experience. Having cornered mob boss Brewster (Carroll O'Connor) at his gadget-infested designer ranch-house, Walker doggedly asks for his ninety-three grand:

> Cash? You think I'd go to some hole in the wall, take out ninety-three thousand dollars and peel it off for you? We deal in millions. We never see cash. I've got about eleven dollars in my pocket.

Primitive though he may be, Walker succeeds in upsetting the carefully-balanced equilibrium of the Outfit precisely because of his unexpectedly direct methods. In turn, the businessmen-mobsters credit him with far subtler motives than he actually has, unable to believe that anyone's reasoning could be so basic:

> 'You're a very bad man, Walker. A very destructive man. Why do you run around doing things like that? What do you want?'

'I want my money.'
'Ninety-three thousand dollars? You'd threaten a financial
structure like this for ninety-three thousand dollars? No, Walker,
I don't believe you. What do you really *want*?'
'I really want my money.'

Like many westerns which preceded it, and the Dirty Harry films which
followed soon afterwards, a major part of *Point Blank's* appeal lies in the
spectacle of one character taking on major odds, and succeeding mostly by
means of a gun and his fists. The bad guy becomes the good guy mainly
because the other bad guys are even worse, and it never hurts that he's
usually a sharper dresser with a laconic, deadpan wit. As a result, when the
film was released in America on 18 September 1967, the character played by
Lee Marvin was hailed in some quarters as a hard-hitting, stylish anti-hero,
while other sections of the press condemned him as a brutal thug, and damned
the film along with him.

Trade newspaper *Variety,* whose reviews generally steer clear of moral
judgements, weighed in first with an assessment that the picture would
probably do very well at the box office. Calling it a 'dynamic, violent, thinly-
scripted film . . . a textbook in brutality and a superior exercise in cinematic
virtuosity', they concluded that 'the real star of the film is the film itself'.
Time magazine's anonymous reviewer, in the 22 September 1967 edition,
was less than impressed, and openly commented on the non-Italian hierarchy
of the Outfit:

> *Point Blank* is one of those forgettable movies in which only the
> settings change – the violence remains the same . . . Perhaps not
> unrelated to Frank Sinatra's new chairmanship of the American-
> Italian Anti-Defamation League . . . it turns out that the big
> shots seem neither to have been born in Sicily nor to be afflicted
> with five-o'clock shadow, but bear names such as Brewster,
> Carter and Fairfax.

Howard Junker in *Newsweek* (25 September 1967) was far more enthusiastic,
and wasn't about to shrink in horror from the scenes of violence like some
other contemporary reviewers:

At last, a symphony of vicious brutality unredeemed by

pretensions to uplift: *Point Blank*. It hits like a fat slug from the .38 Lee Marvin uses as an extension of his fist. It palsies the hands and churns the stomach. It is pure, highly moral violence, based on the simple ethical premise that a crook who withholds a partner's share of a job is liable to death . . . Director John Boorman decorates this stylish exercise in revengemanship with an elegant toughmindedness – assisted by Johnny Mandel's electric score and the trigger-taut editing of Henry Berman. Philip H. Lathrop's compelling photography of the abandoned island of Alcatraz and California's plastic doughnut shoppes, hi-fi dens and discotheques give the film some of the quality of a surrealist documentary.

In February 1968, when *Point Blank* went on general release in the UK as the top half of a double-bill also featuring a 1965-vintage Italian sci-fi production called *Wild, Wild Planet*, the critical response was equally divided. Hitting the cinemas in the same month as Sinatra's private eye thriller *Tony Rome*, Dean Martin's third Matt Helm adventure *The Ambushers* and Michael Caine returning as Harry Palmer in *Billion Dollar Brain*, *Point Blank* was either a new low in screen depravity or a liberating slice of gritty realism – it all depended on which papers you were reading. Oddly enough, it was released at the same time that the British Board of Film Classification finally caved in and gave a certificate to another film which had long been considered amoral and subversive: Laslo Benedek's *The Wild One* (1953). Based in part on the recollections of ex-biker gang member Keenan Wynn (who played Yost/Fairfax in *Point Blank*), the film is pretty much stolen from under Marlon Brando's nose by Lee Marvin. Hence two of the latter's most memorable tough-guy roles could be seen in the West End at the same time, although most reviewers found the biker picture's ability to shock had been severely diminished by the years it had spent sitting on a shelf. And *Point Blank*? In the March 1968 edition of *Films & Filming*, David Austen said:

> When I heard that Lee Marvin was playing the role of Stark's hero in a production for some reason re-titled *Point Blank*, I re-read the book and anticipated the film with pleasure. Alas, rarely have I seen a novel so wilfully destroyed and wasted by film-makers.

Austen, who appears to have been one of the few reviewers to have actually read Stark's *The Hunter*, praised Marvin and Angie Dickinson, before concluding that it was 'a needlessly baffling, though never boring, exercise which is way off target'. Lionel Godfrey, writing in the same magazine a month later, commented, 'Boorman's style is everything; what he depicts is entirely conventional and has been shown countless times before.' A year later, *Films & Filming's* Raymond Durgnat was full of praise for the director's *nouvelle vague* approach: 'This glossy, cold-blooded and satisfyingly nasty tale turns its acreage of sumptuous apartments into a murderous Marienbad.' Over at *Photoplay*, however, the editor Ken Ferguson was moved to attack the film twice in his June 1968 edition, both in his editorial and in an article entitled 'Is there too much VIOLENCE on the screen today?'

> *Point Blank* was for me a totally unnecessary excursion into the mind of a sadist bent on revenge. Its violent content had no real and moral significance. Brutality for the sake of brutality . . . there is too much sickness on our screens today.

Perhaps the most positive review came from Philip French, in the Spring 1968 edition of *Sight & Sound*, who seemed less perturbed about the supposed tidal-wave of filth allegedly about to swamp the nation's cinemagoers:

> *Point Blank* (MGM), a film that is interesting for a variety of reasons, quite apart from the reflection that it would make the late Louis Mayer spin in his tomb . . . It is interesting as a first-class thick-ear that grips from beginning to end; as a dazzling American début by John Boorman; as an even more remarkable case than *Bonnie and Clyde* of the imaginative feedback into Hollywood of New Wave borrowings . . .

In the Autumn 1968 edition of the same magazine, Stephen Farber was moved to compare the picture to Antonioni's *Blow Up* and call it 'the most imaginative, startling, *exciting* American film of the year', while John Lindsay Brown, in a Boorman profile written for *Sight & Sound's* Winter 1969/1970 issue, went even further, dragging the Kennedy assassination and various trendy youth causes into the equation while displaying a blissful ignorance of hardboiled crime fiction:

> . . . *Point Blank* (1967) which he transformed from some

brutalised sub-Spillane origins into what is one of the most important movies about America in the sixties . . . It embodies in Marvin's instinctual violence an increasingly-common American life-style – that spirit of frustration in the face of totalitarian society and of subsequent, compensatory violence, a spirit that unifies Dallas, Detroit and Berkeley, however much the targets may have varied in each case.

By then, Boorman had long since moved on, working with Marvin again in the anti-war two-hander with Toshiro Mifune, *Hell in the Pacific* (1968), and then his dream-like fable *Leo the Last* (1969), in which Marcello Mastroianni grapples with questions of wealth, poverty and race. Marvin himself became an unexpected number-one smash on the pop charts, croaking his way to glory with *Wand'rin' Star* – his party piece from *Paint Your Wagon* (1969), and returning to a variation on his *Point Blank* persona in Michael Ritchie's 1972 mob thriller, *Prime Cut*.

Richard Stark's Parker character continued to show up in various guises in films over the years: in *The Split* (1968, adapted from the 1964 novel *The Seventh*), played by Jim Brown; *The Outfit* (1973, adapted from the 1963 novel of the same name), played by Robert Duvall; and in *Slayground* (1983, adapted from the 1971 novel of the same name) played by Peter Coyote. Donald E Westlake took a break from writing Parker novels under the name Richard Stark after publishing *Butcher's Moon* in 1974, but brought the character back after a refreshing twenty-three-year gap in 1997 with the appropriately-titled *Comeback*, since which time the series has continued at regular intervals. Parker's re-emergence, together with the fact that much of Stark's back catalogue began to be made available once again, very likely prompted the 1999 cinema adaptation of *The Hunter*, under the title *Payback*. It's tempting to conclude that whoever thought Mel Gibson could step into Lee Marvin's shoes in this film was probably the same person that reckoned it was a good idea to give *Get Carter* its recent American makeover, with Sylvester Stallone in the Michael Caine role. Marvin was the real thing: it just took a while for the public to notice. In 1965 while Lee was doing publicity for *Cat Ballou*, two years before *Point Blank*, he said to Howard Thompson: 'I still wonder if audiences will ever line up to watch a mean-looking, damn bastard like me.' Almost from that point onwards and for the rest of his career, they did indeed line up around the block, and rightly so. As mean-looking damn bastards go, he was one of the best.

Bonnie and Clyde

They're young . . . they're in love . . . and they kill people.

Film: Bonnie and Clyde
Director: Arthur Penn
Leading players: Warren Beatty, Faye Dunaway, Michael J Pollard,
Gene Hackman
Year of release: 1967

Real-life events: The short lives and brutal career of 1930s Texas bank
robbers Clyde Barrow and Bonnie Parker

Bonnie and Clyde hit the box office in 1967 like a runaway train, gradually gaining
momentum until by the end of the year it had established itself as one of the
most talked-about gangster films of all time; wildly praised by hippie
counterculture types and the would-be trendy sections of the media, and
roundly condemned in other quarters as heralding a new Dark Ages and a
descent into all manner of depravity. Even the Vatican got in on the act, as the
4 September 1967 issue of the *New York Times* reported:

POPE SCORES DEGENERATION

CASTEL GANDOLFO, Italy, September 3 (AP) – Pope Paul VI
deplored today 'the degeneration of civil and moral customs.'
During a talk from the balcony of his summer residence he also
assailed movies and television programs that 'seem to teach the
art of crime as something bold and brave'.

The Pope certainly wasn't the only one voicing such opinions that month –
indeed, the *New York Times* itself followed this item on 17 September with a
piece entitled 'Arthur Penn: Does His 'Bonnie and Clyde' Glorify Crime?', to
which the public's likely answer, had anyone bothered to ask them, would
probably have been 'Yes, of course it does, or else we want our money back.'
For all the hand-wringing and moralising which took place in the press and on
TV that year concerning *Bonnie and Clyde*, the film itself remained yet another
in a long history of films dating back to the silent era which gave audiences a

sanitised, lovably-unkempt set of bad guys to cheer, whose bullets don't really hurt anyone, and who aren't really *nasty* people, they're just misunderstood.

While *Bonnie and Clyde's* American release may have initially met with some poor reviews and less than remarkable ticket sales, the UK response was wildly enthusiastic from day one, to the extent that its distributor was soon bragging in adverts: 'Never has a film been so unanimously acclaimed by the press!' This British success helped provoke a reissue of the film in the US, some four months after its original outing, at which point it then became the huge all-conquering hit which was to redefine 1960s movie-making and line producer Warren Beatty's pockets with more dollars than he could probably even begin to count, as *Bonnie and Clyde* turned into a genuine pop-cultural phenomenon. Faye Dunaway was seen adorning the fashion pages of *Life* magazine, in a lavish picture spread entitled 'Bonnie Comes On With A Stylish Bang' where it was claimed that she had 'already done for the beret what Bardot did for the bikini'. Featuring 'Depression era' dresses priced at a then jaw-dropping $650, the article was quick to reassure its readers that there was nothing old-fashioned about these old fashions, and that 'many new followers of the Bonnie mode still insist on above-the-knee hemlines of the contemporary mini era'. Meanwhile, Georgie Fame hit the music charts on both sides of the Atlantic with his single, *The Ballad of Bonnie and Clyde*, even reaching the number one spot in the UK, while pop-art legend Robert Rauschenberg had silk-screened Beatty and Dunaway's images for the cover of the 8 December 1967 issue of *Time* magazine, alongside the caption: 'The New Cinema: Violence . . . Sex . . . Art . . . '

Not bad for a couple of long-dead, runty-looking, small-time killers that even John Dillinger said were giving decent bank robbers a bad name, who were often feared by the local population in states where they were active and whose deaths had been greeted by the *New York Herald Tribune* with the words: 'Society is glad that Louisiana rubbed them both out yesterday.'

Their shooting also made the front page of the *New York Times* on 24 May 1934, although the self-mythologising Bonnie Parker might have been a little disappointed at the headline, which read: 'Barrow and Woman are Slain by Police in Louisiana Trap.' These two future heroes of the peace-and-love generation were killed while driving a car found to contain 'three sub-machine guns, six automatic pistols, one revolver, two sawed-off automatic shotguns and enough ammunition for a siege'. Clyde Barrow was described in the article as 'a snake-eyed murderer who killed without giving his victims a chance to draw', and former neighbours from his childhood home in Houston came forward to tell stories of him as a little boy who enjoyed torturing small animals:

'Clyde, they said, would break a bird's wing, then laugh at its attempts to fly.'

Some of the people involved in the making of Arthur Penn's 1967 film based on the activities of Clyde Barrow and Bonnie Parker were keen, like the director himself, to stress that the real-life bank robbers who inspired the characters played by Beatty and Dunaway were a mere starting-point for the movie, and that the legend was far more important than any grubby reality. Others, such as writer Robert Towne, who did uncredited work on the script, formed the view that the outlaws were Robin Hood-type figures, more sinned against than sinning, saying that 'if they were bloody, they never killed in cold blood', an assertion which directly contradicts eye-witness reports of their robberies. So who were they, these mythical gun-toting figures: the good-natured folk-heroes as depicted onscreen; or, in the words of historian John Toland (whose own book *The Dillinger Days* first gave scriptwriters David Newman and Robert Benton a brief description of the Barrow gang), a couple of 'punks' who 'were in the flesh about as loveable as Ilse Koch and Martin Bormann'?

Ever since Arthur Penn's film appeared in 1967, the names of the two outlaws have generally been written with Bonnie's first and Clyde bringing up the rear, but in the early 1930s, the emphasis was much more on Clyde, and the newspapers usually spoke simply of the Barrows. By the time he met Bonnie, he was well into his life of petty robberies and dodging the police, having formed a double act in the late 1920s with his brother Ivan, nicknamed Buck. Members would come and go, but up until their final meeting with 167 bullets in 1934, the outfit was always known as the Barrow Gang.

Clyde Barrow was born on 24 March 1909 in Telice, Texas, to a family of dirt-poor farmers, and by the age of ten had caused enough trouble to get himself sent to a special school in Harris County, roughly the equivalent of the Borstals or Approved Schools in the UK. Once he had served his time, he and his elder brother Buck started stealing pretty much anything around them that wasn't nailed down – chickens, motor vehicles, and eventually guns. During the early 1920s Barrow was part of a minor-league outfit called the Square Root Gang in Houston, mostly robbing people's homes, though he would also mug people in the streets. Somehow Clyde managed to stay out of jail, but then he and Buck moved onto what was to become their lifetime's work – knocking over filling stations and grocery stores at gunpoint, often for just a few bucks and some change. These latter activities are what really brought Barrow and his brother to the attention of the police, who eventually cornered them as they robbed a gas station in Denton, Texas in 1928. Clyde escaped, but Buck was wounded and arrested, drawing a five-year sentence at the Eastham prison farm as a result. All of this activity had taken place in the years before the 1929 Wall Street Crash, so the idea that Barrow only turned to crime as a result of the Depression doesn't really stand up – he and his brother had always stolen things, right back to when they were kids. For instance, when as a child he developed an interest in music, Clyde just went out and stole a saxophone (it was an interest which stayed with him until his death: 'Nestled between guns and ammunition,' said the *New York Times* description of his bullet-riddled car in 1934, 'a saxophone, with several pieces of sheet music, was found in the automobile.')

Clyde continued his life of petty crime, breaking into houses and robbing shops, but then in January 1930 he met a waitress called Bonnie Parker in a Dallas café – 'a hard-faced, sharp-mouthed woman' according to later newspaper reports. At this time, Clyde was only twenty years old, and Bonnie was nineteen and married to convicted murderer Ray Thorton. Ray was then doing 99 years in the same slammer as Buck Barrow, but Bonnie didn't exactly let this interfere with her social life – indeed, she was already known as someone with a voracious appetite for men, and she and Clyde hit it off immediately, despite the fact that he himself was allegedly more interested in sleeping with men. The only slight hindrance to their new-found relationship was the police, who came visiting one day when they were at home and dragged Clyde off to the cells as a result of his carelessness in having left his fingerprints all over the scene of a burglary job he'd recently pulled. He wound up in jail in Waco in March 1930 but Bonnie was able to smuggle a gun in to him when she visited and he escaped, only to be recaptured a week later. This time Clyde was sentenced to 14 years in Eastham prison – the same place from which his brother Buck had only recently escaped – where the regime was so harsh that he opted for having two toes chopped off with an axe by another prisoner as a way of avoiding the punishing work details. During his stay he killed his first man, beating another prisoner, Ed Crowder, to death with a lead pipe because the latter had informed on him to the authorities. Nevertheless, in February 1932, thanks to the efforts of his mother, Clyde Barrow was paroled from prison by Texas Governor Ross Sterling, and during the following two years carried out the series of killings and robberies which were to put him and his gang on the front pages of the nation's newspapers.

Pretty much the first thing he did upon being released was to hook up with Bonnie and steal a car, which he crashed into a tree after a high-speed police chase. Clyde ran for it, but Bonnie was arrested and given a three-month jail term. Barrow filled in his time by raiding filling stations and small shops. Having already killed one man in jail, it soon seemed as if he had developed a taste for it. As the *New York Times* later reported:

> In Hillsborough, Texas, late on the night of 27 April 1932, he awakened John Bucher, a merchant [other reports say he was a jeweller], on the pretence that he wanted to buy some guitar strings. Another man was with him. When Bucher turned his back they shot him. Their loot was $40 in cash.

This set the pattern for many of the heists pulled by the Barrow Gang – pathetic amounts of money stolen, and a willingness to shoot down anyone unlucky enough to be in the vicinity. In the next few months they continued to rob filling stations and general stores, until in August, Clyde was at a barn dance in Atoka, Oklahoma, drinking liquor from a bottle, when he was approached by Sheriff C G Maxwell and his deputy, who objected to this open consumption of alcohol (Prohibition was still in force at this time). Clyde's reply was simply to pull out a gun and kill them both without warning.

Soon, Bonnie was released from jail. She rejoined Clyde, and in addition to breaking into state armouries to steal machine guns, shotguns and ammunition, the pair also began to knock over banks, although here too their takings were distinctly small-time: $1,400 dollars in Abilene, $200 in Orongo, Missouri. In the 1960s, the fact that Bonnie and Clyde robbed banks was generally seen as being a Robin Hood-like act, that of the little people striking a blow for the poor against the big corporations, but this is hard to square with the facts. For instance, two days after the Abilene bank job, they still found time to steal $50 from a small grocery store in Sherman, Texas. Behind the counter was an ordinary working man named Howard Hall, who more than likely came from a similar background to the robbers themselves, and objected to this attempt to redistribute the money in his till by picking up a nearby meat cleaver. In a gesture of proletarian solidarity, they shot him dead. Similarly, on 23 December 1932 in Temple, Texas, the happy couple were in the process of stealing a V8 Ford when the car's owner, Doyle Johnson, jumped on the running board and attempted to remonstrate with them about this. Unwilling to argue the point, they filled him full of holes.

If being a shopkeeper, gas station attendant or a stray member of the public was a hazardous thing to be in the vicinity of Bonnie and Clyde, then wearing a police uniform was like waving a red rag at a bull. On 6 January 1933 they killed Deputy Malcolm Davis, on 13 March they killed Officers Wes Harryman and Harry L McGinnis and on 23 June they killed

Marshal H D Humphrey. By this time, it seemed to have become something of a habit, so much so that on the day they killed Humphrey, while driving through Oklahoma City, they deliberately pulled up at a junction where an officer was directing traffic. Bonnie asked for directions, and then, after the man had finished speaking, she blew his head off with both barrels of a shotgun, at which point, eyewitnesses report, they drove off laughing.

Along the way, the gang had acquired various playmates: Buck Barrow had been paroled from prison on 20 March 1933 after his wife Blanche had begged the Governor for clemency, whereupon they both joined up with Clyde and Bonnie. Meanwhile, a man called Ray Hamilton had become part of the gang in late 1932, helping to rob banks and allegedly sleeping with both Bonnie and Clyde. Hamilton soon wound up in jail, but his place was taken by a filling station attendant named W D Jones, who signed up for their gang when it became clear to him who was robbing the place, and who later gave a lengthy confession to the police detailing his time with the robbers, claiming that he had been forced at gunpoint to do all manner of things, and had often been kept chained up at night. Yet again, the story goes that he was sleeping with both Bonnie and Clyde during this time. In fairness the whole 'Clyde was gay' theory, as outlined by John Toland in *The Dillinger Days*, was later denounced by Nelson Algren in his essay, *After the Buffalo: Bonnie and Clyde*, who claimed that there was insufficient evidence to support such an assertion. Nevertheless, many accounts of the Barrow Gang have Clyde and Bonnie engaging in threesomes with Hamilton and also with Jones.

When not knocking over filling stations, shooting people or taking various hostages, the outlaws appear to have spent most of their spare time photographing each other, posing with a variety of weapons in front of one or other of their stolen automobiles. Many of these pictures, left behind as they fled from one hideout after another, showed up in the newspapers, as they no doubt expected – the resultant publicity helping to inflate their reputation far more than their small-change robberies were ever likely to do. As Patty Hearst and the Symbionese Liberation Army later discovered, there's nothing the media likes more than a picture of a gun-toting young woman to help boost circulation. Ma Barker may have been a much more big-time gun moll, but Bonnie was half her age and half her weight. Not only that, but Bonnie also wrote sentimental, self-justifying poetry about herself and Clyde which was eagerly printed by the newspapers. Headline writers had taken to calling Clyde the 'Texas

Rattlesnake,' and now they were calling Bonnie 'Suicide Sal', so she sent them a lengthy ballad entitled *The Story of Suicide Sal*, part of which read as follows:

> They class them as cold-blooded killers,
> They say they are heartless and mean,
> But I say this with pride,
> That I once knew Clyde
> When he was honest and upright and clean.

Clean or not, in the end, the law of averages just caught up with them – if you kill that many policemen in a short space of time, eventually they're going to send half an army out looking for you. In July 1933 the whole gang was nearly wiped out by a posse which even came equipped with an armoured car. Bonnie, Clyde and W D Jones were all wounded, but Buck and Blanche were captured, and Buck himself died in hospital some days later having been hit six times in the gunfight.

In January 1934 Clyde and Bonnie helped Ray Hamilton, Henry Methvin and Joe Palmer break out of Eastham prison, but they themselves were only a short step ahead of the law. Fate eventually came calling in the shape of an ex-Texas Ranger by the name of Frank Hamer, who had been given a special commission to go ahead and track them down. He and three other Texans followed their trail 15,000 miles through half a dozen states during 1934, but the end, when it came in May, was courtesy of a tip-off from the father of Henry Methvin, on the understanding that Methvin himself would be treated more leniently by the authorities.

On the morning of 23 May 1934, Bonnie and Clyde drove at high speed into an ambush set up by Frank Hamer's Texan lawmen on the road between Sailes and Gibsland (now Highway 154) in the Louisiana parish of Bienville. At a little after 9 am, while some of the policemen lay in wait at the side of the road, other lawmen walked out into the path of the Barrows' speeding grey 8-cylinder sedan, ordering it to stop. According to police reports, Clyde reached instead for a sawn-off shotgun, at which point they let them have it, and kept on firing long after the car had careered off the road and into the embankment. Clyde was dead behind the wheel with his head hanging out of the window. He had $507 on him. One lens of the tinted glasses he was wearing had been shot out. Bonnie was wearing a diamond ring, an expensive watch, a red dress, red shoes and a red-and-white hat. The trigger finger of her right hand had been shot off in the ambush. She'd been eating a sandwich at the time of the attack. The report in the *New York Times* the following day included a quote from the man who'd tracked them down:

> Hamer, a big strapping Texan, gave his comrades credit for bringing down the pair and expressed regret over having to kill a woman. 'I hate to bust a cap on a woman,' he said, 'especially when she's sitting down. However, if it hadn't been her, it would have been us.'

Bonnie always thought they'd be buried side by side, but Clyde Barrow's mother insisted on a separate service for her son. He was buried alongside Buck in the Western Heights Cemetery in Dallas, Texas. Bonnie was buried first in the same city's Fish Trap Cemetery, before being moved at a later date to Crown Hill Memorial Park. For years their bullet-riddled car was a sideshow attraction at state fairs, and these days it is still on display at the annual festival held in Gibsland on the nearest weekend to the anniversary of their shooting.

The demise of the Barrow Gang coincided almost exactly with the onset of tougher restrictions from the Hays Office governing the depiction of criminal activities in Hollywood pictures, but that didn't stop their story from exerting an influence over several key movies of the 1930s and 40s, such as *You Only Live Once* (1937), *They Live By Night* (1948) and *Gun Crazy* (1949). By the time of the late 1950s low-budget gangster cycle (which included such films as *Machine Gun Kelly* (1958), *Baby Face Nelson* (1958) and *Al Capone* (1959)) it was apparently safe to mention Bonnie by name, although the gang which appears with her in *The Bonnie Parker Story* (1958) is renamed the Darrows, and her Clyde is called Guy. However, *Picturegoer's* reviewer, writing in their 30 August 1958 edition, seemed fairly smitten by Dorothy Provine in the role of Bonnie: 'She improves the shining hour by holding up petrol stations, banks, payroll trucks and mows down men with gleeful contempt.' Six years later, however, discussing the current state of crime films in an article in the March 1964 issue of *Films & Filming*, Richard Whitehall dismissed *The Bonnie Parker Story* as a 'strange and uneasy mixture of comedy and violence', while also commenting that 'it seems inevitable, since the [Mafia footsoldier] Joseph Valachi revelations to the McClellan Committee, that another phase of the gangster cycle is due'.

As it turned out, a couple of would-be Hollywood scriptwriters named David Newman and Robert Benton were even at that time researching the life and times of Bonnie Parker, and the film which emerged in 1967 from their script was also said to contain a 'strange and uneasy mixture of comedy and violence'. By the time *Bonnie and Clyde* hit the cinemas the war in Vietnam had spiralled way out of control, there was rioting in many inner city areas, draft-card burning in the streets, assassinations of major public figures and a youth audience for whom figures like the newly-dead Che Guevara were cultural figureheads. Violence was definitely in the air during the 1967 Summer of Love, and a couple of gun-toting young rebels up on the cinema screen fit the bill to perfection: as the advertising campaign said, 'They're young . . . they're in love . . . and they kill people.'

So how did these counter culture pin-ups get to be up there on the big screen in the first place?

David Newman and Robert Benton were young writers on *Esquire* magazine. They were huge fans of the *nouvelle vague* film directors from France, particularly François Truffaut and Jean-Luc Godard. Having spent the first few years of the 1960s avidly watching as many movies as they could track down, by 1964 they had decided to write their own script, and the story of the Barrow Gang appealed to them greatly. The choice is not particularly surprising, given that Truffaut and Godard had both made a huge impression with films based on American crime pictures and pulp novels, in particular *A Bout de Souffle* (1959) and *Tirez sur le Pianiste* (1960). What first attracted Newman and Benton to their own crime couple was a brief mention of Bonnie and Clyde's activities in John Toland's *The Dillinger Days*. Here, it seemed were two characters just crying out to star in their own *nouvelle vague*-style movie. Never having written a script before, Newman and Benton figured they might as well put a lengthy treatment together, and then somehow attract the attention of Truffaut and ask him if he'd like to direct it. Ninety-nine times out of a hundred, this kind of approach would fall flat on its face, but they managed via mutual contacts to get their initial script through to the director himself, and he was interested enough to agree to a meeting. When Truffaut saw Newman and Benton in New York, he gave them encouragement and advice, screened *Gun Crazy* for them by way of inspiration, but said that his schedule was too full for him to become the director. The writers headed for Texas to do more research, finished their script while listening repeatedly to *Foggy Mountain Breakdown* by Lester Flatt and Earl Scruggs, and then sent it off to Truffaut, who passed it on to Jean-Luc Godard, who wanted to begin in three weeks time . . . 'We can make the film anywhere,' he told them. 'We can make it in Tokyo.' As it turned out, Newman and Benton's financial backers were not entirely convinced that one of the world's most futuristic high-rise cities could stand in for the wide-open Texas plains of the Depression era, and the project lapsed into abeyance. However, some time later, François Truffaut was to come through handsomely for the would-be screenwriters, when he mentioned their project to an ambitious young Hollywood matinee idol named Warren Beatty, who promptly unchained his wallet to the value of $75,000 and bought the rights, with a view to producing the film as part of a deal with Warner Brothers.

After a series of less-than-satisfying experiences on movie sets, Beatty had figured out that it might be more enjoyable if he could control more of the process in which he was involved, and had therefore been looking for a film project of his own. Newman and Benton's screenplay seemed to fit the bill: 'I had planned to direct *Bonnie and Clyde*,' he told Gordon Gow in 1975. 'I wasn't going to act in *Bonnie and Clyde* because I was going to direct it.' However, the deeper he delved into the business, the more he saw himself as Clyde, and therefore he needed a director who would help him put this story on film, but wouldn't run away with the whole project to the extent that Warren himself would lose the control he sought, particularly over the script. Unimpressed by the auteur theory which held the director to be all-important, Warren felt rather that 'the writer is more important than the director . . . films are a group experience'. Luckily, Warren had recently had a group experience on a film called *Mickey One* (1965), directed by Arthur Penn – a film which had itself been much influenced by the techniques of the *nouvelle vague*. Penn came up through the theatre and the live television of the 1950s before making his first film, *The Left Handed Gun* (1958), a Method-acting western featuring Paul Newman 'showing Billy the Kid as a kind of navel-scratching, six-gun Lee Harvey Oswald', according to critic Rex Reed, who interviewed the director for the 13 February 1966 edition of the *New York Times*. Describing Penn as 'a small, vanilla-voiced man with big ideas', Reed caught the director at a time when he had just made a fine, violent film down in Texas with Marlon Brando called *The Chase,* but he had suffered a fair amount of interference and re-cutting from his studio bosses, and his sentiments at this time sound very close to those of Warren Beatty: 'Everything I do from now on will be independent, on my own terms,' said Penn. 'I won't touch anything I can't control to the end.' This similarity of feeling is confirmed by comments the director made to Bernard Weinraub in a 1969 interview:

> Beatty and I both had a sense that we were better than we had showed. At first, though, when I started working on the film I wasn't that attracted to it. It seemed dangerously superficial and exploitative rather than meaningful.

Having struck a deal with each other, the first thing to be tackled was the script. While it had all the right ingredients to interest Beatty and Penn, it was deemed still to require a lot of further work. As with the scripts of most successful films, the question of exactly who wrote what is something of a minefield. Penn's later pronouncements generally speak of the finished article as a three-way collaboration between himself and Newman and Benton:

> With *Bonnie and Clyde* there was a completed screenplay by David Newman and Robert Benton in existence when I started to work on the film. There was a reorganised screenplay by the time we actually began to shoot – considerably reorganised, with quite a number of changes made. I laboured over several months with the writers.

Warren Beatty, on the other hand, is more inclusive in his memories, particularly in respect of Robert Towne, who did a fair amount of work at this stage:

> A lot of people worked uncredited on the screenplay of *Bonnie and Clyde*, including myself. I would never produce a film on which I did not concern myself closely with the structure of the script. And although David Newman and Robert Benton had the official credit in that case, what they did was definitely not taken by us as a *fait accompli*.

One thing which was swiftly dropped from Newman and Benton's original script was Clyde's homosexuality and the three-way love triangle between him, Bonnie and C W Moss. The vast amounts of research conducted by the two writers had thrown up many references to Clyde's supposed 'abnormal' sexuality, as they later wrote: 'Some inferred an SM trip. More inferred homosexuality, and one or two ventured the thought that Clyde and Bonnie and one or another of the various men in the gang at different times were involved in a functioning *ménage à trois*, a mini-orgy at every little motel.' Warren Beatty, a long-standing ladies' man who was now set to play Clyde on the big screen, was far from convinced. 'In their original script Clyde had a homosexual relationship with C W Moss, the character Michael J Pollard played,' he recalled. 'Nobody knows if that was true, but I doubt it.' François Truffaut, who had obviously read the original script, prior to any rewrites, told the *New York Times* in 1970:

I liked Arthur Penn's *Bonnie and Clyde*, but I would have preferred another actor to Warren Beatty, because Beatty had no genuine innocence, no authenticity. He distorted the script, out of a fear of being ridiculed. Originally, Clyde was to have had a homosexual relationship with the other fellow, the one played by Michael Pollard. But Beatty wanted to be more important than Pollard and, after all, he *was* the producer of the film.

In *Easy Riders, Raging Bulls*, Peter Biskind (who also repeats the story that Beatty is supposed to have literally kissed studio boss Jack Warner's feet to get the financing for the film) alleges that Beatty simply said, 'Let me tell you one thing right now: I ain't gonna play no fag.' In the end, they settled for making him impotent, but even so, they wrote in a scene towards the close of the film where the two young outlaws have a classic Hollywood 'did the earth move for you too, darling?' encounter, in which Clyde does right by his gal in the bedroom department.

Straight, bi or gay, they now had their Clyde, so it followed that a Bonnie would soon be required. Initially, when Warren had only planned to direct but not to appear in the picture, he'd intended the Bonnie role for his sister, Shirley MacLaine, but once he himself joined the cast it became clear that this wouldn't work, and that even in the swinging 60s they'd have baulked at the idea of a love story that kept things quite that much in the family. Tuesday Weld apparently turned it down, but Arthur Penn was convinced that an upcoming young actress called Faye Dunaway was just right for the part, having talked it through with her for three hours. The real-life Bonnie and Clyde never made it past their early twenties, so 26-year-old Faye was probably just about right, and wouldn't make the 30-year-old Beatty look too old. Still, she was hardly a big box office name, as this profile in the November 1967 edition of *ABC Film Review* makes clear:

> This month's colour pin-up is Faye Dunaway. Never heard of her? Neither had we until we saw *Hurry Sundown* one week and *Bonnie and Clyde* the next . . . Hailed by the film critics as 'exciting', 'sensual', 'subtly sexy with acting ability as a bonus', Florida–born Faye was discovered by film producer Sam Spiegel when she was acting on the New York stage.

Beatty himself, though, wasn't convinced. According to Faye, 'Warren likes to woo the ladies. He was taking all the pretty actresses to dinner and giving them his routine, including promising them a part in his movie.' In the end, Penn got his way, despite the fact that Beatty and Dunaway apparently had no mutual attraction. Indeed, the February 1968 issue of *Modern Screen* ran an article by Carole Robbins entitled: 'Faye Dunaway: The Girl Who Wouldn't Say Yes To Warren Beatty' in which the lady in question – 'wise and hip and mod and 'very now'' – is quoted as saying 'I don't want to sound like an unfeminine freak, but Warren Beatty and I didn't even raise a quiver much less a riptide.' Given the impotence angle that had now been built into the storyline, perhaps this was just as well.

For the third part of the *ménage à trois*-that-wasn't – the role of C W Moss, a composite figure based on three or four of the lesser Barrow Gang members – they chose an old friend of Warren's, 28-year-old Michael J Pollard, who, in the immortal words of *Time* magazine, 'had a few minor parts to his credit before *Bonnie and Clyde*, usually playing an ungainly amalgam of chagrin and Silly Putty'. He himself knew that there was open derision being expressed around Hollywood about the chances of success for a gangster picture produced by Warren Beatty – 'I mean he was only 29 years old and who was going to give him two and a half million dollars to make a film?' – but the two of them went way back to the days when they'd both been appearing on the New York stage in a play called *A Loss of Roses*, and the script looked like the best thing he'd seen in a long while.

Arthur Penn meanwhile was still unhappy with things, and allegedly had to be persuaded by Beatty not to quit the project less than a month before shooting. Nevertheless, the summer of 1966 found him on location all around Texas in places like Dallas, Waxahachie (where the teenage Jerry Lee Lewis had been thrown out of Bible college back in the early 1950s), Ponder, Garland and Midlothian. Filming also took place in Louisiana, Iowa and Montana, and in most places where they travelled the cast and crew would be met by curious locals with their own memories of the Bonnie and Clyde days, as Beatty told Stefan Kanfer in *Time* magazine shortly after the film was released:

> A huge waiter came in and said to me, 'Hey Warren, at trew yew gonna play Clahd Barra? Sheee! I knowed Clahd Barra, and he wuz much better lookin' than yew are.' As it happens, Clyde Barrow was not much better looking than Mr Hyde . .
> .

This was a natural consequence of using real locations for the filming, but all the principals agreed that it would give the movie a far more naturalistic look than anything they could achieve on a studio back lot in Los Angeles. The production also benefited greatly from the fact that some banks which had closed during the Depression years were still standing, and had remained virtually unchanged since those days, such as the one at Pilot Point, to the north of Dallas.

From the opening scenes of the film, the script sets out to make the audience like Bonnie and Clyde, which ties in with Arthur Penn's comments that the film is more about the myth than the reality, and in many ways reflects events as the outlaw couple would have liked them to have been, rather than how they actually were. The opening robbery is a pretty harmless affair, and although Clyde fires his gun, he points it up in the air, and only uses it in order to scare the storekeeper. Then, when he's asking Bonnie about her background, she is presented as a girl who has mostly just worked in a café, and nearly married a guy who worked in a cement plant, whereas the real Bonnie already had a husband in jail for murder. Soon after this comes a scene in which Clyde and Bonnie encounter a farmer whose home has been repossessed by the bank, and, after giving the man a chance to put a few bullet holes in his former property, Clyde proudly tells him 'We rob banks,' thus setting the pair up as Robin Hood figures, avenging the wrongs of the Depression. Similarly, after the pair rob a general store, and the butcher behind the counter has taken exception to this and attacked him with a meat cleaver, it is Clyde who is offended by the injustice of the whole thing:

> Why'd he try to kill me? I didn't want to hurt him. Try to get something to eat round here and some son-of-a-bitch comes up on you with a meat cleaver. I ain't against him. I ain't against him.

(This is based on the October 1932 killing of butcher Howard Hall, less than a month after a hungry Clyde had raided the National Guard Armoury at Forth Worth, emerging with machine guns, automatic rifles and shotguns, but apparently no food.) Hence, even the film's first shooting is presented as a reasonable act of self defence, rather than one of aggression, and Clyde's man-of-the-people credentials are also emphasised. The film is also keen to show a later scene of the wounded butcher sitting up in a hospital bed, having survived the shooting.

Shortly after this comes the first bank robbery, which initially plays like a Keystone Kops routine as C W Moss mistakenly parks the getaway car and has trouble extracting it from its space, but then the mood changes dramatically as the bank teller jumps on the running board and is shot in the face, *Battleship Potemkin*-style. Clyde is obviously horrified, and later, as the robbers watch *Golddiggers of 1933* in a cinema, he says to Moss:

> You ain't got a brain in your skull. On account of you I killed a man. And now we're all gonna be wanted for murder and that's you too boy.

Yet again, the violence is shown as something used almost accidentally, and in self-defence. Just to reinforce the point, when Buck (Gene Hackman) and his wife Blanche (Estelle Parsons) show up to join the gang, as soon as he gets Clyde alone he asks, anxiously:

> The guy that you killed. You had to do it, didn't you? It was either you or him.

In reality, by the time Buck was paroled and came to rejoin the Barrow Gang with his wife Blanche, Clyde had already killed one fellow prisoner, two shopkeepers, three policemen and the owner of a car he was trying to steal, so few people, least of all Buck would have been worrying about the details of the latest shooting.

The gang are then shown kidnapping and holding hostage Texas Ranger Frank Hamer (Denver Pyle) – who, in real life never fell into their hands, although they did kidnap several other policemen at one time or another. He is described as a bounty hunter, a lackey of the landowners and the banks, and they tie him up and photograph him. The description of Hamer at this point in the published screenplay gives a clear indication of the film's attitude to this character:

> Hamer is tall and strong with a frightening face, a face that can impart evil. He is a man tightly under his own control. He holds on to whatever rages inside him. He is very aware of his position, professional and egoistic.

Eventually, when he can stand no more of being humiliated at gunpoint, he spits in Bonnie's face, at which point Clyde attacks him, and the sympathy of the audience is supposed to be entirely with the gang members. (Descendents of the real Frank Hamer later took legal action against the film company concerning the way he was portrayed in the film.)

During their next bank raid, Clyde tells a frightened customer to keep his money, because they're 'only after the banks', a real-life event for which John Dillinger was famous, rather than the Barrow Gang, and then, just to reinforce his good-guy persona, he only blows a hole in a bank guard's hat when the other man reaches for his gun, merely saying 'next time I'll aim a little lower'. All in all, it's not hard to see why audiences emerged from the film having been rooting for the plucky outlaws, since the script stacks the odds so heavily in their favour right down the line that when they are blown to pieces in the dazzling set-piece slow-motion finale, it's as if the squares have triumphed over the hip people, and the forces of repression have regained control – which is why a variant on this same ending proved so popular two years later, when Hopper and Fonda were blasted with a shotgun in the final scene of *Easy Rider*.

Bonnie and Clyde premiered as the official US entry at the Montreal Film Festival on Friday 4 August 1967, and five days later *Variety* handed down its verdict, calling it 'Rough stuff but box office,' saying that it was far from perfect, but with the right promotion they predicted good-sized audiences. Penn's direction was described as 'uneven,' as was the characterisation: 'Scripters Newman and Benton have depicted these real-life characters as inept, bumbling, moronic types, and if this had been true they would have been erased in their first try.' Beatty's performance was held to be 'inconsistent', but Dunaway was 'a knockout', and Burnett Guffey's colour camerawork 'excellent'. The overall mixture of comedy and violence seems to have not been judged a success, particularly in regard to the choice of uptempo hillbilly music on the soundtrack.

If *Variety* thought that the film was uneven but a likely success, Bosley Crowther, writing in the *New York Times* on 14 August was far less impressed, calling it a 'cheap piece of bald-faced slapstick comedy that treats the hideous depredations of that sleazy, moronic pair as though they were as full of fun as the jazz-age cut-ups in *Thoroughly Modern Millie*'. Not to be outdone, *Time* magazine weighed in on 25 August, under the title 'Low-Down Hoedown', with a review that spoke of Warren Beatty's 'long-unawaited debut as a producer', calling it a 'strange and purposeless mingling of fact and claptrap that teeters uneasily on the brink of burlesque. Like Bonnie and Clyde themselves, the film rides off in all directions and ends up full of holes.' This review prompted a letter to the editor from comedian Jerry Lewis, who said, 'I can't remember being as upset with anything you've written about films as I am with this unjust, unfair and just plain unkind rap at one of the finest films ever projected on the American screen,' but failed to mention that Arthur Penn used to be the floor manager on the Martin & Lewis TV show back in the 1950s. Meanwhile, Joseph Morgenstern in *Newsweek*, called it a 'squalid shoot-'em-up for the moron trade' one week, and then published a retraction the following week, calling his own review 'grossly unfair'.

Luckily, help was at hand, and *Bonnie and Clyde*, like Jimi Hendrix, found that becoming a big hit in London paved the way for an equivalent success back home in the States. From the time that the film opened at the Warner Theatre in Leicester Square, there were queues around the block, and the press reception was hugely enthusiastic. Tom Milne, writing in *Sight & Sound*, pinpointed the film's *nouvelle vague* influences, and seemed to have no problem with its blend of comedy and violence, adding, 'Penn drives unerringly through a mood and milieu which look like the result of a shotgun marriage between *Cat Ballou* and *Bande à Part*.' Dunaway, Beatty and Denver Pyle even made the cover of the October issue of *Films & Filming*: 'Bringing nostalgia to heel, sharply and superbly, Arthur Penn's *Bonnie and Clyde* is a film for now, and perhaps for posterity,' said Gordon Gow's lead review. 'Tormented spirits of the 1960s, seeking release amid a bewilderment of flower petals, are eschewing the dubious manifestations of progress to wallow defiantly in romantic conceits of the past.'

One unlikely flower child who caught the picture at the Warner Theatre was actor Kenneth Williams, who called in to see it on 14 September after a hard day on-set filming *Carry On Doctor*. Later that night he recorded his impressions in his diary:

> The film is certainly v. daring. A scene showing an unsuccessful attempt at intercourse with Warren B rolling off the girl and lying there crestfallen, and then she tries to go down on him for the old fellatio and he looks appalled and stops her. The entire cinema welcomed this episode – in the W/End! – and there were cries of approval from the auditorium.

By this stage, after a shaky start in the US, it was becoming clear that the film was likely to make some money, at least overseas. Arthur Penn was busily engaged in directing a new Broadway musical, winningly entitled *How Now, Dow Jones,* but found time to deny accusations that his film glorified violence, and acknowledged that Hollywood's opinion of him had risen somewhat since the days of *The Chase,* two years before: 'Now it's as if they'd just discovered that my parents were married,' he remarked. The immediate difficulty lay in the fact that Warner Brothers had recently been sold to Seven Arts, and the cinemas across the US which were currently showing *Bonnie and Clyde* were contractually due to replace it with another film. As Warren Beatty watched this happen, he was convinced that his film was going to disappear without trace. However, Pauline Kael weighed in with an extremely lengthy review of the film which was mostly full of praise, and this, along with the glowing UK press, helped Beatty put sufficient pressure on to get an agreement for the film's re-release in December 1967, luckily coinciding with a very high-profile *Time* magazine cover story about violence in cinema which put Beatty and Dunaway's faces on the news-stands across America. By Christmas, it wasn't just a hit, it was a sensation, and a major talking-point, with its relevance to all manner of contemporary issues being hotly debated. 'Planted firmly in the Thirties,' wrote Philip French in the Winter edition of *Sight & Sound, 'Bonnie and Clyde* has much to tell us of the current ghetto explosion and the milieu that produced Lee Harvey Oswald.' Oddly enough, Billie Jean Parker, having taken offence at the film-makers' alleged 'blackening' of her dead sister Bonnie's name, engaged the same lawyers who had acted for Oswald's assassin Jack Ruby to help her when she attempted to sue Warner Brothers for $1,025,000. Meanwhile, John Toland started getting letters from ageing convicts in prisons across America, whom he'd interviewed some years previously for his book *The Dillinger Days,* asking why in hell anyone would want to make a film about 'a couple of small time hoodlums like Bonnie and Clyde'?

Throughout December 1967, in the letters page of *Time* magazine, readers fought it out in an attempt to declare the picture either a moral disaster area or a triumph of the film-maker's art: 'Bonnie and Clyde is a victory if the battle was to rape senses, offend dignity, and threaten the thin threads of humanity some of us are still tenaciously holding on to in spite of the Mr Beattys of this age,' said one, yet an 18-year-old student wrote in claiming that adults just wouldn't understand the movie anyway, and that her generation – the television generation – were the only ones properly equipped to deal with it: 'The reason it was so silent, so horribly silent in the theatre, was because we liked Bonnie Parker and Clyde Barrow, we identified with them, and their deaths made us realize that newspaper headlines are not so far removed from our quiet dorm lives.' Incredibly, this debate continued all the way through 1968 in newspaper and magazine articles on both sides of the Atlantic, while the film's influence spread onto the fashion pages and into the music charts. One aspect of the film's publicity that drew much comment, both favourable and unfavourable, was this text which appeared on some of the posters and in adverts:

> Clyde was the leader. Bonnie wrote poetry. C.W. was a Myrna Loy fan who had a bluebird tattooed on his chest. Buck told corny jokes and carried a Kodak. Blanche was a preacher's daughter who kept her fingers in her ears during the gunfights. They played checkers and photographed each other incessantly. On Sunday nights they listened to Eddie Cantor on the radio. All in all, they killed 18 people. They were the strangest damned gang you ever heard of.

This prompted a, perhaps inevitable, letter from a London reader of *Films & Filming* called Malcolm Silver, which began as follows: 'Tired of the constant publicity for the film *Bonnie and Clyde*, may I now suggest a film based on World War Two and called *Adolf and Eva*. To ensure its success we'd introduce it with this bit of exciting publicity: 'Adolf was the leader. Eva read magazines. Goebbels was a Fritz Lang fan who had a swastika on his arm. Goering told political jokes and carried a baton . . . ' Indeed, even John Coleman's favourable review of the film in the *Observer* asked whether a similar treatment could have been applied to another couple of killers recently in the news, Moors Murderers Ian Brady and Myra Hindley. Mostly though, it was party-time all the way in 1968, as the film was nominated for a stack of Golden Globes and Oscars, although in the event it only picked up two of the golden statuettes (Estelle Parsons for Best Supporting Actress and Burnett Guffey for Best Colour Photography), prompting Dunaway to complain: 'We're all disappointed. As a bunch of bank robbers, we was robbed.'

Debating the thorny question 'Are the Movies Teaching Us To Be Violent?' in the pages of the *New York Times*, 30 June 1968, Fredric Wertham ('psychiatrist and author') stated: 'If I should meet an unruly youngster in a dark alley, I prefer it to be one who has not seen *Bonnie and Clyde*,' but Warren Beatty argued, 'The task is not to censor the movies . . . The underlying problems are Vietnam and the domestic ghettos.' However, in the same month's issue of *Photoplay* magazine, reader Mrs B McDermott from Cheshire was writing in to complain of a howling error she'd spotted in the film: 'Clyde's sister-in-law wore pink pearl nail polish, and the undertaker's girlfriend pink pearl lipstick. Surely it should have been bright red?' A thorny question indeed . . .

By this stage, Bonnie and Clyde had become a bestselling poster staring down from the walls of student bedrooms all over the world, and the pair had been co-opted to stand alongside Ho Chi Minh, Che Guevara and cuddly old Chairman Mao as heroes of the youth revolution; a fact reflected in the following anguished letter to the trendy *Evergreen Review* from a New York reader in August 1968:

> You motherfuckers bug me right out of my tree. Because I am white, forty-six years old, and out of jail, I am, in your book, a stone square. Why is it absolutely necessary that a person be a spade, under twenty-five years of age, or something out of *Bonnie and Clyde* to be anything but lost?

The September newspapers even brought forth calls for the banning of *Bonnie and Clyde* in the wake of the assassination of Senator Robert Kennedy, a question even asked in such pro-cinema quarters as the pages of *Films & Filming*, while Bonnie's sister Billie Jean, fresh from her lawsuit with Warner Brothers, decided to storm the album charts with an LP on RCA Victor entitled *The Truth About Bonnie & Clyde*, in which she enlightened interviewer Jud Collins with fascinating insights about the dead couple, such as 'They were always clean. They had good clothes.' However, it was left to *Evergreen Review* to provide the last word in film criticism, psychoanalysing the famous bank robbers by means of their choice of transport. The article, by Jean-François Held, was entitled 'A Car for Bonnie', and it lovingly eulogised one of the many vehicles stolen and driven by the Texas outlaws – the Packard 626, a sporty little number capable of 95 mph:

> Bonnie and Clyde killed and drove by instinct. For them, the machine gun and the car were less tools than liturgical objects half way between concrete reality and insane hallucination. At once a kind of asceticism, a transfiguration, and an absolute deviation from the norm, their cars had to be fast to keep ahead of their pursuers . . . The cigar lighter on the dashboard has a long wire attached to it that allows you to take it wherever you want to and it still stays red hot. Very practical, when a bound and gagged victim stubbornly refuses to tell you where his dollars are hidden.

The following year Serge Gainsbourg and Brigitte Bardot got together to record an album entitled simply *Bonnie and Clyde,* but renowned author Henry Miller, who'd only just caught up with the film, wrote an article for *Penthouse* magazine called 'Make Love Not Gore', denouncing Arthur Penn's movie as 'a toccata for half-wits'. The author of *Tropic of Cancer* called for a rash of down-to-earth pornographic films by way of an antidote to all the violence – 'the more censorable the better . . . what a relief it would be to see some real warm-hearted honest-to-God intercourse on the screen'. Evidently, Henry wasn't a follower of Yippie activist leader Jerry Rubin, busy collecting his wisdom together in a book entitled *Do it! Scenarios of the Revolution* (1970), which declared that 'Bonnie Parker and Clyde Barrow are the leaders of the New Youth', and went on to predict that, come the revolution, 'barbers will go to rehabilitation camps where they will grow their hair long', 'the Pentagon will be replaced by an LSD experimentation farm', and 'kids will lock their parents out of their suburban homes and turn them into guerilla bases, storing arms'.

The long-running argument about *Bonnie and Clyde* and screen violence gradually faded, and the film itself was enshrined as one of the top box office earners of all time. Still, however, Penn and others involved in the movie found themselves continually on the defensive regarding the picture's historical accuracy, which in many ways is understandable. In 1964, when Benton and Newman set about researching the lives of Bonnie and Clyde, the events which they were describing were only thirty years in the past – closer in time to them than the 1960s are to us now – and very many of the families of those killed by the Barrows were still alive. Under the circumstances, it's not hard to see why Penn's film stirred up controversy – some arguing that it glorified violence, and others saying that it whitewashed a couple of cold-blooded killers. Many of those connected with the film have spent the years since it appeared promoting the view that Barrow and Parker were 'enormous folk heroes', and that they never shot at anyone who hadn't fired at them first. Arthur Penn said at the time that they may have been inaccurate in small details 'but not in the big ones', and that 'we don't purport to tell the exact truth, but we do tell a truth'. As a piece of film-making, *Bonnie and Clyde* is remarkable; as a piece of history it doesn't really stand up, but then, neither do most movies.

The moral of the story would seem to be: 'Live fast, die young, and have a much-more-photogenic Hollywood star provide the good-looking corpse.' Perhaps Spinal Tap were onto something with *Saucy Jack,* their proposed musical based on the life of Jack the Ripper: 'He *may* be young . . . he *may* be in love . . . and he kills people.'

Get Carter

What happens when a professional killer violates the code?

Film: Get Carter
Director: Mike Hodges
Leading players: Michael Caine, Britt Ekland, Ian Hendry, John Osborne
Year of release: 1971

Book: Jack's Return Home
Author: Ted Lewis
Year of publication: 1970

Sex and thuggery unlimited, narrative disjointed, rewards few.
Halliwell's Film Guide, Fifth Edition, Paladin 1986

Britain in 1970. The 'swinging' 60s had disappeared down the drain, leaving the average working-class bloke with longer hair, an epidemic of unflattering facial fungus and clothes apparently designed in the dark by someone with a job-lot of flower-patterned man-made fibres they needed to shift in a hurry. 'Women's Lib' was some new thing from America which people were reading about, but in the UK most females under forty were still referred to as 'birds' and were walking around in mini-skirts, while the new tabloid-style *Sun* newspaper was celebrating its first anniversary by introducing their first topless Page Three girl, Stephanie Rahn. 'The *Sun*,' they explained, 'like most of its readers, likes pretty girls.' Official film censor John Trevelyan, apparently not a *Sun* reader, was complaining about the increasing amount of onscreen sex, saying 'the sad fact is that there are simply not enough U and A films around', and, in June 1970, introduced a new classification – AA – in an effort to cut down the number of X ratings being given out. The most popular programme on any of the nation's three television channels was *On The Buses,* pulling in around eight million viewers a week, in which a handy geezer (Reg Varney, aged fifty-four at the time) regularly has to fight off lust-crazed, nubile young women whilst trying to outwit a crusty old bus inspector (Stephen Lewis, then in his early thirties).

1970 was also the year that a writer named James Moffat, using the name Richard Allen, published a book called *Skinhead,* which sold like wildfire among schoolkids up and down the country, while some of the spare money the skins themselves had left after buying Crombies and Doc Martens helped put reggae singles by Desmond Dekker and Jimmy Cliff into the charts. Sharing the musical spotlight on the BBC's *Top of the Pops* programme on Thursday nights – along with the likes of Des O'Connor and *Dad's Army* refugee Clive Dunn – were the England World Cup Squad, singing *Back Home*, which is exactly where they wound up after being knocked out of that year's competition in Mexico. Cinema admissions were down, and the industry was keeping a wary eye on an invention which Philips had just announced called the VCR, due to be available in 1971, but exactly who was supposed to be able to afford such an expensive piece of gear apart from the seriously rich was anybody's guess. Unemployment was rising, and, according to the media, half the people who actually *did* have a job spent most of their time on strike anyway, particularly the electricity workers, which meant that random power cuts had become a familiar feature of life.

A decade after smug Tory Prime Minister Harold Macmillan had told the plebs, 'You've never had it so good,' and five years after smug Labour Prime Minister Harold Wilson had come up with a load of flannel about Britain forging ahead with the 'white heat of technology', the country was slowly waking up to the fact that 'modern' high-rise buildings didn't necessarily mean progress, and that the good times might not be just around the corner. Enter Ted Lewis, a writer who'd grown up through the optimism of the 60s (he even worked as a freelance illustrator on the Beatles cartoon film *Yellow Submarine*), but who, in *Jack's Return Home*, using the quintessentially American form of the hardboiled crime novel, nailed down some of the best descriptions of what it was like to live in Britain as the decade of hippie optimism finally rolled over and died.

Ted Lewis was born in Manchester on 15 January 1940, but grew up near Hull in a small town called Barton-on-Humber, close to the southern end of the Humber Bridge, the iron and steel mills of Scunthorpe and the fishing port of Grimsby. He developed an early interest in both writing and the attractions of the local pubs, while at the same time taking a keen interest in the visual arts, which prompted his decision to study at Hull Art School. Lewis then moved to London, and in 1965 he published his first novel, *All the Way Home and All the Night Through*. During that same year he also drew illustrations for a children's book and an edition of *The Bridge on the River Kwai*. Ted's first novel looked back to his Art School days for inspiration, but his next book, which he wrote in the late 1960s while earning good money as an animator, turned to the field of crime fiction, blending the twin influences of his northern upbringing and the London gang subculture of the Krays and the Richardsons. Lurid tales were emerging at that time, of Ronnie and Reg Kray stabbing Jack 'The Hat' McVitie or ventilating George Cornell in an East End pub called the Blind Beggar. In 1967 Charlie and Eddie Richardson's trial gave rise to charming newspaper headlines such as 'They Broke My Toes With Pliers, Says Man' and it became clear that English criminals weren't entirely the ineffectual, 'It's a fair cop, guv' softies that films and books had always portrayed. Ted Lewis managed to build his new novel around a character who moved easily in this violent world; a man named Jack Carter, working for a pair of London brothers, Gerald and Les Fletcher, who were a thousand times more frightening than anything the TV coppers from *Z Cars* or *Dixon of Dock Green* were ever likely to come up against.

As a crime novel, *Jack's Return Home* (1970, republished the following year as *Carter*, then finally as *Get Carter*) is simply one of the finest ever to have emerged from the UK. A classic revenge tragedy of a London-based hard-man visiting the small northern town of his youth in order to investigate the mysterious killing of his brother, it's sharply written, direct and pleasingly devoid of sympathetic characters. It's hard to think of anything quite like it among the British crime fiction which had come before – in fact, its closest spiritual predecessor is probably Paul Cain's US hardboiled masterpiece *Fast One* (1936); another nihilistic train-wreck of a book where virtually every character comes to a bad end. Here is a world of self-made men who came up the hard way, starting trouble with phrases like 'Now then, cuntie, let's be having you,' and no-nonsense pubs, where there's 'singing till ten, fighting till eleven'. If you're a stranger in town visiting one of the local hostelries, your chances are split 50/50 between dying of boredom and getting your head kicked in. Or both:

> You had to give the landlord credit. He'd really tried to make it look the kind of place that married couples in their forties would want to come to for the last hour on a Saturday night . . . There were a couple of yobboes playing a disc-only fruit machine. There was an old dad with a half-a-bitter and the *Racing Green*, and sitting next to him there was a very old brass in a trouser suit leaving her lipstick all over a glass of Guinness.

As a social document the novel is so in tune with its time that given another twenty years it'll probably need a lengthy glossary, like some medieval text, otherwise half the subtle references in the descriptions of people and places will be lost. Here's Jack Carter on his first visit to see the big local boss, Cyril Kinnear:

> The girl called Joy brought my drink. She was strictly Harrison
> Marks.

That's a needle-sharp one-line character sketch, which falls flat on its face if the reader doesn't know the style of photo model favoured by Britain's 1960s king of the soft-core pin-up, George Harrison Marks, who in magazines such as *Kamera* and feature films like *Naked as Nature Intended* (1961) and *The Nine Ages of Nakedness* (1969), boldly went, as far as most schoolboys were concerned, where only those naughty French and Scandinavian types had been before. Harrison Marks might not have been a name to drop in 'respectable' society, but your everyday pub-going geezer would most certainly have known about George's particular contribution to British culture. (Oddly enough, *Naked as Nature Intended* was brought to the screen by a company called Compton-Cameo Films, run by Tony Tenser and Michael Klinger. Klinger would eventually buy the film rights to *Jack's Return Home* during the manuscript stage and go on to produce *Get Carter*.)

Another reference which has moved from mass market to obscure with the passing of time shows up in this description of the 'entertainment' available for customers in a bar called The Cecil:

> While we'd been talking the band had drifted on to the stage.
> There was an old fat drummer in an old tux and a bloke on an
> electric bass, and at the organ, with all its magic attachments, sat
> a baldheaded man with a shiny face, a blue crewneck sweater and
> a green cravat. They struck up with *I'm A Tiger*.

Tatty pub combos like this, tormenting the locals, are generally a thing of the past these days, but the sting in the tail here comes with the song which they choose to play – a desperately chirpy record from 1968 by Scots singer Lulu, who at that time had her own TV show. In an age before videos, satellite TV or computer games, songs which were plugged on television would have reached a huge slice of the population, regardless of whether they happened to be followers of the music scene, and anyone unlucky enough to be stuck at home on a Saturday night was a captive audience. Ted Lewis, who was at the very end of his twenties while writing the novel, throws in all these mainstream family entertainment references with an implied air of sarcasm – 'Margaret was lying on the sofa watching Rolf Harris and smoking' – and an eye for detail born of hundreds of nights locked in watching any old rubbish that the TV had to offer. In what is possibly the book's most depressing location – Albert Swift's one-family brothel on a piece of waste ground in the grotty part of town – the television is blasting out the relentlessly cheerful voice of a celebrity sports commentator, whose northern accent was so famous at the time that it formed part of every TV comedian's roster of vocal impressions:

> I opened the kitchen door but Albert wasn't there any more. Just Eddie Waring and Hull Kingston Rovers and St Helens and their supporters making a lot of noise in the corner.

Swift's house is a pigsty ('On the kitchen table amongst the plates from at least half a dozen meals was a carrycot'), yet the expensively-decorated homes and the brand-new buildings in the novel are also a pretty uninspiring bunch, usually decorated in the height of bad taste and crammed full of tacky accessories. The house of Cliff Brumby, the 'fiddling slot machine king', is a monument to then-current trends in modern home decoration, with a wall-to-wall carpet whose 'floral pattern was far too big to fit into the space it occupied'. There are banister railings of 'white-glossed wrought iron,' a red telephone, and on the walls, 'a print of the green-faced Oriental Girl in a white frame' and 'a pair of plastic duelling pistols'. As for sinister Mr Big, Cyril Kinnear, he runs a gambling joint wittily named The Casino, which presumably also won numerous architectural and design awards:

> It looked like the alternative plan to the new version of Euston Station. White, low and ugly. A lot of glass. A single piece of second storey that was a penthouse. A lot of sodium lighting. Plenty of phoney ranch-house brickwork. Probably the worst beer for seventy miles.

By the time he was working on this novel, Lewis had already spent a couple of years working in the very heart of 'swinging' mid-60s London, and so when he was describing all of these locations from the point of view of big city Jack

Carter back in the small northern town of his youth, he could draw directly on his own experience. The streets, houses and pub interiors are not viewed through the eyes of someone who lives there, but rather from the standpoint of someone who used to belong, but is glad that they left:

> It all looked as it had eight years ago when I'd seen it last. A good place to say goodbye to.

Clearly, though, this landscape haunted him. In Lewis's next novel, *Plender* (1971), sleazy photographer Knott is a character who has spent some time down in London after having attended Art School, but then moves back to his (unnamed) home town by a river, within striking distance of Scunthorpe and Grimsby. (In a nod to a character from his previous book, one of the local villages in *Plender* is called Brumby, just as the opening sentence of his 1974 novel *Jack Carter's Law* begins in Plender Street.)

If the descriptions of places in *Jack's Return Home* are harsh and unforgiving, the scenes of violence are equally direct. It's not something employed by these characters for pleasure, but usually as a method of getting results or handing out punishment. As such it is applied without mercy, and women as well as men can wind up horribly disfigured or dead if they have offended those in control. If by some chance any of these characters had ever bought a copy of the Marquess of Queensberry's Rules, it's clear they'd have been wasting their money – heads are butted, eyes are gouged, and below the belt is very far from off-limits:

> Con had both hands in his pockets. One on the shooter, one on the knife. I stopped the car and pulled the handbrake on. Then I flashed my hand between Con's legs and grabbed his balls and squeezed hard. Con opened his mouth to scream, but before any sound could come out I pulled his hat over his face and stuffed as much of it as I could into his mouth. I let go of his balls and gave him one in the throat. He began to choke so I hit him on the temple with my elbow and pulled the hat out of his mouth. He fell forward and cracked his forehead on the dashboard. With a little assistance from myself.

Just as many of the book's characters seem to have abandoned any concept of 'fair play' when it comes to fighting, it also appears that the Age of Chivalry

158

has long since past. Escaping from the police along with alcoholic porn actress Glenda in a white Triumph TR4, Jack slugs her in the mouth and leaves her lying in the road in order to slow down the pursuing cops. This is probably no more than she would have expected, since this is a macho world in which Jack's former sister-in-law is dismissed as 'plain as buggery', his brother's girlfriend is worse – 'I'd say she was a whore . . . what would you say?' – and the repartee between men and women as the drinks are being poured is equally coy and restrained:

> 'Glenda,' he said, 'Your fanny's in Jack's face.'
> Still leaning over, Glenda screwed her head round to look at me.
> 'I don't see him complaining,' she said.

This kind of language in an English novel would have been hard to imagine only ten years before, but much had changed in the social scene during the previous decade. The well-publicised *Lady Chatterley's Lover* obscenity trial in 1960 (during which both the *Guardian* and the *Observer* decided that their readers were adult enough to read the word 'fuck' printed in a newspaper without the benefit of asterisks), had radically shifted the boundaries of what was held to be permissible. The influence of the 'kitchen sink' school of English drama popularised at the Royal Court Theatre, together with the subsequent success of films like *Saturday Night and Sunday Morning* (1960) and *A Kind of Loving* (1962), led to stories with a working-class and particularly northern background being considered hot properties both in the book trade, among TV drama producers and with film companies. Director Ken Loach had brought gritty realism into the homes of the nation in December 1966 when the BBC screened his drama *Cathy Come Home*, and the following year he'd moved into the cinemas with *Poor Cow*, further signalling that the age of the upper-class drawing-room comedy had long since past. Measured against this background – despite the efforts of the one-woman moral crusade being waged at the time by Mary Whitehouse, who would have felt more at home in the England of the early 1800s, when they were happily censoring all kinds of filth like *Gulliver's Travels*, Pepys' *Diary*, the Bible and Shakespeare – it's not surprising that a book company such as Michael Joseph were impressed enough in 1968 with the manuscript of *Jack's Return Home* to accept it for publication.

In fact, during the two years before the novel hit the shops, there was a further relaxation of restrictions upon what was deemed permissible in the arts generally. Censorship of stage productions in the UK was abolished in

1968, and films such as Peckinpah's *The Wild Bunch* (1969) and *I Am Curious – Yellow* (1969) showed how rapidly the boundaries in the cinema were changing. In this increasingly liberal climate, it is easy to understand why film producer Michael Klinger optioned a hard-hitting story like *Jack's Return Home* for cinema adaptation before the book had even been published. As things turned out, it proved a useful property to have available when an old friend of Klinger's approached him about forming a production partnership. He was a famous actor with an urge to branch out, and to have more control over the kinds of films he was making. His name was Michael Caine. As the actor himself recalled in his 1993 autobiography, *What's it All About?*:

> This decision was based on the rather negative conclusion that as I had worked with several allegedly great film-makers and gone straight down the drain with them, I might as well go that route on my own for a change.

By 1970, Michael Caine, who had recently alerted the cinema-going public to the joys of driving a Mini down staircases and over factory roofs in *The Italian Job* (1969), was a household name around the world. Starting out in the 50s, he'd come up the hard way through bit-parts in stage plays and B-features, and in an April 1969 *Films & Filming* interview with David Austen he had this to say about the moment when he finally hit the big time:

> Looking back, people imagine that my break came with *Zulu*. But quite honestly, that's just what *didn't* happen, it was a year later. *The Ipcress File* made me a star.

The Ipcress File (1965) and *Alfie* (1966) brought Caine to the attention of all sorts of people, not least the *New York Times*, who sent Gloria Steinem to interview him (published in December 1966 under the headline 'Maurice Joseph Micklewhite – What's 'E Got?'), and he also wound up on TV explaining to Merv Griffin, 'Cockneys used to be looked on kindly, like Mickey Mouse or dwarves, but we decided to be people instead.' He later claimed that the French had responded badly to *Alfie*, refusing to believe that any Englishman could possibly sleep with that many women, 'because as far as the French are concerned we're a nation of homosexuals, so my character to them was entirely and utterly false,' but, this minor drawback aside, by the time he decided to branch out into production with *Get Carter*, Caine was in a position to set things up entirely his own way.

One thing that he and his partner Michael Klinger were determined about was that they wanted to portray English gangsters in a far more realistic fashion than was usual in films, and that the violence should be equally convincing. 'In real life,' as Caine pointed out, 'every single punch in the face tears skin and cartilage and often breaks bones.' With *Jack's Return Home*, they had the ideal story with which to put across this tough, unflinching approach: now all they needed was to find the right director. Sitting at home one night, Michael Caine happened to watch a new crime drama called *Rumour*, by a television director called Mike Hodges. Caine rang Michael Klinger as soon as the end titles rolled, convinced that he'd found the man they were looking for, only to find that Klinger was already calling him on the other line to say exactly the same thing. In the memorable words of film critic Alexander Walker, *Rumour* 'revealed a vividly-conceptualised view of life as a state of constantly impending doom only tempered by periods of grievous bodily harm', which would seem to be a fairly appropriate calling card for a man about to direct *Get Carter*.

Mike Hodges was a veteran of ITV's *World in Action* programme, and had also produced a series of short films for ABC television in 1967, which *Town* magazine's reviewer raved about as 'the sort of material which I would like to see accompanying feature films at my local cinema'. Still, for a 38-year-old first-time cinema director, working with a major star like Caine was certainly a step up in the world. Hodges was also contracted to write the script, although Caine's autobiography implies that there was already some kind of screenplay in existence before the director was chosen. ('We had a script and all we needed now was a director.') One thing is certain, Ted Lewis himself wasn't given the opportunity to write the script, although, as his ex-wife remembered, 'he would have done it for nothing, even, but he wasn't given the opportunity'. In many ways this is a shame, since he had created these characters and their world, and a fair amount of Lewis's dialogue was lifted verbatim from the book anyway. In the feature-length commentary that Hodges later prepared for the DVD release of *Get Carter*, he fails to mention Ted Lewis at all, and only namechecks the book in order to point out scenes where the film differs from the novel. Similarly, in his article 'Getting Carter' (*Crime Time* Issue 9, 1997), Hodges is keen to stress how many things he changed, and doesn't mention anything praiseworthy about the original novel at all. A favourite story he has told over the years involves the first appearance of Carter in a pub, where Jack asks for a pint 'in a thin glass'. Hodges remarks that in the book, Carter adds the word 'please' to the end of this request, and that, by omitting this from his script, he has had to endure 'twenty five years of macho men, on learning that I made the film, snapping their fingers at me with the same sinister authority'. Fair enough, you might think, except that in the book, Carter first says the words 'Pint of bitter,' and only says 'in a thin glass please' some time later, deliberately to annoy the slow barman once he has already begun pouring the drink. 'Why didn't you bloody well say?' complains the barman. 'I was going to, but you were too fast for me,' replies Jack. In the film, Carter is just looking for a drink, in the book, he's also looking for an argument, and yet Hodges's version of events seems designed to suggest that the Jack of the novel is something of a wimp, and that the character created for the film is a different kind of man altogether. To support this theory, in his article for *Crime Time*, he also quotes the following passage from the book:

> I was the only one in the compartment. My slip-ons were off.
> My feet were up. *Penthouse* was dead. I'd killed the *Standard* twice.
> I had three nails left. Doncaster was forty minutes off.

Hodges then writes: 'That's the third paragraph of the novel; but already my script was deviating. Caine's Carter doesn't bite his nails.' Neither does Ted Lewis's Carter: the nails in question are cigarettes – 'coffin nails' – standard working-class slang for most of the twentieth century. He's on a long train journey and he's simply wondering if he's going to run out of cigarettes, which eventually he does, and the subject crops up four or five times in the next few pages until he finally cadges a smoke from a taxi driver. Ted Lewis's Jack Carter isn't a nail-biting worrier, nor did the film transform this character from a mild-mannered bloke into a tough guy. Hodges wrote a very fine script, and did a magnificent job of directing the picture, so it's a shame that he seems unwilling to credit his source material in any terms other than this.

One major contribution that Mike Hodges made to the film was his choice of Newcastle and its outlying districts as a location. Not only is it much larger and more visually striking than the novel's fictionalised version of Barton-on-Humber, but it was also a city in the throes of major reconstruction, as producer Michael Klinger told *ABC Film Review*: 'Newcastle is in an incredible state of transition at present, changing from the old to the new. Buildings are being demolished and new ones are going up all over the place and we took advantage of the resulting, often highly dramatic locales, when shooting the film.' Given that one of the dodgy 'businessmen' in the film – slot-machine mogul Brumby – is ploughing his money into a high-rise car-park and restaurant, the choice of city was more appropriate than anyone knew, since a series of corruption trials (which began in the year of *Get Carter's* release and would eventually lead to the resignation of Tory Home Secretary Reginald Maudling) soon revealed that the head of Newcastle City Council, T Dan Smith, had been dishonestly involved with local architect John Poulson and others, and that a lot of backhanders and bribes had been affecting the course of the city's building boom.

Another item of real-life criminal activity in the Newcastle area that had a more direct effect upon the making of the film was the January 1967 murder of Angus Sibbett, whose bullet-riddled body was found in his car beneath a bridge in South Hetton, County Durham. The dead man was involved in collecting money from fruit machines in working men's clubs in the area, and it was alleged that he had been skimming the take. Sibbett had been working for a man named Vincent Landa, the local slot-machine king, as had Dennis Stafford and Michael Luvaglio (Landa's brother), the men who were eventually jailed for the murder. Landa himself had fled the country at the time of the trial, but Hodges discovered that his former mansion, Dryerdale Hall, County Durham, was still on the market, and available for use as a film location; with the minimum of props it became fictional villain Cyril Kinnear's home. (Strangely enough, the Sibbett murder hit the headlines again in May 2002, when the European Court of Human Rights at Strasbourg ruled that the British Home Secretary had kept Dennis Stafford in jail longer than was necessary and ordered compensation paid. By this time, the papers had taken to calling it the '*Get Carter* murder'.)

While Hodges was investigating the Newcastle gangland scene, Michael Caine had been doing his own research in London, tracking down a suitably authentic role model on which to base his portrayal of Jack Carter. 'I didn't want to play the cliché heavy, the hardcase with a soft centre,' he said at the time. 'Actors have been doing that since Paul Muni's *Scarface*. I wanted, very simply, the truth now.' In an article entitled 'Inside the Mind of a Villain', published in the January 1971 edition of *Club* magazine, he described how he'd spent three months locating a suitable hoodlum, and had interviewed the man at length about his life and opinions, so that he would feel he knew how Jack Carter might behave in any given situation. The bulk of the article consists of excerpts from these tape-recorded interviews, with Caine asking the questions and his subject identified only as 'Jack'. This real-life Carter turns out to be a fan of right-wing politician Enoch Powell, hates 'ponces' and wants to see 'concentration camps in this country for pimps and drug pushers'. As for romance: 'I've got a smashing flat, near the King's Road, and pull fantastic birds. Not any old slags. It's got to be a bit special. I think I've had birds of every nationality – and I've never been abroad.' He tells Caine that he is unafraid of death, and is certainly not a sadist:

> Nobody likes violence. I'm not a psychopath like geezers you read about in books, the Marquis de Sade and all that. I don't get any pleasure out of hurting people . . . I am a reasonable sort of bloke, I would say a gentle sort of bloke in a way. I go and tell them what I want. If they don't see eye to eye with me . . . that's the unhappy time. The happy time is when I meet someone who has as much intelligence as me; he listens to my proposition and sees the sense in it – and he also sees the stupidity in getting himself hurt.

As Caine said in 1997, after having played another villain in Bob Rafelson's *Blood and Wine*: 'I was born in an area that was full of seedy characters . . . I always have a different take on the attitude of criminals than most people, because most people's knowledge of criminals and villains comes from what they've seen in films, which they think is true. I know what criminals are like in real life.'

After an initial couple of days shooting in London, most of *Get Carter* was made on location in and around Newcastle in the late summer and early autumn of 1970. Publicity material at the time suggests that the filming took nine weeks, although Hodges's records indicate a slightly quicker timespan of forty days. Extensive use was made of actual buildings, with lighting cameraman Wolfgang Suschitzky and his crew backing into corners of rooms and using available light where possible, which helped enormously in achieving the downbeat, realistic look of the picture. However, a studio was used for some interior scenes, which were shot on the EMI-MGM sound stages at Elstree, on a set next door to Vincent Price filming *The Abominable Doctor Phibes*. (Other cultural landmarks under construction at Elstree that year included *Up Pompeii*, Hammer's *Lust For a Vampire*, the *Double Deckers* TV series, *The Railway Children* and Britain's first penis-transplant comedy, *Percy*.) Advance publicity material listed the film's name as *Carter*, which was also the title under which Pan Books republished Ted Lewis's book – with a fine still of a shotgun-toting Caine on the cover. Curiously enough, the list of current UK films in production in the November 1970 issue of *Films & Filming* mistakenly shows

Carter as being 'directed by Ted Lewis'.

If Caine was perfect casting for the part of Jack Carter, the film's other roles were also filled by a remarkable selection of character actors – indeed, together with Mike Hodges's choice of locations, it is the strength of the cast that he assembled which contributed enormously to the film's success. World-renowned playwright John Osborne, playing the part of Newcastle's main gang boss, was certainly far removed from the character's description in the novel – 'Cyril Kinnear was very, very fat. He was the kind of man that fat men like to stand next to. He had no hair and a handlebar moustache that his face made look a foot long on each side' – yet he brought a convincingly sleazy malevolence to the part. Likewise, Brian Mosley (who was later to become known to millions of soap fans as Alf Roberts in Granada TV's *Coronation Street*) did a fine job portraying Cliff Brumby, whose late night confrontation with Jack Carter prompted the film's most-quoted lines: 'You're a big man, but you're in bad shape. With me it's a full-time job. Now behave yourself.' (In the book, the threat is slightly different: 'Cliff, you're a big bloke – you're in good shape. But I know more than you do.') For the key role of Eric Paice, Ian Hendry was another inspired choice – a veteran of 60s cult TV programmes such as *The Avengers*, and *The Saint*, he was a hard-drinking, deadpan customer and utterly believable in the part. Ironically, while most of the cast were actors playing tough guys, for the part of Sid Fletcher (called Les in the book) the film-makers employed John Bindon, a genuine hardman and friend of the Krays, who had turned to acting on the suggestion of director Ken Loach, but later wound up in court on various counts of alleged violence, including a gangland murder charge in 1978.

In a macho world such as that of *Get Carter*, the women's roles are inevitably somewhat less rewarding, particularly in the case of Britt Ekland, whose principal task as Gerald Fletcher's girlfriend Anna (called Audrey in the novel) is to writhe around on a bed, telephone in hand, as Caine tells her: 'Take your bra off. Now, hold them, gently.' Geraldine Moffatt is given much more scope as Glenda, the permanently-drunk woman in the white sports car who divides her time between Brumby and Kinnear, but even she is not spared some heavy-handed moments suggestively caressing a gear stick as the speedometer revs into overdrive. Pub singer Denea Wilde makes it through a couple of verses before having a beer poured over her head by a jealous rival, but at least she gets to keep her clothes on – unlike her counterpart in the novel, who is down to a G-string and dunking portions of her anatomy in pints of beer before the catfight begins. Rosemarie Dunham – as Edna, the landlady of the

Las Vegas guesthouse – has the obligatory roll in the hay with Carter, but still delivers some nice sarcastic lines, pointing out to him the box of ashes which has been delivered by someone from the local crematorium:

Edna: That was left for you this evening. What is it?

Carter: My brother Frank.

Edna: Is he staying the night?

Petra Markham, playing Jack's teenage niece Doreen, comes across as less jaded and somehow more wholesome than her counterpart in the novel, but this is perhaps not surprising, since the porn film in which she stars – *Teacher's Pet* – has to be one of the most innocuous examples of the genre ever filmed, in which all concerned are desperate to keep their clothes on, recalling nothing so much as the *St Trinians* comedies of the 1950s. The Doreen of *Jack's Return Home* is a far tougher customer, but then she'd probably have to be, since *her* fifteen minutes of celluloid fame is a charming item entitled *Schoolgirl Wanks*, in which she is sent off the deep-end by looking at pictures of pop sensation Engelbert Humperdinck.

In general, although the location has changed and so have various minor plot details, it's remarkable how faithful the film stays to the spirit of the book. Most of the changes are insignificant – characters' names are altered, Eric Paice drives a Cadillac instead of a Rolls, the main pub becomes the Half Moon rather than the Cecil, Edna's underwear changes from green to purple – while others, such as the shifting of a key gunfight from Albert Swift's house to the ferry terminal, are mostly there in order to take advantage of visual opportunities offered by the Newcastle locations. Nevertheless, anyone seeing the film after reading the book, or vice versa, would instantly recognize it as the same story. Ted Lewis was photographed on location with the unit in the back streets of Newcastle, and although he had no part in the screenplay, he must have been justifiably proud of the way his novel was brought to the screen.

Right from the start, as soon as Roy Budd's stunning title theme kicks in and the train heads into a tunnel, this is a film that sinks its teeth into your leg and won't let go. Caine is shown sitting in a carriage, reading a copy of Chandler's *Farewell, My Lovely*, while the sniper who will eventually kill him sits opposite, seemingly engrossed in a tabloid newspaper whose front page headline is 'GAMING CHIEFS WARN OF GANG WAR'. Somehow, you just know that there won't be a conventional Hollywood happy ending this time. As Michael Caine points out in the audio commentary on the DVD release of the picture, one thing distinguishing him from most American stars at the time was his willingness to play a character who dies in a movie. These days, such behaviour seems to have disappeared from mainstream film-making, but – as Hitchcock demonstrated when he killed off Janet Leigh barely a third of the way through *Psycho* – the advantage of employing a method of storytelling in which the principal characters are by no means indestructible is that the audience is continually alert, and the narrative seems almost as random as real life. Hodges has said that he always knew that Carter would die at the end of the film, but that's hardly a revelation, given that he dies at the end of the book. Still, as Caine has said, if the film had been made a few years later, Jack would have lived, and we'd have all had to endure *Carter 2, 3, 4* and maybe *5*.

For its time, the violence in the film was not particularly extreme. Audiences had already been treated to Sam Peckinpah's slow-motion bloodbath finale in 1969's *The Wild Bunch*, and yet it was the cold, matter-of-fact killings such as the knifing of Albert Swift that gave *Get Carter* such impact. Even so, the language is toned down from that in the novel, where the final exchange is as follows:

Jack, for Christ's sake. . .

Don't be a cunt, Albert. You knew what I'd do.

This particular onscreen stabbing is sickeningly real, and it's worth noting that in the book, Jack himself is killed with just such a knife, at the hands of Eric, who then dies himself as a shotgun backfires while he's attempting to finish off Carter. In the novel, the two opponents bring about their own destruction, whereas the film allows Jack his moment of revenge in killing Eric, before his own death at the hands of a hired killer. Either way, the intended moral is clear, and in neither version does Carter ever get to fire the shotgun which has become so much a part of the film's iconography; dying just as he attempts to throw it into the sea, on a bleak and desolate beach similar to the one in Roman Polanski's *Macbeth* (also released in 1971).

Get Carter had its London premiere on 11 March 1971, and Caine himself also filmed a message for those attending a special Newcastle showing of the

167

picture. MGM's publicity people had done a comprehensive job of building up the figure of Jack Carter as the archetypal new anti-hero for the 1970s – a tougher guy for a tougher decade. As *Photoplay* dutifully reported:

> Carter is, not to put too fine a point on it, a crook, a criminal, a hoodlum, a thug, and generally a nasty piece of work . . . He goes in for mid-blue, three-piece mohair suits made by a showbiz tailor in Shepherd's Bush. Made-to-measure, of course. With them he favours high-collared pale-blue shirts from Turnbull and Asser set off with black, figured ties by Christian Dior. His black shoes are decorated with a gold band on the instep and made by Bally of Switzerland. He displays an inch-and-a-half of shirt cuff and always carries a clean handkerchief.

Journalists were obviously encouraged to present Carter as a hard-bitten descendent of 60s icons such as James Bond and Matt Helm. Vincent Firth wrote in *ABC Film Review*:

> They were good, very good, and they filled the cinemas of Britain and America with millions of movie fans who thrilled to their exploits. Now comes the decade of the seventies and where shall we look for their successors? No further, in my opinion, than Jack Carter, who is brilliantly brought to vibrant, pulsating life by Michael Caine.

In later years, Caine has often remarked that the press gave the film a hard time, particularly over its depiction of violence, but it certainly had its supporters, and Vincent Firth's article goes on to say that Carter is the 'part of a lifetime for Michael Caine' and that he 'bestrides the screen like a colossus'. *Variety's* reviewer called it an 'excellent drama of criminal vengeance', praised the acting, direction and photography, compared the film favourably to *The Maltese Falcon* and *Bullitt* and felt that Carter was Michael Caine's 'best role in years'. Even the journalists who weren't quite as taken with the picture as a whole generally had some positive things to say. Tom Milne, writing in the Spring 1971 edition of *Sight & Sound*, wondered 'why none of the crew seem to be present during the shoot-out on a ferry which has just docked', and 'who is operating the mechanical dredger on the empty beach which allows Caine to dump Hendry's body in the sea'. Nevertheless, he also wrote that 'the English setting is brilliantly exploited . . . Mike Hodges screws his direction up tight against his hero, clamping him in a bright, shiny vice of sex and sadism, and (apart from a couple of appallingly vulgar montages) looking a likely bet for better things to come'. Meanwhile, in the May 1971 issue of *Films & Filming,* Richard Weaver gave the film a generally positive review, and linked its approach to that of a couple of other upcoming British crime pictures:

> This film may well herald the beginning of a spate of hard-hitting thrillers; with Albert Finney's *Gumshoe* and *Villain*, starring Richard Burton, to follow, this could possibly indicate a trend for the early seventies . . . This is crime at its most blatant, breeding a successful degree of tension from the knowledge that not all violence is likely to occur down dark alleys.

Several other contemporary reviewers quite justifiably also made this connection between Caine's performance and Burton's gangland role in *Villain*. 'It's a hard, ruthless world, we're told, and we must believe it, if films like *Get Carter* and *Villain* have any grain of truth,' wrote Susan d'Arcy in that year's *Photoplay Film Annual*, but the London cinemagoers who queued up at the Ritz in July 1971 to see *Get Carter* obviously didn't seem to mind. Competing for their hard-earned ticket money that same week across the big metropolis were such tasty items as *The Sexy Dozen* at the Cameo-Royal, *On the Buses* at the ABC Edgware Road, a double bill of *Blood On Satan's Claw* and *The Beast in the Cellar* at the New Victoria and *The Language of Love* at the Jaycey, Charing Cross – the latter being an example of a new trend in feature-length continental sex-instruction films, whose title music was newly available on an album entitled *Soldier Blue & Other Film Themes* played by *Get Carter's* own Roy Budd.

The film did respectable business in the UK, but Michael Caine's memory of the US release was that it was basically thrown away as the bottom half of a double bill, playing second fiddle to a Frank Sinatra western called *Dirty Dingus McGhee* – 'so we went in the toilet in two weeks'. America aside, the picture was certainly judged enough of a success even during its initial London run to warrant a news item in the August 1971 edition of *Photoplay* claiming that the team of Caine, Klinger and Hodges would be getting together shortly to work on another film, which was to be called *Scandal*. This was eventually retitled *Pulp*, and was shot in Malta during the spring of 1972. *Photoplay* magazine had a reporter on set, who filed an article entitled 'There Are Devils Inside Me says Michael Caine' and, although it transpired that *Get Carter* could not have been shown on the island due to tough censorship restrictions, the team's previous film appears to have been much on everyone's minds. Caine commented that 1971 had been 'a heavy year for me, I did *Get Carter*, *Zee & Co* and *Kidnapped*. I wanted something lighter. This was specially written for me,' while producer Michael Klinger added that *Get Carter* 'was made for a million dollars and has already made seven million'. In May 1974, ostensibly promoting his new film *The Marseilles Contract*, Michael Caine was still talking to journalists from magazines like *Film Review* and *Photoplay* about *Get Carter*, adding that it was one of his favourites among his own films. 'The public didn't really go for *Carter* the way we expected. We didn't put any salacious sadism into it but the critics said it was too violent. What they should have said was that it was too realistic.' By the time he published his autobiography in 1992, his high opinion of the film had justifiably not diminished:

> Mike Hodges did a great job on the picture, maybe too great since when it came out we were slammed by most of the critics for the violence. It was too realistic for these people who had become used to the choreographed nonsense you usually saw in those days. I happen to think that *Get Carter* is an excellent movie and I am very proud of it. It didn't make a great deal of money but it didn't lose any either, so nobody got hurt. Mike Hodges unfortunately did not live up to the promise that Klinger and I saw in him and *Carter* is still the best movie he ever made, but he is still a young man and he has time to prove us right.

At that time, the film had long enjoyed a high reputation among a hardcore of crime film enthusiasts, but was less well known among the general public, and film reference works in the 1980s such as *Halliwell's Film Guide* had been happy to write it off in a couple of sarcastic sentences. Caine's publishers included various stills drawn from throughout his career to illustrate his autobiography, but nothing from *Get Carter*. Had the book been published even five years later, they may well have wound up using an image of Caine as Jack on the cover – so much has the film's profile risen in recent years. Mike Hodges may have had an uneven career, as anyone who's ever sat through *Morons From Outer Space* (1985) would probably be the first to tell you, but in *Get Carter* he managed to direct what many consider to be the finest British gangland film of them all.

And Ted Lewis? *Plender*, his next novel after *Jack's Return Home*, was published in 1971 with a front cover credit that read 'Author of *Get Carter*', and the back dustjacket was largely taken up with a photograph of Ted taken at one of the film's Newcastle locations. For a while, things looked very good for him, and the June 1973 edition of *Films & Filming* carried the following news item:

> Cupid Productions has bought the rights to *Billy Rags*, for production here later this year. It will be the third Ted Lewis novel to be filmed: *Get Carter* was made by MGM and *Plender* is now being prepared by an independent production company.

Sadly, the other film projects stalled in the planning stage, and, in addition to writing books such as the police thriller *Boldt* (1976) and *G.B.H.* (1980), Ted also brought back Jack Carter in two other novels – *Jack Carter's Law* (1974) and *Jack Carter and the Mafia Pigeon* (1977), evidently hoping to have the same kind of success which he'd experienced at the start of the decade, but it wasn't to be. As his alcohol consumption increased, his health began to deteriorate, his marriage collapsed, and he died of a heart attack in 1982 aged only 42. It took another fifteen years, but eventually all of his novels were reissued in the UK, and the man who wrote *Get Carter* has now been afforded a little of the respect that he should have been shown in his lifetime. By combining contemporary London gangland mythology with large doses of his own northern upbringing, he managed to lay the basis for a whole new tradition of crime novel, quite unlike anything this country had produced before. As *American Publisher's Weekly* said at the time of *Jack's Return Home*:

> Ted Lewis writes like a British Mickey Spillane, with one big difference, Spillane writes entertainment, Lewis writes literature . . . The story is completely believable, and Lewis introduces us to a vivid parade of wildly vulgar and foul-mouthed people, both sexes, all ages.

Ted, like Jack and the England 1970 World Cup Squad, may have long since returned home, and the world of tatty Victorian boozers with 'singing till ten, fighting till eleven' has all but vanished in an epidemic of plastic theme-pub makeovers, but his remarkable, uniquely English strain of hardboiled books and their 'wildly vulgar and foul-mouthed people, both sexes, all ages', lives on.

Dillinger

Nobody Did it Like Dillinger – He Was the Gangster's Gangster.

Film: Dillinger
Director: John Milius
Leading players: Warren Oates, Ben Johnson, Michelle Phillips, Harry
Dean Stanton, Geoffrey Lewis, Cloris Leachman
Year of release: 1973

Real-life criminals: John Dillinger, Pretty Boy Floyd, Machine Gun Kelly,
Baby Face Nelson
Active: 1933-4, USA

John Dillinger's life was tailor-made for the movies. He knew it, and the
public knew it. Hell, even the FBI knew it. He kicked up such a media storm
over the course of one short year that by 1934 J Edgar Hoover had officially
named him Public Enemy Number One, and when Dillinger sensationally
broke out of the heavily-guarded Crown Point jail armed only with a self-
made wooden pistol, Hollywood's chief wet blanket, censor Will Hays, was
moved to personally veto any likelihood of the popular bank robber's exploits
showing up on the silver screen:

> Ban on Dillinger Escape as Film Thriller Theme
>
> The interest of motion picture studios in the escape of John Dillinger
> from prison was discouraged yesterday by an announcement from
> Will H Hays, president of the Motion Picture Producers and
> Distributors of America, declaring that the board of directors would
> not countenance a film based on the Dillinger episode.
>   'No motion picture based on the life or exploits of John
> Dillinger will be produced, distributed or exhibited by any
> company member,' Mr Hays' statement said. 'This embraces all
> the major companies in the motion picture industry. The decision
> is based on the belief that such a picture would be detrimental to
> the best public interest.'
>
> *New York Times*, 21 March 1934

Dillinger's high-profile series of unauthorised cash withdrawals came at the height of the Depression and at the very start of the Hays Office's attempts to persuade Hollywood to make cops, rather than hoodlums, the heroes of their urban shoot-em-up sagas. Henceforth, it was still fine to show cars screeching round corners on two wheels as their occupants blazed away with a tommy gun out of the shattered back window, just so long as the guy with the Chicago piano also happened to have a G-Man badge as well. That, apparently, constituted a moral approach to film-making. Trouble was, despite the best efforts of the censor and his buddies, Joe and Jane public still seemed to be continually cheering the bank robbers. As Herbert Corey wrote in *Farewell, Mr Gangster! – America's War on Crime,* his very pro-Hoover 1936 book about the then-recent exploits of the FBI:

> More people knew the mob leaders by name than could identify the Vice President . . . Sappy sentimentalists wrote of criminals as sick men to be pitied . . . The urban public sneered at law-enforcement officers. Movie producers issued sentimental pictures of gangsters.

Corey's book, published only two years after Dillinger's crime spree and eventual slaying outside Chicago's Biograph Theatre on 22 July 1934, is dominated by the shadow of America's most famous bank robber. Although the book reads at times more like a love-letter to J Edgar than a serious study of law enforcement ([Hoover] is forty years old, erect, swarthy, not quite six feet tall, with a strong, compact body . . . his black hair glistens . . . '), it was written with the FBI chief's full co-operation, and provides an interesting contemporary snapshot of official attitudes to the lives and recent deaths of the likes of Dillinger, Pretty Boy Floyd and Baby Face Nelson. While Hollywood had lately resigned itself to making films like *Public Hero Number One* and *G-Men* (both 1935), Herbert Corey's book was also at pains to point out that there was nothing glamorous about gangsters, or their women for that matter:

> Most of the men who have gained notoriety are ignorant and sullen louts . . . When they are in funds, criminals relax their over-strained nerves in drunken debauches with women who rank little higher than sows.

With character references like that, it's hard to imagine Tinseltown's finest trampling each other to death in the rush to play such glamorous roles, but Corey's view was very much at odds with the public perception of Dillinger and his gang. This wasn't a vicious, petty little killer like Clyde Barrow or Bonnie Parker – indeed, there's no hard evidence that Dillinger ever killed anyone at all, while his frequently-noted resemblance to the film star Douglas Fairbanks Sr, his laconic good humour and habit of giving his getaway hostages a few dollars for the ride home all helped make him something of a national hero. As the 4 March 1934 edition of the *Chicago Tribune* put it: '[Dillinger] is today what Dick Turpin, the English highwayman, and Jesse James, the American road agent, were to the public of their day.' In the depths of the Depression, few people had cause to love the banks, and it was Dillinger who famously told a customer during a heist to pick up the cash which was on the counter in front of him because 'We don't want your money, we only want the bank's', an incident later hijacked by Arthur Penn's *Bonnie and Clyde*.

John Herbert Dillinger was born in Indianapolis on 22 June 1903, and had his first brush with the law while still at school, charged with stealing coal from a railroad yard. He and his family then moved from the big city to a farm near Mooresville, Indiana, but on leaving school Dillinger had little enthusiasm for the prospect of life as a farmer. He played a lot of pool, worked for a while as a machinist, stole a car and then signed up for the US Navy. Evidently, somewhat less than impressed with a life on the ocean wave, he demonstrated the escape techniques for which he was later to become famous, running away several times from the *USS Utah* before going permanently AWOL in December 1923. Returning to Indiana, Dillinger devoted himself once more to some serious pool playing, and found time to get married before falling foul of the law once again. This time, however, without the aid of a lawyer, he came up against a judge looking to throw the book at someone, and wound up being sent to the slammer for armed robbery, remaining there from 1924 to 1933. By the time Dillinger was paroled, having been locked away for years with the cream of the bank-heist set, he'd met just about everyone he'd ever need in order to form the gang that would help write his name all over the front pages of America's newspapers.

Within a year of his release, John Dillinger was so famous that President Roosevelt mentioned him in one of his famous 'fireside chats', commenting that he was 'shocked by the public adulation of a vicious criminal', but by then the bank robber's face was already appearing on a series of chewing-gum cards, and the 7 May 1934 edition of *Time* magazine carried a four-page special on the outlaw, complete with a pull-out map which could be used to play a game called *Dillinger Land*. It wasn't just that he was robbing bank after bank, typically jumping Fairbanks-style over the counter to get at the loot, or even that he seemed forever one step ahead of the Feds, slipping away from their ambush at the Little Bohemia resort, and breaking out of Crown Point prison only days after telling newsreel cameras, 'No jail can hold me.' In an era where jobs were nowhere to be found but bootleggers were seen to be making fortunes, someone like Dillinger, who rode into town and just took what he wanted, was doing something which some of the ordinary people reading the newspapers might have wished they could do. No wonder the Hays Office and the FBI didn't want Hollywood putting him up there on the big screen.

Eventually, the FBI got their man, outside a movie theatre just as he was leaving a showing of *Manhattan Melodrama* – a film in which gangster Clark Gable pays for his sins with a one-way trip to the electric chair. 'Dillinger was just a yellow rat, and the country may consider itself fortunate to be rid of him,' J Edgar Hoover told the newspapers, who printed photos of the corpse in the Cook County morgue, surrounded by grinning sightseers. The following day's edition of the *Chicago Tribune* summed things up a little differently:

> No other criminal in American history ever so captured the imagination of the public. His insouciance, his cynical attitudes, his put-on good humour when bullets did not serve the immediate purpose he had in mind, were as much a part of the legend of this supercriminal as his uncanny ability to shoot his way out of traps or his unfaltering courage in battle.

Unable to make a film that might be said to be glorifying the dead bank robber, the Hollywood studios nevertheless managed to incorporate significant episodes from Dillinger's career into their new series of pro-police movies, such as *G-Men*, *Public Hero Number One*, *Men Without Names*, and *Let 'Em Have It* (all 1935). In essence, everything was fine as long as the Dillinger character wasn't actually *called* Dillinger, was shown throughout to be an utter sleazebag who'd sell out his own mother just for the hell of it, and met a suitably grim fate at the hands of the forces of law and order.

The years rolled by, with the censors still firmly set against flattering biopics of criminals, but then World War Two came along, giving Hollywood a different background for their tough-guys-with-guns pictures, and, as it drew to a close, the success of previously 'unfilmable' subjects like *Double Indemnity* created a situation where a producer was prepared to risk a picture based on the life of

America's favourite heist-merchant. Released in 1945, Max Nosseck's film was called, logically enough, *Dillinger*, and starred Lawrence Tierney in the title role. Although the screenplay mixed in more than a little fiction along with the facts, the picture was a solid commercial hit, and helped pave the way for many crime biopics that were to follow.

During the 1950s, it was mostly Dillinger's contemporaries who received the big screen treatment – Al Capone, Baby Face Nelson, Ma Barker, Machine Gun Kelly, Bonnie Parker – but then in 1965, came Terry O Morse's *Young Dillinger*: 'The raw, brutal, bullet-riddled story of the young punk whose name became the most dreaded in America.' This time it was James Dean's old buddy Nick Adams who got the chance to wave a tommy gun around and leap over bank counters, but the picture was no more historically accurate than the 1945 version. A year or so later, however, when Warren Beatty and Faye Dunaway proved that 1930s Depression-era hoods could look and dress like film stars and meet every situation with a wisecracking, ironic humour, it couldn't be long before someone decided to do a proper job on the life story of the biggest of them all.

In early October 1972 a small news item in *Films & Filming* announced: 'Warren Oates is to play the title role in American International's *Dillinger*, which starts October with screenwriter John Milius directing.'

Milius was then a 28-year-old ex-surf bum who had drifted into film courses at the University of Southern California and wound up co-writing a biker picture called *The Devil's Eight* for AIP in 1969 (the same year in which he also wrote a script that no one would put into production called *Apocalypse Now*, for another young film hopeful named Francis Ford Coppola). He quickly gained a reputation as a skilful script doctor, making a sizeable contribution to *Dirty Harry* (1971), and pitching a story called *Liver-Eating Johnson*, which went through several other hands to emerge in a more sanitised form as *Jeremiah Johnson* (1972). What really made his reputation, though, was the $300,000 he was paid *not* to direct *The Life and Times of Judge Roy Bean* – a script he had originally written with Lee Marvin in mind. Add to this the fact that he had a clause in his various contracts stipulating that he should receive exotic weapons such as Purdey shotguns in part-payment of his fee, and it's not surprising that he began attracting attention. In 1973, when the press started scratching at his heels in earnest, John Milius showed he was hardly tongue-tied when it came to giving them a good outrageous quote:

'The world is divided into vassals, serfs and kings,' Milius told *Newsweek's* Malcolm MacPherson in February 1973. 'I would definitely be a king . . . I have been labelled a crypto-Fascist, a right-wing reprobate and the house hardhat. But I am caught up with people who live by their own code of honour and chivalry.'

Given his admiration for the ancient Japanese warrior code of *bushido*, his tendency to label himself a 'Zen Fascist', and his often-voiced approval of such two-fisted, meat-eating types as Genghis Khan and General George Patton, it's hardly surprising that John Milius was drawn to the story of America's most famous bank robber.

'I deliberately chose Dillinger,' he said later, 'because he was a pure criminal. Robbing banks to right social wrongs did not come into it. Dillinger and his opponent are building their legends, building an event. Dillinger actually says: 'You would do what I do, if you had the nerve.'

At this time, John's office was decorated to resemble a Vietnam-style military outpost, and he spoke lovingly of the motorcycle gang which he had recently formed, named Mobile Strike Force Paranoia: 'There aren't enough of us yet to sweep down and terrorise small towns.' Producer Peter Bart, who worked with Milius in the early 1980s when he was developing *Red Dawn* (a quiet, understated picture in which the tooled-up youth of America form ad-hoc militia gangs in order to gun down the invading Commie hordes), has written of him as 'the sort of man who could lovingly describe the proficiency of a Gatling gun with the good-natured smile of a man discussing his pet terrier. He knew he was outrageous; he clearly relished that role.'

Obviously a very talented scriptwriter, in 1973 Milius was a natural for the dual role of writing and directing a story based on Dillinger's life. Sure there'd been a barrel-load of 1930s gangster pictures in the wake of 1967's *Bonnie and Clyde*, but the public was showing little sign that they were growing weary of seeing hoods with howitzers drilling holes across the silver screen, and 1973 was, after all, to be the year of the biggest gangster picture of them all – Coppola's *The Godfather*. Milius might have had only a fraction of the latter's budget available to him, but he couldn't have wished for a better cast. To give one of Sam Peckinpah's *Wild Bunch*, Warren Oates, the role of Dillinger was a stroke of genius, but then to have another, Ben Johnson, playing his FBI nemesis, Melvin Purvis, set the film up with a riveting double-act around which to spin the tale.

Studio publicity stills were taken showing Warren Oates in the same poses as the official 1934 prison mugshots of Dillinger, and the likeness is startlingly close – as one reviewer commented, Oates seemed to have 'infiltrated the skin and bones of the true man'. It's hard to imagine anyone doing a finer job of playing Dillinger, and, after watching Milius's film, it's difficult to watch original newsreels of the bank robber without thinking that it's really Warren Oates in some skilfully-faked footage. If you stop to consider that Oates was only a few years on from *The Wild Bunch* and one year away from his grimy tour-de-force in *Bring Me the Head of Alfredo Garcia*, it becomes clear what a remarkable era for films the early 1970s were, and that most 'action' films made in the last twenty years would be better reclassified as comedies or fitness-instruction tapes.

While the real-life Melvin Purvis was in fact a good deal younger, and shorter, than actor Ben Johnson, it's still a powerhouse performance, effectively capturing the driven, relentless spirit of the early FBI operatives, as summed up in Herbert Corey's 1936 discussions with J Edgar himself:

> One of the reasons Hoover feels as he does toward the criminals with whom he deals is that they have shot down seven of his men . . . The crook who murders an agent should know that to the end of his life he will be pursued by a man who does not know how to forgive that crime.

In keeping with this statement of intent, Milius uses the notorious Kansas City Massacre, in which four FBI agents and their prisoner, Frank 'Jelly' Nash, were ambushed and killed by unknown assailants, as the film's driving motivation, with Melvin Purvis and his men becoming the instrument of J Edgar Hoover's vengeance. The story is told partly by means of a voice-over from Purvis, and his opening speech makes his feelings abundantly clear:

> On June 17th 1933 in Kansas City, five of my finest men were ambushed escorting convicted bank robber Frank Nash to the Federal penitentiary. My men died like dogs in the gutter and I swore personal vengeance. Mister Hoover told me he wanted those rats that did it exterminated, and that was my only job. Charles Arthur 'Pretty Boy' Floyd, George 'Machine Gun' Kelly, Lester 'Baby Face' Nelson, Wilbur Underhill the Tri-State Terror, Handsome Jack Klutas, and, of course, John Dillinger.

While several of the above-named were at one time part of the Dillinger gang, there's little evidence to suggest that he, or indeed any of them, were involved in the Kansas City killings. Still, as Tom Milne pointed out in his review of

Dillinger for *Sight & Sound*, the director was always more interested in the myth than the precise facts of the life in question:

> 'If this story is not the way it was,' John Milius wrote by way of preface to the published script of *The Life and Times of Judge Roy Bean*, 'then it's the way it should have been and furthermore the author does not give a plug damn.'

Certainly, when he then shows Purvis telling Agent Samuel Crowley, 'Shoot Dillinger and we'll find a way to make it legal,' Milius is giving a pretty accurate summary of the attitudes displayed at the time by law enforcement officials, as exemplified by Assistant Attorney General Joseph R Keenan, who told *Time* magazine on 7 May 1934: 'I don't know where or when we will get Dillinger, but we will get him. And you can say for me that I hope we will get him under such circumstances that the government won't have to stand the expense of a trial.'

Dillinger's character is established in his opening robbery, seen from the bankteller's point of view, as he smiles at the camera, polite, and completely in control of the situation: 'You're being robbed by the John Dillinger Gang, that's the best there is. These few dollars you lose here today, they're gonna buy you stories to tell your children and great-grandchildren. This could be one of the great moments in your life. Don't make it your last.'

Later, in a bar, he meets a girl called Billie Frechette (Michelle Phillips, formerly of the Mamas and the Papas, in her first acting role). Managing to chat her up and rob the customers at the same time, he displays the same self-mythologizing tendencies as during the earlier heist: 'Look at my face you sons of bitches. You're gonna remember this face. I'm John Dillinger and I don't want you to ever forget it.' Billie, who seems more intrigued than bothered by this kind of behaviour and who willingly follows Dillinger back to his hideout, is based on his real-life girlfriend, Evelyn 'Billie' Frechette, a Chicago nightclub singer who was part Menominee Indian, and had little capacity for alcohol.

> Dillinger: They don't serve Indians in here. You said you was an Indian.
>
> Billie: Yeah, I'm half Indian. The other half's French, and that side drinks.

179

In the film, Billie is simply a whore, with few ties except to her mother, whereas the real Billie had a husband doing time in Leavenworth for bank robbery, so Dillinger's profession would have been something very familiar to her.

Milius's script shows Melvin Purvis and his boys in a relentless hunt for the gangsters supposedly behind the Kansas City Massacre, with Dillinger left until last, for maximum dramatic tension. As Purvis says: 'I'd get my chance at him, but there were plenty of other public rats on the federal list, and they had to be cleaned out first.'

First up in the shooting gallery is Wilbur Underhill, the Tri-State Terror, trapped in a heavily-armed FBI stakeout in a lonely farmhouse in Northern Missouri in 1933 with his new wife. In the film, Purvis ritually straps on his bullet-proof vest, picks up his automatics and strides off alone into the gunman's lair, cigar clenched between his teeth. After thirty seconds or so of shooting, he emerges, carrying the body of the gangster's wife, while Underhill staggers out to die from his wounds in the dirt. In reality, a whole posse full of Feds caught up with Underhill in Shawnee, Oklahoma, on New Year's Day 1934, and riddled his house with more than a thousand bullets. Before the fatally-wounded Tri-State Terror left for his deep-six holiday, he denied any involvement in the Kansas City Massacre.

Next, the action of the film switches to a heist at the First National Bank in East Chicago, 1933, where the Dillinger gang are shown escaping in a hail of bullets, shooting it out with guards, and running over a pedestrian. 'Dillinger killed his first man in East Chicago,' says Purvis's voice-over. 'A bank guard named O'Malley.' Gang member Charley Mackley is shown to have been shot in the stomach, and eventually dies. (Although blamed at the time by the FBI and the newspapers for the robbery and killing, there's no proof that Dillinger was within five hundred miles of East Chicago at the time, while the real Mackely died during an attempted jailbreak with fellow gang member Harry Pierpont, some months after Dillinger's own death, having carved fake guns out of soap in a Woody Allen-style bid for freedom.)

'The next big break I had was in Memphis,' says Purvis. 'George Machine Gun Kelly.' Here the picture dramatises the famous story of Kelly being arrested while yelling, 'Don't shoot, G-Man!' and certainly the latter name (short for 'Government Man') became current around that time. However, during Kelly's long years in prison, he always denied using the phrase, claiming that he had merely said, 'I've been waiting for you.' Significantly, although Herbert Corey's 1936 book uses the term 'G-Man' elsewhere, it makes no mention of the phrase in it's recounting of the arrest, claiming that Kelly's words were: 'Don't shoot. I'm through. I've quit.'

Next, Handsome Jack Klutas is given the six-gun send-off, and Milius then shows Dillinger being rounded up by the local cops in Tucson, Arizona, having been recognised from the pictures printed in a *True Crime* magazine. This is more or less the way that it happened, although what really blew the whistle on the gang was their willingness to offer a wad of greenbacks to firemen attending a blaze at their hotel in return for rescuing their suspiciously heavy (and machine gun packed) luggage. However, Milius's script has a fine and logical justification for the law's initial suspicions of the well-dressed group of men: 'They're all criminals. Decent folks don't live that good.'

The scenes showing Dillinger's 'press conference' at the heavily-guarded Lake County Jail, Crown Point, Indiana, and his subsequent escape with the aid of a hand-carved wooden gun, are especially well handled. The press seem to love him, and he flatly denies responsibility for the East Chicago shooting – 'I never killed anybody in my life. I just steal money.' Freeing a fellow convict, Reed Youngblood (Frank McRae), who says he's awaiting trial for killing his wife and a Bible salesman after catching them 'in flagrant dee-lecto', Dillinger bluffs his way to the armoury and overpowers the guards. Stealing the Warden's car, they take along the Deputy Warden and a mechanic as hostages, stopping on their way out of town in order to knock over a bank – 'I'm John Dillinger, most recently on display down at your local jail. Sack it up, honey . . . ' Out in the wilds, Dillinger is shown sharing out the money with Youngblood and the astonished hostages (who eventually accept it), and his fellow convict opts to join up with the bank robber's gang. In reality, there was no impromptu bank heist after the escape, the hostages were given just a couple of bucks for cab-fare, and the real Youngblood (whose first name was Henry) split up with Dillinger just a few miles down the road, and died swapping lead with the police in Port Huron, Michigan just a few days later.

At this point, at a holiday resort known as Little Bohemia, the film introduces two of the most famous members of the Dillinger gang – Pretty Boy Floyd (Steve Kanaly, smooth and charming) and Baby Face Nelson (a supremely bratty performance from Richard Dreyfuss). Floyd and Dillinger swap tales about the recently-deceased Bonnie and Clyde – 'Small-timers get into it, ruin it for everybody' – while Nelson outlines his Cro-Magnon approach to the bankrobbing business: 'I come in shooting, I kill everyone in sight. I grab the dough. It's very easy and it works very well.' The real Nelson was apparently every bit as unlikeable as he is portrayed here, and his enthusiasm for gunning down innocent bystanders was well known. At a raid in Sioux Falls, South Dakota (changed in the film to South Bend, Indiana) he opened up with a tommy gun from inside the bank because he'd spotted an off-duty policeman through the window, shouting 'I got one of them!' as the man fell.

Purvis and the FBI's disastrous raid on the gang's hideout at the Little Bohemia Lodge at Rhinelander, Wisconsin, from which Dillinger and his associates slipped away almost unnoticed while the Feds mistakenly gunned down three innocent civilians, is changed in the film into a tense gun battle between crooks and lawmen. One of the picture's great strengths is its realistic handling of the shoot-outs – hardly surprising, given a director so thoroughly familiar with so many different types of weapon, whose name credit in the opening titles is set against a background of tommy guns and ammunition clips. Whether it's the wounded gang member slowly bleeding to death from a stomach wound, or the injured Homer Van Meter (Harry Dean Stanton) surrounded by a bunch of vigilante farmers – 'I've been shot in the lung. Will someone get a doctor, please?' – being blasted to death by a circle of shotguns, this is certainly a film which takes firepower and its consequences seriously. Pretty Boy Floyd is cornered by the Feds in a cornfield and mown down like something earmarked as breakfast on a Scottish grouse moor, but manages as he lays dying to refute any suggestion that he had a part in the Kansas City Massacre. Floyd's demise is presented much as it happened in real life, as is Baby Face Nelson's mutually-fatal final shoot-out with two FBI men.

The climax of Milius's story comes with the FBI stakeout at Chicago's Biograph Theatre on the night of 22 July 1934. This almost ended up as a Little Bohemia-style fiasco, as the legendary Chicago journalist Studs Terkel (who was at school with junior members of the Capone gang) recalled in his 1977 autobiography, *Talking to Myself*:

> Consider this. Melvin Purvis, the tiny Virginian in charge of the FBI Chicago Bureau, almost blew the Dillinger kill. A battalion of Chicago police came within seconds of a bloody shootout with suspicious characters hanging around the Biograph Theatre. The FBI, its mind on an exclusive, had neglected to inform the locals of the stakeout.

The Feds are supposed to have been tipped-off that Dillinger would be attending the cinema that night, having been given the word by a local brothel madam Anna Sage (played here by Cloris Leachman, nearly two decades after her high-decibel appearance as Christine in Aldrich's *Kiss Me, Deadly*). Sage, later immortalised by the media as the 'Lady in Red', had approached a Chicago detective called Martin Zarcovitch, looking to bargain with the law, since she was under threat of deportation as an undesirable alien. Zarcovitch brought in Purvis, so that when Public Enemy Number One (using the false name James Lawrence), Sage and another woman called Polly Hamilton emerged from the cinema, the FBI were waiting and Dillinger was shot dead. At least, that's the story . . .

In some versions of the tale, Purvis, Agent Sam Crowley and Zarcovitch are credited with the killing. Other sources name Agents Herman E Hollis, Clarence O Hurt and Charles B Winstead as the ones who pulled the triggers. The FBI always maintained that Purvis shouted a warning to Dillinger, and that the bank robber had made a move for his gun before being shot, whereas civilian witnesses at the scene denied hearing anything before the gunfire. In the lengthy report of the incident printed in the following day's edition of the *New York Times*, titled 'Dillinger Slain in Chicago', Melvin Purvis denies having seen the Lady in Red or any other women with Dillinger, credits two of his men, rather than himself, with the shooting, and is quick to spread the story of Dillinger's alleged facelift to account for the body's strange lack of resemblance to the known pictures of the outlaw – 'I was surprised to notice that the scar on the left side of his face had been removed without a trace, a nice piece of plastic surgery.'

It's certain that two women bystanders were wounded in the shooting, and that several onlookers dipped handkerchiefs and newspapers in the outlaw's fresh blood on the pavement for souvenirs. However, author Jay Robert Nash has put forward a convincing theory that the 'James Lawrence' gunned down outside the Biograph that night wasn't Dillinger at all, but a substitute lured into the role by Sage and Zarcovitch, so that the real Dillinger could disappear. Certainly, the body displayed at the Cook County morgue the following day bore only a vague resemblance to the man described on the FBI's official $10,000 wanted posters: 'Marks and scars: half inch scar back left hand, scar middle upper lip, brown mole between eyebrows.' These distinguishing features were nowhere to be found, and the FBI insisted that Dillinger and several of his gang had undergone plastic surgery while on the run, in an effort to disguise themselves. Unfortunately, the chief witness to the facelift story took a one-way flight out of the window of an office building in Chicago a few days after the shooting, but, given the primitive state of such procedures in the 1930s, it's hard to account for the number of changes in the body in question.

Crucially, the corpse had brown eyes, whereas Dillinger's were blue, and an autopsy revealed evidence of a chronic and long-standing heart condition hardly consistent with the ability to leap tall bank counters at a single bound. If the FBI really did get the wrong man, then Dillinger's escape stands as one of the great disappearing acts of the twentieth century.

Dillinger may or may not have been shot down like a dog, but popular rumour was certainly convinced that he'd been hung like a horse, and that the FBI had posthumously removed the member in question and consigned it to a jar at the Smithsonian. What's certain is that J Edgar Hoover had a display case outside his office containing Dillinger's death mask, hat and glasses which remained there for the rest of his career. As the film's end titles point out, Melvin Purvis shot himself in 1960, either with the gun he used on Dillinger, or with a gun which his colleagues in the FBI presented to him in honour of the occasion. Anna Sage was deported to her native Romania, and died of liver disease in 1947, Billie Frechette died on an Indian reservation in 1969, and, as the film's final caption says: 'John Dillinger now adorns the combat silhouette targets used by the FBI.'

Although John Milius's later verdict was that he'd been a much better scriptwriter than director at the time of making *Dillinger*, this may have been a response to the film's lukewarm reception at the box office. The press reaction was pretty much split down the middle, and the film became caught up in the then-common argument over whether cinema in the age of *Straw Dogs* and *A Clockwork Orange* was becoming too brutal. The 13 June 1973 edition of *Variety* praised the performances of Oates, Johnson and Phillips, together with the realism of the gunplay, saying, 'There can be no criticism of Milius's ability to keep such action sequences at top-heat.' Gordon Gow in *Films & Filming* called it a 'real-seeming evocation of the gangster's activities in the America of 1933 and 1934' with 'raw colour photography which has the look of life observed by chance', but *Photoplay* found it too near the knuckle:

> Audiences, it seems, cannot get enough violence in their films. Right now there are only two kinds of motion pictures that are making money in the USA: films catering to the blacks and films filled with stomach-churning violence . . . In order to avoid the criticism of 'too much violence' they turn to true stories like Dillinger because they can answer the critics with 'How else can I make such a picture but violent?'

Photoplay may have been attempting to take the moral high ground, but Jay Cocks in the 10 September 1973 edition of *Time* magazine was downright snotty, calling the film 'slack and derivative,' and evidently wouldn't know a great Warren Oates performance if he tripped over it in the dark:

> Sounding in interviews like a combination feudal lord, Texas land baron and bawdyhouse piano player, Milius proclaims the glories of guns, the beauties of blood lust and the masculine honour of big money. Affectation like this makes good copy and, judging from *Dillinger*, bad movies . . . He has two surpassing leading actors: Warren Oates as Dillinger and Ben Johnson as the G-man who finally does him in. His most singular accomplishment is that he manages to make them both look bad.

Perhaps the last word should go to Lynn Minton, whose 1984 book, *Movie Guide for Puzzled Parents,* offers a selection of reviews designed to keep youngsters from straying into temptation, but which could almost be used as slogans on the cover artwork of video nasties:

> There are enough blood-spurting, twitching, groaning and bullet-riddled deaths to satisfy the most bloodthirsty. Not for children.

Milius in later years went on to fill the silver screen with anti-Communist vigilantes, surfer dudes and Arnie Schwarzenegger's biceps, but with *Dillinger*, he left behind a worthy successor to the no-nonsense hardboiled crime films of the 1930s and 40s, a low-budget gem that deserved a far wider audience. It would be good to see him tackle another subject like this today, but times have changed so much, that it's hard to know who would even put up the money for such a thing. Like the man himself once put it: 'Maybe I should do pornography. As George Lucas says, it's a warm room and the props aren't that important . . . '

LA Confidential

Everyone is Suspect . . . Everyone is for Sale . . . and Nothing is What it Seems.

Film: LA Confidential
Director: Curtis Hanson
Leading players: Kevin Spacey, Russell Crowe, Guy Pearce, Kim Basinger,
Danny DeVito
Year of release: 1997

Book: LA Confidential
Author: James Ellroy
Year of publication: 1990

Real-life events: LAPD's Bloody Christmas, *Confidential* magazine, Mickey
Cohen and the 1950s LA underworld.

*In 1988 and '89 I wrote LA Confidential. It was big, it was epic, it was huge, it was
a book for the whole family, if the name of your fucking family is the Charles Manson
Family . . .*

James Ellroy

There are a million James Ellroy stories in the naked city, and he's told most
of them better than anyone else is ever likely to: how his father 'poured the
pork' to Rita Hayworth; how his mother was strangled when he was ten years
old; how he used to break into houses in his neighbourhood as a teenager to
steal drugs from bathroom cabinets and sniff panties in girls' bedrooms; how
he lived rough on the streets, lifting wallets, occasionally falling foul of the
cops, drinking his way through the 1960s and early 70s until he quit the booze
and pills and reinvented himself as a world class novelist. It's hardly surprising
that he can depict the sleazy underbelly of post-war America with such accuracy,
given how much of it he seems to have witnessed at first hand.

'I am a fiend for darkness, sleaze, groovy twisted sexuality,' Ellroy told Paul
Duncan. 'I'm especially interested in this around the late fifties, early sixties,
at the time of my emerging sexuality. I recall being holed up with a copy of
Confidential magazine looking at a picture of Corinne Calvet for about three
hours on a hot summer night before I even knew what masturbation was.

And I like to go back and relive those times, the time of darkness in my life and explicate it.'

The darkness in his life came knocking with a vengeance in 1958 when his mother was killed by an unknown assailant – strangled and left at the side of the road one night. Six months later, on his eleventh birthday, Ellroy's father gave him a copy of a new book called *The Badge*, by actor Jack Webb, star of the hit TV cop show *Dragnet*. It was packed full of real-life stories of the LAPD and their most notorious cases – the most famous of which was the unsolved brutal slaying of good-time-girl Elisabeth Short some ten years before, who became known to the media as *The Black Dahlia*. Short's body had been horrifically mutilated, entirely drained of blood, sliced neatly in half and then left on a patch of waste ground. Webb's book devoted nine pages to a detailed description of the killing and the police attempts to solve the case. For 1958, it was pretty strong stuff, and, as a birthday present for a young boy whose mother had very recently been murdered, it was bizarre in the extreme, but then, as Ellroy later said of his father, 'he was a twisted motherfucker'.

The Badge, however – with its real-life stories of LAPD Chief William H Parker, crime lab technician Ray Pinkner, mobsters like Jack Dragna and the tabloid sleaze-rag *Confidential* – had, like his mother's murder, a huge influence upon the writer Ellroy was to become. Although the book is at pains to present the police in an unremittingly flattering light, it also contains much solid factual information, and includes diagrams showing the various LAPD departments, as well as a thorough glossary of police terms then in use, such as:

311	Indecent exposure – Penal Code Section 311
CODE 3	Red light and siren
FISH	New man in prison
HOP SQUAD	Narcotics division
R & I	Records and identification

This language – in which the cops are forever chasing PVs (parole violators) on suspicion of 240PC (assault) or 459 (burglary) – shows up time and again in James Ellroy's novels, although the fact that the term 'blow job' was used in the book to mean 'where explosive is used on a safe' would probably have raised a smile with that particular 11-year-old reader, who was already hip to some of the ways of the world. With Hollywood all around him, and two parents both hooked on the glamour and the dirt, he knew damn well that things weren't as squeaky-clean as Webb's book tried to paint them.

I grew up in LA and my father was a sleazebag on the edge of the movie biz. I knew that Rock Hudson was a fag in 1959 – it was no newsflash when he finally caught AIDS and died . . . I'm voyeuristically curious about people's sex lives, about their inner moral workings, and here you have a cast of – usually very good looking – characters, both men and women, and all I want to know is who's a homosexual, who's a nymphomaniac, who's a sader, who's got the biggest wang in Hollywood, who's got the smallest, who's impotent, who's the underhung, who's the snap-diver, who's the sword-swallower, who's the peeper, who's the prowler, who's the pimp, who's the pederast and who's the panty-sniffer?

One man who felt that the world had a God-given right to read this kind of vital information over their bowl of breakfast cereal was Robert Harrison, who launched a scandal magazine in 1952 called *Confidential*, which aimed to give the Great American Public a grandstand view right up the collective *unterhosen* of Tinseltown's finest. It was cheap, it was nasty, it was muck-raking – and its first issue shifted 250,000 copies. Within a couple of years that figure had risen to four million, and celebrities were running for cover, fearful that Harrison's rag would reveal to their fans that they spent weekends in Tijuana having threesomes with underage farmyard animals whilst dressed up in drag and belting out choruses of *How Much is That Doggie in the Window*. *Confidential* had it all – mobsters, junkies, hookers, film stars – and for the first five years, astonishingly, none of them sued, although Harrison wisely reported on the excesses of Hollywood from an office way over on the other side of the country in New York. The magazine dished the dirt while using a kind of breathless hipster-speak which set the pattern for a slew of tabloid imitators that followed. The cover of the January 1957 issue of *Confidential* offered the lowdown on one of Hollywood's biggest female stars ('Joan Crawford's Back Street Romance With A Bartender') while also taking a swipe at the brand new king of rock'n'roll ('Girls! Beware Of Elvis Presley's Doll-Point Pen'). The latter was an in-depth feature devoted to the Pelvis's habit of signing his name across the chests of young female fans – 'Elvis on the righty. Presley on the lefty . . . You've never read it in your local gazettes but reporters in the know can tell you there are any number of chicks who've sported Presley print on their superstructure.'

Confidential and its imitators were feeding an insatiable appetite on the part of the public for Hollywood gossip, but obviously they weren't the first people in this racket, merely the most blatant. Columnists Hedda Hopper and Louella Parsons had long been sitting in judgement over the private lives of the stars and picking over scraps of gossip about their private lives like a pair of overpaid vultures, but they had the backing of some very powerful people, and their victims very rarely fought back. *Confidential's* dubious newsgathering methods, however, attracted the attention of the LAPD, as Jack Webb reported in *The Badge* over several pages devoted to the magazine:

> For months one Lieutenant did nothing except run down the tie-ins between scandal mags, private eyes, and strongarm collection agencies. He turned up the scabrous story of Confidential magazine's dirt-collection system in which gossip fed by prostitutes was double-checked by private investigators. One admitted having hidden in the bushes and secretly shot fifty feet of coloured film of an actress at her Bel Air home . . . The undercover work which had been done primarily by Parker's team led in turn to a grand jury investigation and even further disclosures about the love-and-tell-for-pay activities of call girls and bit actors.

Of course, actors and actresses weren't the only people who made good copy – the mob could always be relied upon for some sordid column inches, particularly in the wake of Senator Estes Kefauver's heavily-televised Senate Crime Investigating Committee hearings between 10 May 1950 and 1 May 1951, which 'the Nation's Number One crime buster' then capitalised upon with the rush-release of a book entitled: *Crime in America – Trial Before Television of America's Leading Thugs* (1951). Based on testimony given to the committee, Kefauver's book helped to make LA mobsters like Mickey Cohen and Jack Dragna household names throughout America, while also pointing the finger at some of the more suspect police officials:

> The committee, however, was not impressed by the Los Angeles County sheriff's office, particularly after hearing the remarkably uninformed Under-Sheriff Arthur C Jewell testify . . . When Chief Counsel Halley asked Jewell if he could tell the committee of any illegal activities of which Mickey Cohen was suspected, the under-sheriff replied: 'Personally, I cannot, sir; that is honest and sincere.'

In a section entitled 'Murder of a Mouthpiece', Kefauver relates the story of how Mickey Cohen's lawyer, Samuel Rummel, was mysteriously gunned down shortly before he was due to testify before the committee – 'killed by a close-range shotgun blast as he walked from his garage to the front door of his home'. People unfortunate enough to be seen in the company of Mickey Cohen had a disturbing tendency to wind up on the wrong end of a shotgun blast, as *Newsweek* reported in a particularly sarcastic article entitled 'Les Mickeyrables' (20 February 1950):

> Mickey Cohen is a much misunderstood man, who always has been much more sinned against than sinning. He never killed anyone except Maxie Shaman, and that's Maxie's fault, really. Maxie had pulled a gun on him first, and besides he was a 'welsher.' As for the accident that happened to 'Hooky' Rothman in the plush haberdashery that Mickey used to own just off Sunset Strip in Hollywood, Mickey's 'absolutely clean on that.' Just prove he isn't. Maybe it did look bad that he should have ducked into the washroom only a split second before someone entered the shop and tore Hooky apart with a shotgun, but there's no denying it: coincidences do happen, particularly to Mickey.

Anyone labouring under the misapprehension that Cohen was merely an unfortunate businessman with a habit of being in the wrong place at the right time would have certainly had their eyes opened by a section of Kefauver's book, entitled 'The Gang World of Mickey Cohen', in which he is described as 'a gambler and bookmaker, with far-flung interstate connections, an extortionist and all-round rackets boy'. Kefauver also noted that there had been at least five attempts to assassinate Cohen, which had led him to purchase a $16,000 bulletproof Cadillac. Quite apart from his links with organised crime, prostitution and a selection of LA's most prominent leg-breakers, it seems that it was Mickey's physical appearance and zoot suit threads which most offended the senator and his committee:

> Cohen, a simian figure, with a pendulous lower lip, thinning hair, and spreading paunch, appeared before us dressed in 'sharp' clothing, including a suit coat of exaggerated length, excessively padded at the shoulders, and a hat with a ludicrous broad brim.

On this evidence, it's surprising they didn't send him up the river for ten years on a charge of felonious Cab Calloway impersonation. The committee also questioned Cohen about 25-year-old Johnny Stompanato, 'described to us by police as one of his closest lieutenants and strong-arm men'. Johnny was alleged to have been blackmailing wealthy LA businessmen, but Mickey denied this to the committee, describing Stompanato as 'a nice fellow . . . a good boy.' Stompanato later found public fame in 1957 when he began dating Lana Turner, shortly after her split from Tarzan actor Lex Barker. He already had a different kind of fame among Hollywood insiders due to the allegedly award-winning dimensions of his penis, which had earned him the nickname Oscar, but it was his habit of conducting discussions with Lana by means of his fists which made him front page news in April 1958 when he was stabbed to death by Turner's 14-year-old daughter Cheryl, apparently seeking to protect her mother. A few days later, censored versions of Lana's love letters to Johnny showed up splashed across the front pages of the tabloids, thoughtfully supplied to the gentlemen of the press by a Mr Cohen of Los Angeles, no doubt for a not-so-small fee. By the time of Johnny's murder, things were getting tough for Mickey and many of those around him. The *Chicago Daily News* carried the following announcement one day in February 1957:

> Jim Vaus, former wire tapper for Los Angeles hoodlum Mickey Cohen, will open a week-long series of nightly demonstrations of electronic equipment at 7 p.m. tomorrow in Bethel Community Church (Evangelical Free), Foster and Oriole.

Perhaps inspired by this novel alternative to his usual more shady ways of earning a dollar, Mickey himself discovered the power of the spoken word, as this item from the 13 July 1959 edition of *Newsweek* explains:

> Hoodlum Mickey Cohen, who has devoted his life to disproving the maxim that 'Crime Doesn't Pay,' found a new racket – and, this time, a legitimate one. He's going to talk about the evils of crime – for fees ranging from $1,000 to $2,500. Mickey said he decided to make a swing of the lecture circuit at the suggestion of columnist Drew Pearson, who put him in touch with the Edna Stewart Agency in Beverly Hills, Calif. 'Our clients are all top men,' said an agency spokesman. 'After all, Mr Cohen, in a sense, was a captain of industry in his field.'

191

By this stage, even to be seen in public with Cohen was getting to be a liability, as actress Liz Renay discovered when she was hauled in front of a grand jury to testify about her links with Mickey and another ex-boyfriend, Anthony 'Coppy' Coppola, who just happened to have been the late Mafia kingpin Albert Anastasia's bodyguard. Unsurprisingly, the sordid details were rounded up and thrown at the public by one of *Confidential's* many imitators, in a crusading piece of journalism called 'Have the Hoods Put a Hex on Mickey Cohen's Moll?' in the December 1960 edition of *Vice Squad* magazine. Liz – described here as 'a smart tart with a bagful of tricky talents and a slick chick with almost highbrow interests' – apparently adhering to the line that all publicity is good publicity, is shown sitting at the side of a pool in a swimsuit, smiling and waving her grand jury subpoena at the camera:

> She posed pleasantly for the photographers: alone in a pink nightgown in her New York hotel room; after a hush-hush appearance before a grand jury; holding hands with her Coppy in a mid-Manhattan club; slumming with Mickey Cohen in an all-night Los Angeles ice cream parlor.

Throughout the 1950s in Los Angeles, the public face of law and order was LAPD Chief William Henry Parker, a deeply controversial figure bleached whiter-than-white in Jack Webb's *The Badge*, but even in those pages, Parker's public utterances make for uncomfortable reading. Responding to a complaint that the police department had been wiretapping citizens' phones without having first obtained a search warrant, Chief Parker said: 'The voice of the criminal, the Communist and the self-appointed defender of civil liberties cries out for more and more restrictions upon police authority.' Webb sees Parker in the tradition of the 'direct-action philosophy of the Old West', for whom the end result usually justifies the methods:

> Parker is an essentially simple man who believes with all his soul that crime and Communism are the twin scourges of America and their suppression, by almost any means, the greatest challenge of our era.

Even while he was waving a flag for Parker, there was still no way that Webb could avoid mentioning the biggest police scandal of the decade – the 1951 'Bloody Christmas' episode in which seven unarmed Mexican-American prisoners were beaten senseless by drunken officers at Los Angeles Central police station in the early hours of Christmas morning. Webb told the story in this way, conveniently avoiding embarrassing words such as 'drunk', 'cell' or the fact that the victims were Latinos:

> Ironically, it all began with Christmas cheer, both in Central where about one hundred policemen were enjoying a party and in a small bar in the rough part of town. Two policemen, rolling on a 'trouble' call to the bar, tried to eject two holiday celebrants. A brawl broke out, and the outnumbered officers were beaten up, one so badly he had to be hospitalised. Reserves rushed seven of the merrymakers off to Central, booked them and put them in a waiting room. So far, routine, for Christmas Day. Then, among the police celebrants, the story spread that the more seriously injured officer was going to lose an eye. Immediately, the enraged policemen began taking turns to work over the seven prisoners. Before they were through, the floor was blood-covered, the walls were splattered red.

Chief Parker initially denied any police wrongdoing, but the controversy became too great, and the scandal led directly to the first grand jury indictments of serving officers and convictions for use of excessive force in the history of the LAPD. The case became a rallying-point for the Mexican-American community, leading to the formation of several Latino rights groups such as the CSO, whose membership included the activist Cesar Chavez.

For James Ellroy, Bloody Christmas was the starting point for the book which was to become *LA Confidential*, just as Webb's account of the Black Dahlia case had first triggered his fascination with the murder which was to become the central subject of his novel of the same name. In the BBC Arena documentary *James Ellroy's Feast of Death* (2001), he said of *The Badge:*

> To this day, the cases in there continue to drive me. Here it is, forty one years later, I remain driven, morally and psychically, by what I got out of that book. It's fucking astonishing.

The novel, *LA Confidential* (1990), forms the third part of James Ellroy's *LA Quartet*, which began with *The Black Dahlia* (1987) and *The Big Nowhere* (1988), and concluded with *White Jazz* (1992). Beginning with the murder of Elisabeth

193

Short, the series trawls through post-war Los Angeles, lifting up various rocks and seeing what kind of life-forms crawl out from underneath them, weaving in numerous real-life characters such as Howard Hughes, bandleader/murderer Spade Cooley and the ever-present Mickey Cohen – all of them now dead, to avoid litigation. Through them all walks the deeply disturbing figure of Dudley Smith, a man whose behaviour does for the reputation of the LAPD roughly what the Borgias did for the Papacy. As an evocation of the sleazy underbelly of Hollywood in the 40s and 50s, the *LA Quartet* is pretty much unbeatable, as Ellroy himself told Paul Duncan:

> It is considered a monument of some sort – I consider it a great monument, like Mount Rushmore, and so does my dog, my wife, my agent and my current publisher. Others are not so charitable, but fuck 'em, because they don't have to be. The bottom line is this: if you don't like my books you can kiss my ass.

LA Confidential runs to 480 pages – which is a fair size, but practically a novella compared to the 809 page version which Ellroy originally wrote. The main action covers a series of events which run from the 1951 Bloody Christmas beatings up to 1958 around the time of Johnny Stompanato's murder, although there is a prologue from 1950 dealing with the motel gunfight in which an ex-employee of Howard Hughes, Buzz Meeks, is gunned down by Dudley Smith and his thugs. The narrative of the novel – seen through the eyes of three police officers: Ed Exley, Willard 'Bud' White and 'Trashcan' Jack Vincennes – includes, among other things, call-girl vice-rings, a shotgun massacre at an all-night café, the building of a theme park by a cartoon-film mogul, a series of brutal sex-killings, the dirt-digging activities of a shakedown-orientated scandal magazine, and various attempts to control the LA drug trade. With a large cast of characters ranging from the morally ambiguous to the downright evil, and a plot that twists and turns like a switchback railway, it should be obvious that any attempt to explain the story of *LA Confidential* in a couple of paragraphs would be a futile exercise. It's a wild ride, and the reader has to pay attention every step of the way or find themselves getting hopelessly lost.

'I grew up in the film noir era in the film noir epicentre,' wrote Ellroy in *Bad Boys in Tinseltown,* his October 1997 GQ article about the filming of his novel. 'I read *Confidential, Whisper* and *Lowdown* magazines before I learned to ride a two-wheel bike.' The shadow of these scandal rags hangs over all the events in the novel, in a world where pretty much everyone has something to hide, and the threat of public revelations in *Hush Hush* magazine – Ellroy's fictional version of *Confidential* – can either keep people in line or ruin their careers. Sleazebag writer Sid Hudgens keeps extensive files on all kinds of public figures, but there's far more dirt and guilt floating around than even he realises. The three policemen at the heart of the novel are all compromised in one way or another: war-hero Ed Exley faked his medal-winning exploit on Guadalcanal by lining up a trench full of already-dead Japanese and frying them with a flamethrower to make it look as if he'd killed them all single-handedly in battle; Jack Vincennes gunned down two innocent people back in 1947 and a dead criminal took the blame; Bud White is a borderline psycho beating hell out of people on Dudley Smith's orders up at the Victory Motel, whose interrogation methods also include shoving a pimp's hand down a kitchen garbage-disposal unit – 'SCREEEE – the sink shot back blood, bone. Bud yanked the hand out minus fingers.' Needless to say, in Ellroy's world, these guys are among the more sympathetic characters.

The Bloody Christmas scandal drags the reputation of the LAPD through the dirt, so that when six people are blown to pieces in a massacre at the Nite Owl café, the pressure from the public and the media for a quick solution to the case is intense. Given the condition of the victims, this is no easy task:

> Bodies – a blood-soaked pile on the floor. Brains, blood and buckshot on the walls. Blood two-feet deep collecting in a drainage trough. Dozens of shotgun shells floating in blood . . . No discernable faces.

The Nite Owl massacre has similarities to a real-life case in which six people were killed at an all-night joint in LA called the Mecca café, near the corner of Normandie and 59th Street, by several men who tipped a bucket of petrol on the floor and then lit it. The killings, initially reported as a bombing, received enormous press coverage, and four men were eventually arrested and convicted. In *LA Confidential*, the Nite Owl killing prompts a major police manhunt, and three suspects – Raymond Coates, Tyrone Jones and Leroy Fontaine – are brought in on suspicion. Exley's grilling of the prisoners brings out the fact that they have spent most of the previous evening abducting and raping a Mexican woman called Inez Soto, at which point Bud employs his subtle Russian roulette-style interrogation technique to discover that she is being held captive by a man named Sylvester Fitch. Never one to show mercy where woman-beaters are concerned – having been forced to watch his father kill his mother with a tyre iron – Bud rescues Inez and kills Fitch, rearranging the crime scene post-mortem to suggest that the rapist had been armed:

> Bud shot him in the face, pulled a spare piece – bang bang from the coon's line of fire. The man hit the floor dead spread – a prime entry wound oozing blood. Bud put the spare in his hand; the front door crashed in. He dumped Rice Krispies on the stiff, called an ambulance.

Exley, too, proves himself capable of handing out frontier justice, when he corners the unarmed escaped Nite Owl suspects and their hideout man Navarette, and blows them all away with a shotgun after being called a sissy:

> Ed jerked the trigger: once, twice – buckshot took off Coates' legs. Recoil – Ed braced against the doorway, aimed. Fontaine and Navarette stood up screaming; Ed SQUEEZED the trigger, blew them up in one spread. . . . He saw Jones make the elevator. He ran after him: slid, tripped, caught up. Jones was pushing buttons, screaming prayers – inches from the glass, 'Please Jesus.' Ed aimed point blank, squeezed twice. Glass and buckshot took his head off.

Clearly, this is a world where the line between the good guys and the bad guys barely exists, and just about anyone could wind up in jail if the skeletons in their own particular closet are brought to light – a situation summed up in the old saying (quoted by Ellroy in *Bad Boys in Tinseltown):* 'LA: come on vacation; go home on probation.'

The sleazy underside of the Hollywood dream factory is probably exemplified by the call-girl stable run by millionaire pornographer and *Fleur-de-Lis* head honcho Pierce Patchett, whose girls are given plastic surgery in order to resemble movie stars. He too is in the film business, but his bestselling titles – *Locker Room Lust, Blow the Man Down, Jesus Porks the Pope, Cocksuckers Paradise, Cornholers Meet the Ramrod Boys, Rex the Randy Rottweiler* – aren't exactly the sort that receive a star-studded premiere at Grauman's Chinese. Meanwhile, in the wholesome world of children's entertainment, animation pioneer Raymond Dieterling (who is building, as Ellroy later wrote, a 'theme park disingenuously designed to remind readers of Disneyland'), has already conspired to murder one of his own sons, while deliberately hiding the fact that his other son has turned into a psychopath along the lines of real-life 1950s bondage-photo killer Henry Glatman.

Then of course, there's Dudley Smith, a fine upstanding police officer, who enjoys nothing more than meeting visiting mobsters as they come to town and whisking them off to the abandoned Victory Motel for intensive discussions involving brass knuckles and buckshot-weighted leather saps designed to persuade them to cut short their stay in sunny Los Angeles. This pro-active method of discouraging out-of-town mobsters from moving to California has a solid basis in fact, although Jack Webb's version of these procedures is much milder, consisting of a short conversation at an airport, in which the hood is threatened with nothing more frightening than seeing his own name in the papers:

'There's a plane taking off for Chicago in an hour. Be on it, Eddie.'
'What for? I'm clean, copper.'
'That's not what our files say, Eddie.'
'Files! Listen you, I'm a businessman. I got nothing to be afraid of.'
'You're a celebrity, Eddie, not a businessman. You got a big name. The kind the newspapers might like to get hold of – in Chicago as well as Los Angeles. Now whadda ya' say?'
The swarthy gent winces.
'Okay, pal. You win.'

Throughout Ellroy's book, broadcasting an uplifting message to the public about the fight for law and order and how the coppers always get their man, is the *Badge of Honor* TV show, closely modelled on the real-life *Dragnet* series, its name inspired by the title of Jack Webb's book. The original show, which did indeed have an LAPD officer working as special advisor, is credited with popularising many authentic police terms, and set the pattern for most of the TV cop shows which followed. While the *Dragnet* stars were constantly asking the public for 'Just the facts, ma'am, just the facts,' the fictional cast and crew of *Badge of Honor* are more concerned with keeping secret the less-than-savoury facts of their own private lives. Looking to raise money for corrupt DA Ellis Loew, Trashcan Jack Vincennes, the show's police advisor, shakes the *Badge of Honor* team down for contributions, under threat of revelations in *Hush Hush* magazine.

197

In a world populated by fine upstanding characters such as these, it's not surprising that virtually the only sympathetic character in the whole book is the hooker, Lynn Bracken, who works for Pierce Patchett as a Veronica Lake lookalike, but even she, having got involved with Bud White, ends up sleeping with the man he hates most, Ed Exley. As a whore working for a well-connected millionaire in Beverly Hills, Lynn knows almost as much as *Hush Hush's* Sid Hudgens about the private lives of the stars, in much the same way that real-life Hollywood madam Brenda Allen got to know the secrets of the Tinseltown elite in the immediate post-war years, and also enjoyed the backing of a rich benefactor. Jack Webb wrote that Allen paid corrupt police officials for protection for her stable of call girls, and the case was also recalled in the December 1960 issue of *Vice Squad* magazine:

> By early 1948, there were 14 'stringers' going out on calls, while a dozen girls entertained guests at Brenda's house-that-wasn't-a-home. She had elaborate and tricky 'arrangements' for guests to 'entertain' each other. And her special little gadgets are still preserved in the property room of the LA Police Department, where they are viewed with admiration by visiting firemen . . . Though Brenda catered exclusively to the movie trade, business was so brisk that she had to move to bigger quarters – into the Moroccan-style villa of a well-known millionaire, on swanky Harold Way. By then all Hollywood was beating a path to Miss Allen's elegant man trap.

Somewhat further down the evolutionary chain come the *Fleur-de-Lis* delivery boys like Lamar Hinton, a man-mountain with, as Tom Waits used to say, the IQ of a fence post. He drives around Hollywood distributing Patchett's custom-order care packages, which contain all the essential ingredients for a quiet evening at home after a hard day on the movie back lot:

> Absinthe, 190 proof on the label, viscous green liquid.
> Hashish.
> Black-and-white glossies: women in opera masks blowing horses.
> 'Whatever you desire.'

Pimps, whores, drug-dealers, rapists, corrupt cops, sex-killers, extortionists, sadists, pornographers, leg-breakers, hit-men – from the cast of characters it's relatively certain that James Ellroy didn't set out to write a novel in the Jane Austen manner. He was also damned sure that Hollywood would never be interested in turning his book into a film, and he couldn't have cared less about the prospect. When he appeared in London in February 1995, giving a talk at the Museum of the Moving Image (after a showing of Jules Dassin's 1948 noir classic *The Naked City*), he advised anyone in the audience thinking of selling their own novels for cinema adaptation to just take as much money as they could get and run, while trying never to see the finished picture, because it was bound to be a disaster. Ellroy's 1984 novel *Blood on the Moon* had been filmed in 1987 by James B Harris under the title *Cop*, with James Woods in the starring role of Lloyd Hopkins, but the results hadn't left him eager to repeat the experience. Since that time, the narratives of his books had become ever more complex and dark, and the characters in them were hardly standing up and yelling, 'Look how appealing I am, wouldn't I be perfect for Robin Williams or Tom Cruise?' As Ellroy commented in the documentary included in the DVD release of the film version of *LA Confidential*:

> My agent and I laughed like hell because we thought this fucker was movie-adaptation proof. It was big, it was bad, it was bereft of sympathetic characters. It was unrestrainable, uncontainable, unadaptable . . .

Many would have considered the novel to be exactly that, but little did James Ellroy and his agent know that someone would take his novel and actually stay true to the spirit of it, and still make it into a movie for the multiplex crowd in an era when most crime films had been reduced down to 90 minutes of cars and buildings exploding with an airbrushed hero who repeats bargain-bin tough guy dialogue and then practically grins himself to death during the obligatory cheerful finale. If that seemed unlikely, then consider the actors playing Ed Exley, Pierce Patchett and the very frightening Dudley Smith: Guy Pearce had found fame in the ultra-cheesy daytime soap *Neighbours*, and then as a drag queen in *The Adventures of Priscilla, Queen of the Desert* (1994), David Strathairn was a graduate of the Ringling Brothers Clown College, and James Cromwell was a veteran of *Revenge of the Nerds IV: Nerds in Love* (1994) and had played lovable old pig-farmer Hoggett in *Babe* (1995). The director/co-screenwriter aiming to weld these disparate elements into a neo-noir walk down the mean streets was a man whose previous film had been the Meryl Streep family-against-the-elements movie *The River Wild* (1994), and his writing partner was

199

a former commercial fisherman who'd packed in the nautical life 'following a big storm at sea on Thanksgiving 1985'. Given James Ellroy's generally low opinion of most attempts to film crime stories ('I like movies as cheap entertainment. To me they're like hamburgers. I've ate about ten profound hamburgers in my life and I've probably seen ten profound movies'), it's hard to imagine him thinking that anyone could take the basic elements of his novel and put it on the screen. However, it worked out better than anyone had any right to expect, and he was happy to go on the record and say so:

> Here was a compatible vision, unique on its own terms, of a book that I wrote, characters and a milieu that I created, they assumed a brilliant alternative life and I was flabbergasted and staggered by the experience.

Self-evidently, the film is nowhere near as dark as the book – if it had been, no Hollywood studio would have touched it with a ten-foot pole, the budget would have been somewhere in the region of thirty-five bucks and it'd probably have played for just one week at some concrete bunker video installation in a trendy loft on New York's Avenue A to fifteen people, most of whom were the cast. Sure, you can get away with pretty graphic violence and a lot of swearing and still stay in the mainstream, but certain little details in the book were never likely to impress the majors – such as teenage school truant Daryl Bergeron, who's 'too tired to cause trouble: fucking your mother on roller skates takes a lot out of a kid'. Add to that the fact that if you try to film every last word of a 480-page novel you'll wind up with a picture with a running time of maybe twelve to fifteen hours, so if you want to get the finished movie onto any of the major distributors' release schedules, a large amount of something has to be cut. The obvious drawback here is that James Ellroy's novels are so densely plotted, with important pieces of information on every page that help to drive the narrative along, that when you start removing things the whole structure is in danger of collapse.

The brave men taking on this challenge were Curtis Hanson (director/co-screenwriter) and Brian Helgeland (co-screenwriter), who had not known each other before they came to work together on this film. (In fact they had both been going around Hollywood individually trying to persuade various studios to let them have a crack at adapting *LA Confidential* for the screen and this is what eventually led to people suggesting that they collaborate.) Hanson had grown up in LA, with a father who'd been thrown out of his job at a school when movie mogul Darryl F Zanuck complained that someone who'd been a wartime conscientious objector shouldn't be teaching kids (presumably this was only one step away from being a Commie spy as far as Mr Z was concerned). However, it was Hanson's Uncle Jack, who ran a hip clothes shop and a Beverly Hills dance club, that gave the young Curtis an intro to the world of movies, and bankrolled him when he took over the running of 60s movie magazine *Cinema*. From there, he gradually made the move into scriptwriting and then directing.

Executive Producer David Wolper optioned the film rights to *LA Confidential* in the early 90s after his wife had recommended it to him, and he'd tried unsuccessfully to interest the major US broadcast networks in developing it as a television series. He was receptive when Curtis Hanson approached him wanting to direct and adapt the book as a feature, and it was arranged that Brian Helgeland would be brought in as co-writer. Both writers explained their approach in the DVD documentary:

> Curtis Hanson: It just seemed that we both felt the same way – that extraordinary liberties would have to be taken with that convoluted, dense plot of Ellroy's, but that there'd be a way to let the characters guide us through that.'

> Brian Helgeland: Right. To try to preserve the people and not the plot.'

Many characters are recognisably the same as their counterparts in the book, while others have disappeared altogether, and some names or speeches are given over to entirely different characters. To list all of the changes would take a book almost as long as the original novel, but a few examples should suffice. Ed Exley's father Preston, who features heavily in the book – firstly as a model policeman and later as a far more compromised figure who eventually commits suicide – becomes in the film an entirely offstage figure, gunned down before the action begins at the hands of an unknown pickpocket, his only function being that of heroic role model for Ed. Similarly, there is no mention at all of Ed himself having faked his war heroics, nor of Jack Vincennes having killed two unarmed bystanders in 1947 or threatening the *Badge of Honor* team with *Hush Hush* revelations if they don't come up with some cash. Buzz Meeks, the fictional mister fixit for Howard Hughes who features heavily in Ellroy's previous novel, *The Big Nowhere*, is gunned down at an abandoned motel during the prologue to the book, as he attempts to run for the border having hijacked a shipment of heroin at a summit meeting between Mickey Cohen and Jack Dragna which was being guarded by Dudley Smith. In the film version, the motel shoot-out is moved to the end of the story, and it is Bud and Ed who are up against Dudley and his minions. Buzz Meeks now becomes a minor character working for Pierce Patchett (and Patchett is made up to look strangely like Howard Hughes), who meets an early death and winds up under the floorboards at the Lefferts' house – whereas in the book the subterranean stiff is a pimp by the name of Duke Cathcart. Meanwhile, the novel's dog-shagging rapist-murderer singing-bass player in Spade Cooley's Western Swing band, Deuce Perkins, disappears from the film but his name lives on, transferred to a character described only as Mickey Cohen's narcotics lieutenant, who enjoys a whole three or four seconds of screen time before being blasted all over the soft furnishings by a two-man shotgun team. And so it goes.

Changes like these are inevitable, given the huge task of compressing the many strands of the novel down to fit the available space in a two-hour film. Overall, Ellroy's cast of uniformly 'unsympathetic' characters has been made more box office friendly and lovable. Curtis Hanson's instruction to Kevin Spacey for the role of Jack Vincennes was that he play it as Dean Martin, and this appears to be exactly what he did. Everybody digs Jack, or so it seems, and there's little remaining of the guilt and fear underneath the character's surface which is present in the book – here instead is a man whose world falls apart if he is taken away from his favourite TV show. Ed Exley (Guy Pearce) is more squeaky clean and less compromised – 'All I ever wanted was to measure up to my father' – and only shoots the Nite Owl suspects after they have shot at him first, whereas in the book he kills four unarmed men on the slimmest provocation. Bud White (Russell Crowe) comes across as far less of a sadist, but it's Dudley Smith (James Cromwell) who has been toned down the most, although in fairness it's hard to imagine anyone matching the machiavellian brutality and sinister malevolence of the character which Ellroy had been developing since he first introduced him in the 1982 novel *Clandestine*. Physically, the actor does not resemble the figure of Smith as described in the novel, but then, as Ellroy later wrote, neither did several of the other lead actors, and it didn't particularly matter:

> My Exley was tall and blond. Guy Pearce, the film Exley, is medium size and dark haired. My Smith was burly and red-faced. James Cromwell, the film Smith, is pale and imperiously tall.

However, even though he kills Sid Hudgens and shoots Jack Vincennes without warning (two killings which, incidentally, are the work of other people in the novel), somehow the film version of Dudley still seems a little too *nice*, and it's difficult to imagine the one in the novel being stupid enough to walk out of the motel at the end leaving a man with a grudge and a loaded gun behind him. Still, embodying a character onscreen about whom millions of readers already have pre-conceived ideas is never going to be an easy task. Russell Crowe, having read the novel was aware of that when Hanson asked him to play the role of Officer White, as he tells Bella Fiscal:

> I thought Curtis was totally insane. In the book it says that Bud is the largest man in the LAPD. I rang him up and said, 'Listen, mate, I don't know what you've seen but it must have been smoke and mirrors – I'm not that sort of fellow.'

Crowe looks handy enough in the muscle department to be convincing, but, oddly enough, it was Guy Pearce, who plays the much less macho role of Ed Exley, who in real life back in Australia won the junior Mr Victoria body-building competition when he was fifteen years old. For Pearce, an Australian born in England, the main concern was to sound convincingly American – not that he had any real doubts about being able to pull it off, but for the first part of his career, he says that casting directors had continually told him, 'Well, we know you can act, but can you do an accent?' With Kim Basinger, playing a woman who's mostly playing Veronica Lake, it was more a question of hair. She told Anwar Brett:

> Curtis said I could wear a wig if I want to, but wigs make me look like I'm wearing a football helmet. I decided to get the Veronica Lake look by dyeing my own hair, which was very long at the time. This was a week prior to the movie starting, and that afternoon all I remember was my head burning up. They said it would burn a bit, but by the end of it my hair was literally falling apart.

Perhaps that's why when Guy Pearce was later asked for his main impression of Kim on the set he replied: 'I was amazed at her entourage, a little mystified to tell you the truth. There were babies, babysitters, make-up artists and hairstylists around all the time.' In fact, she could have done worse than to have consulted co-star and ex-hairdresser Danny DeVito, whose role as sleazebag Sid Hudgens from *Hush Hush* magazine also triggered hair-related memories:

> When I was a kid in New Jersey, when you went to a barber shop, that's when you'd see these gossip magazines. We modelled the type and layout of our *Hush Hush* magazine on *Confidential* magazine. That was great – you'd see someone running out of a hotel with a hat over his face. The great thing was, you'd find out how many times people were married. A guy married four times! That was big news with us in New Jersey. Not the fact that he was married four times, but the fact that he *scored* four times.

Great attention was paid to the look of the film, and most of the locations were authentic LA buildings which match the mood of the novel perfectly: the Formosa Cafe, a 1929-vintage restaurant at 7156 Santa Monica Boulevard, which was used several times, notably when Ed Exley confronts Johnny Stompanato and Lana Turner; the Hollywood Center Motel at 6720 Sunset Boulevard, where failed actor Matt Reynolds is found murdered; the Lovell House at 4616 Dundee Drive, built by Richard Neutra in 1929, which is used in the film as Pierce Patchett's residence. The abandoned Victory Motel where Dudley Smith batters the hell out of various suspects, which is also the site of the final showdown between him and Bud and Exley, was purpose-built for the film at the Baldwin Hills oil field close to Culver City. This is understandable, given that they needed to blast the place to pieces with shotguns during the latter scenes.

If the buildings are exactly right for the era, the precise timeframe of the film is more loose. From most of the evidence onscreen and in the dialogue, the action appears to be taking place in 1953 – in particular, all the newspaper front pages which are flashed up onscreen have this date. (The events in the novel take place between 1951 and 1958, with a prologue from 1950.) However, the real Bloody Christmas happened in 1951, and the film *When Worlds Collide*, which is billed on the front of the El Cortez cinema during the 'Movie Premiere Pot Bust', also dates from that year. Yet if it really is 1951, and not 1953, Bud and Lynn couldn't be at the cinema watching Audrey Hepburn in *Roman Holiday* (1953), and the songs which Jack and Sid watch Chet Baker and Gerry Mulligan perform at the *Badge of Honor* party all date from '53 and '54. Mind you, Lana Turner and Johnny Stompanato are shown enjoying a quiet date in the Formosa, and in real life they didn't meet each other until 1957. In the final analysis, none of this matters much, because the moods of all these film and music references are right for the story, and, as an historical document, *LA Confidential* is a model of accuracy compared to efforts such as *The Buddy Holly Story* (1978), a film so riddled with factual errors that they even have the singer performing his last gig a day late, at a time when he was already in the morgue.

All in all, the film adaptation of *LA Confidential* turned out to be one of the finest crime pictures of the 1990s, and even though the final resolution looks a little too much like the classic modern-day 'Hollywood ending', it still comes about as close to the feel of Ellroy's novels as any major studio picture is ever likely to get. Reviewers seemed in general to be delighted with the results: Roger Ebert in the *Chicago Sun Times* gave it the four-star treatment, calling it 'seductive and beautiful, cynical and twisted' and comparing it favourably with Polanski's *Chinatown* (1974); over in the UK, *Neon* magazine gave it five out of five and called it the best picture of the year.

And Mister Ellroy? He was happy to go on the record telling journalists how pleased he was with the adaptation, and when he published *Crime Wave*, his 1999 collection of pieces from *GQ* magazine, the book was dedicated to director Curtis Hanson. In addition, it contained stories such as *Hush Hush* (written in 1998) which revolves around the stabbing of Johnny Stompanato and has an LAPD officer called Sergeant Helgeland, while *Hush Hush* magazine shows up again in the story *Hollywood Shakedown,* along with Johnny Stompanato, Mickey Cohen, Jack Webb, the *Dragnet* show and Sheriff William H Parker. These days, James Ellroy's novels no longer concern themselves with 1950s Los Angeles, and he's pretty much said all that he's got to say about the 1997 film version of his book, but in the Arena documentary *James Ellroy's Feast of Death* (2001), after calling the movie 'the best thing that happened to me in my career that I had absolutely nothing to do with', he did offer what he says is his final word on the subject:

> I go into a video store in Prairie Village, Kansas. The youngsters who work there know me as the guy who wrote *LA Confidential.* They tell all the little old ladies who come in to get their G-Rated family flicks. They come up to me. They say, 'Oh, you wrote *LA Confidential.* What a wonderful movie. Kim Basinger was so beautiful. Is she a nice person?' 'Yeah, she's alright.' 'It was a wonderful movie. Oh what a wonderful movie. Is Kevin Spacey really gay? Oh, what a wonderful, wonderful movie. I saw it four

times. You don't see storytelling like that on the screen any more.' I smile. I say, 'Yes, it's a wonderful movie, and a salutary adaptation of my wonderful novel, but listen, granny, you loved the movie – did you go out and buy the book?' And granny invariably says, 'Well . . . no, I didn't.' And I say to granny, 'Then what the fuck good are you to me?'

Evidence

Books

Nelson Algren	*Chicago: City on the Make*, Chicago: University of Chicago Press, 1987 (first published 1951) *The Texas Stories of Nelson Algren*, Austin: The University of Texas Press, 1995
Geoff Andrew	*The Films of Nicholas Ray*, London: Charles Letts & Co., Ltd., 1991
Kenneth Anger	*Hollywood Babylon*, New York: Dell Publishing Co., 1980 (first published 1975)
Sam Arkoff with Richard Trubo	*Flying Through Hollywood by the Seat of my Pants*, New York: Birch Lane Press, 1992
Edward T. Arnold & Eugene L. Miller	*The Films and Career of Robert Aldrich*, Knoxville: University of Tennessee Press, 1986
Lauren Bacall	*By Myself*, London: Coronet Books, 1980 (first published 1978)
Mark Baker	*Nam*, London: Abacus, 1987 (first published 1982)
Peter Bart	*Fade Out: The Calamitous Final Days of MGM*, New York: William Morrow & Company, Inc., 1990
Laurence Bergreen	*Capone: The Man and the Era*, New York: Simon & Schuster, 1994
Jack Bilbo	*Carrying a Gun For Al Capone: The intimate Experiences of a Gangster in the bodyguard of Al Capone*, London: Putnam 1932
Peter Biskind	*Easy Riders, Raging Bulls: How the Sex'n'Drugs'n'Rock'n'Roll Generation Saved Hollywood*, London: Bloomsbury, 1998
Robert Bloch	*Psycho*, New York: Simon & Schuster, 1959

Peter Bogdanovitch   *Who the Devil Made it?*, New York: Alfred A. Knopf, 1997

Marlon Brando   *Brando: Songs My Mother Taught Me,* Toronto: Random House
with Robert Lindsey   of Canada, 1994

William B. Breuer   *J. Edgar Hoover and His G-Men*, Westport, Connecticut: Praeger
Publishers, 1995

Gene Brown, ed.   *The New York Times Encyclopedia of Film,* New York: Times
Books, 1984

Edward Bunker   *Mr Blue: Memoirs of a Renegade,* Harpenden: No Exit Press, 1999
No Beast So Fierce, Harpenden: No Exit Press, 1993
(first published 1973)

W.R. Burnett   *Little Caesar*, New York: Bantam Books, 1959 (first published 1929)
Vanity Row, London: Corgi Books, 1956 (first published 1952)

James M Cain   *The Postman Always Rings Twice,* London: Jonathan Cape, 1934

Michael Caine   *What's it All About?,* London: Arrow Books, 1993 (first
published 1992)

Ian Cameron, ed.   *The Movie Book of Film Noir*, London: Studio Vista, 1992

Kingsley Canham   *The Hollywood Professionals, Volume 5: King Vidor, John Cromwell,*
& Clive Denton   *Mervyn LeRoy,* London: The Tantivy Press, 1976

Truman Capote   *In Cold Blood*, London: Abacus, 1989 (first published 1966)

Sean Dennis Cashman   *Prohibition: The Lie of the Land,* New York: The Free Press, 1981

Raymond Chandler   *The Big Sleep,* London: Penguin Books, 1992 (first
published 1939)
Trouble is My Business, New York: Pocket Books, 1951 (first
published 1950)
Killer in the Rain, London: Penguin Books, 1966 (first published
1964)

Raymond Chandler *Selected Letters of Raymond Chandler*, London: Macmillan, 1981
(Frank McShane, ed)

Connery Chappell, ed. *Picturegoer Film Annual*, London: Odhams Press Ltd., 1953

Citizens' Police *Chicago Police Problems,* Chicago: University of Chicago Press,
Committee, (Dir., 1931
Bruce Smith)

Al Clark *Raymond Chandler in Hollywood*, London: Proteus, 1982

Max Allan Collins *One Lonely Knight: Mickey Spillane's Mike Hammer,* Bowling
& James L Traylor Green, Ohio: Bowling Green State University Popular Press, 1984

Herbert Corey *Farewell, Mr Gangster!: America's War on Crime*, New York:
D. Appleton-Century Company, 1936

Roger Corman *How I Made a Hundred Movies in Hollywood and Never Lost a*
with Jim Jerome *Dime,* New York: Random House, 1990

Peter Cowie *The Godfather Book*, London: Faber & Faber, 1997

John Cummings *Mobster: The Astonishing Rise and Fall of a Mafia Supremo and*
& Ernest Volkman *his Gang*, London: Warner Books, 1993 (first published 1990)

William L. DeAndrea *Encyclopedia Mysteriosa*, New York: Macmillan, 1997 (first
published 1994)

Thomas Doherty *Pre-Code Hollywood: Sex, Immorality, and Insurrection in American
Cinema 1930 – 1934*, New York: Columbia University Press, 1999

Paul Duncan, ed. *The Third Degree: Crime Writers in Conversation*, Harpenden:
No Exit Press, 1997

Bernard Eisenschitz *Nicholas Ray: An American Journey,* London: Faber & Faber, 1993

James Ellroy *Clandestine*, New York: Avon Books, 1987
The Black Dahlia, London: Arrow Books, 1991 (first published 1987)

James Ellroy	*The Big Nowhere*, London: Arrow Books, 1990 (first published 1988) *L.A. Confidential*, London: Arrow Books, 1994 (first published 1990) *White Jazz*, London: Century Books, 1992 *Dick Contino's Blues and Other Stories,* London: Arrow Books, 1994 *Crime Wave*, New York; Vintage Crime/Black Lizard, 1999
Francis Edwards Faragoh	*Little Caesar,* Wisconsin: University of Wisconsin Press, 1981
Ken Ferguson, ed.	*Photoplay Film Annual 1971*, London: The Illustrated Publications Co. Ltd., 1970 *Photoplay Film Annual 1972*, London: The Illustrated Publications Co. Ltd., 1971 *Photoplay Film Annual 1974*, London: The Illustrated Publications Co. Ltd., 1973
Marshall Fine	*Bloody Sam: The Life and Films of Sam Peckinpah,* New York: Donald I. Fine Ltd., 1991
John Follain	*A Dishonoured Society: The Sicilian Mafia's Threat to Europe*, London: Little, Brown & Co., 1995
J.B. Foreman, ed	*Collins Albatross Book of Verse*, London: Collins, 1977 (first published 1933)
Peter Fryer	*Mrs Grundy: Studies in English Prudery,* London: Dennis Dobson, 1963
Dorothy Gardiner & Kathrine Sorley Walker, eds.	*Raymond Chandler Speaking.* Berkeley: University of California Press, 1997, (first published 1962)
Bernard Gordon	*Hollywood Exile or How I Learned to Love the Blacklist*, Austin: University of Texas Press, 1999
Val Guest	*So You Want to Be in Pictures?,* London: Reynolds & Hearn, 2001
Leslie Halliwell	*Halliwell's Film Guide, Fifth Edition*, London: Paladin 1986 (first published 1977)

Richard Hammer *Playboy's Illustrated History of Organised Crime*, Chicago: The Playboy Press, 1975

Phil Hardy, ed. *The Aurum Film Encyclopedia: Gangsters,* London: Aurum Press, 1998

Dorothy B. Hughes *The Bamboo Blonde,* New York: Pocket Books, Inc., 1946 (first published 1941)
Ride the Pink Horse, New York: Dell Publishing Inc., 1958 (first published 1946)
In a Lonely Place, Harpenden: No Exit Press, 1990 (first published 1947)

Tom Johnson & *Hammer Films: An Exhaustive Filmography*, Jefferson, North
Debbie Del Vecchio Carolina: McFarland, 1996

Ephraim Katz *The Film Encyclopedia*, New York: Thomas Y. Crowell, 1979

Senator Estes Kefauver *Crime in America: Trial Before Television of America's Leading Thugs*, London: Four Square Books, 1951

Arleen Keylin & *Crime as Reported by the New York Times,* New York: Arto Press,
Arto DeMirjian Jr., eds. 1976

James E. Kibler, Jr., ed. *The Dictionary of Literary Biography, Volume 6: American Novelists Since World War II, Second Series*, Detroit: Bruccoli Clark Books, 1980

Paul Kooistra *Criminals as Heroes: Structure, Power & Identity*, Bowling Green, Ohio: Bowling Green State University Popular Press, 1989

Leonard J. Leff *The Dame in the Kimono: Hollywood, Censorship and the Production*
& Jerold L. Simmons *Code from the 1920s to the 1960s, New York:* Grove Weidenfeld, 1990

Janet Leigh, with *Psycho: Behind the Scenes of the Classic Thriller*, London: Pavilion
Christopher Nickens Books, 1995

Ted Lewis *Jack's Return Home* (aka Carter), London: Pan Books, 1971 (first published 1970)

211

Ted Lewis

Plender, London: Michael Joseph, 1971

Jack Carter's Law, London: Allison & Busby 1993 (first published 1974)

William Luhr

Raymond Chandler and Film, Florida: Florida State University Press, Second Edition 1991 (first published 1982)

Joseph McBride

Hawks on Hawks, Berkeley: University of California Press, 1982

Patrick McGilligan, ed.

Backstory: Interviews with Screenwriters of Hollywood's Golden Age, Berkeley: University of California Press, 1986

Backstory 2: Interviews with Screenwriters of the 1940s and 1950s, Berkeley: University of California Press, 1997

Backstory 3: Interviews with Screenwriters of the 60s, Berkeley: University of California Press, 1997

Doug McClelland

Star Speak: Hollywood on Everything, Boston: Faber and Faber, 1987

Peter Maas

The Valachi Papers, London: Panther Books, 1976 (first published 1968)

Peter Manso

Brando, New York: Hyperion, 1994

John Miller, ed.

Chicago Stories, San Francisco: Chronicle Books, 1993

Lynn Minton

Movie Guide for Puzzled Parents, New York: Dell Publishing Co., 1984

Robert F. Moss, ed.

The Dictionary of Literary Biography, Volume 253: Raymond Chandler – A Documentary Volume, Detroit: Bruccoli Clark Layman, 2002

Jeffrey Myers

Bogart: A Life in Hollywood, Boston: Houghton Mifflin Company, 1997

J. Robert Nash

Bloodletters and Badmen: A Narrative Encyclopedia of American Criminals from the Pilgrims to the Present, New York: M. Evans and Company, 1973

David Newman & Robert Benton

Bonnie & Clyde, London: Faber & Faber, 1998 (first published 1972)

Fred D. Pasley *Al Capone: The Biography of a Self-Made Man*, New York: Books for Libraries Press, 1971 (first published 1930)

Albert Pierrepoint *Executioner: Pierrepoint,* London: Coronet Books, 1977 (first published 1974)

Nicholas Pileggi *Wiseguy: Life in a Mafia Family*, New York: Pocket Books, 1987 (first Published 1985)

Frank Richard Prassell *The Great American Outlaw: A Legacy of Fact and Fiction*, Norman, Oklahoma: University of Oklahoma Press, 1993

Stephen Prince *Savage Cinema: Sam Peckinpah and the Rise of Ultraviolent Movies*, Austin: University of Texas Press, 1998

Maurice Procter *Hell Is A City,* London: Arrow Books, 1957 (first published 1954)
Devil's Due, London: Panther Books, 1966, (first published 1960)

Mario Puzo *The Godfather*, London: Pan Books, 1972 (first published 1969)
The Godfather Papers & Other Confessions, New York: G. P. Putman's & Sons, 1972

Michael Pye & Lynda Myles *The Movie Brats: How the Film Generation Took Over Hollywood*, London: Faber & Faber, 1979

Stephen Rebello *Alfred Hitchcock and the Making of Psycho,* London: Marion Boyars, 1990

Tony Reeves *The Worldwide Guide to Movie Locations,* London: Titan Books, 2001

John M. Reilly, ed. *Twentieth Century Crime and Mystery Writers*: Second Edition, London: St. James Press, 1985

John Roeburt *Al Capone*, London: Panther Books, 1959

Jerry Rubin *Do it! Scenarios of the Revolution,* New York: Ballantine Books, 1970

Thomas Schatz   *The Genius of the System: Hollywood Film-making in the Studio Era*, London: Faber & Faber, 1996 (first published 1989)

Harold Schechter   *Deviant: The Shocking True Story of the Original Psycho*, New York: Pocket Books, 1989

Murray Schumach   *The Face on the Cutting Room Floor: The Story of Movie and Television Censorship*, New York: William Morrow & Co., 1964

Percy Bysshe Shelley   *Poetical Works*, Oxford: Oxford University Press, 1978 (Thomas Hutchinson, ed.) (first published 1905)

Alain Silver &   *Whatever Happened to Robert Aldrich: His Life & His Films*, New
James Ursini   York: Limelight Editions, 1995
            The Noir Style, London: Aurum Press, 1999

Alain Silver &   *Film Noir: An Encyclopedic Reference to the American Style*, Woodstock,
Elisabeth Ward   N.Y.: The Overlook Press, 1992 (first published 1979)

Garner Simmons   *Peckinpah: A Portrait in Montage,* New York: Limelight Editions, Revised edition, 1998 (first published 1976)

Robert Sklar   *City Boys: Cagney, Bogart, Garfield,* Princeton, N.J.: Princeton University Press, 1992

F. Maurice Speed, ed.   *Film Review: 1959-1960*, London: MacDonald & Co., 1959
            Film Review: 1961-1962, London: MacDonald & Co., 1961
            Film Review: 1963-1964, London: MacDonald & Co., 1963

A.M. Sperber &   *Bogart*, New York: William Morrow & Company, Inc., 1997
Eric Lax

Mickey Spillane   *Kiss Me, Deadly,* New York: Signet Books, 1954 (first published 1952)

Donald Spoto   *The Dark Side of Genius: The Life of Alfred Hitchcock*, London: Plexus 1994

Dwight C. Smith, Jr.   *The Mafia Mystique,* New York: Basic Books, Inc., 1975

Richard Stark *The Man with the Getaway Face*, New York: The Mysterious Press, 1998 (first published 1963)
The Hunter (aka *Point Blank*) London: Allison & Busby, 1986 (first published 1962)

Studs Terkel *Division Street America*, London: Allen Lane, The Penguin Press, 1968 (first published 1966)
Hard Times: An Oral History of the Great Depression, London: Allen Lane, The Penguin Press, 1970
Talking to Myself: A Memoir of my Times, New York: Pantheon Books, 1977
American Dreams: Lost & Found, London: Hodder & Stoughton, 1980
Coming of Age, New York: The New Press, 1995

Jim Thompson *The Getaway,* London: Sphere Books, 1973 (first published 1958)

Frederick M. Thrasher *The Gang: A Study of 1,313 Gangs in Chicago*, Chicago: University of Chicago Press, 1947 (first published 1927)

John C. Tibbets & James M. Welsh eds. *The Encyclopedia of Novels into Film,* New York: Facts on File Inc., 1996

John Trevelyan *What the Censor Saw*, London: Michael Joseph, 1973

Francois Truffaut *Hitchcock,* New York: Touchstone/Simon & Schuster 1985 (Revised edition first published 1983)

J. K. Van Dover, ed. *The Critical Response to Raymond Chandler*, Westport, Conn.: Greenwood Press, 1995

Alexander Walker *Stardom*, London: Penguin Books, 1974 (first published 1970)
National Heroes, London: Harrap Ltd, 1985

Patricia Warren *Elstree: The British Hollywood,* London: Columbus Books, 1988

Jack Webb *The Badge*, London: Ace Books, 1960 (first published 1958)

Michael Webb, ed. *Hollywood: Legend and Reality,* London: Pavilion Books Ltd., 1986

Charles Williams *The Hot Spot* (aka *Hell Hath No Fury*), New York: Vintage Crime/ Black Lizard, 1990 (first published 1953)

Kenneth Williams *The Kenneth Williams Diaries*, London: Harper Collins, 1994 (ed. Russell Davies)

Clarence Winchester, ed. *The World Film Encyclopedia,* London: The Amalgamated Press, 1933

Charles Winecoff *Split Image: The Life of Anthony Perkins,* New York: Plume Books, 1997 (first published 1996)

Neal S. Yonover *Crime Scene USA*, New York: Hyperion Books, 2000

Donald Zec *Marvin: The Story of Lee Marvin*, London: New English Library, 1979

Various Authors *Star T.V.& Film Annual 1967*, London: Odhams Books Ltd., 1966

Articles, etc.

Renata Adler, 'The Movies Make Heroes of Them All', *New York Times,* January 7th 1968

Robert Aldrich, 'The High Price of Independence', *Films & Filming,* June 1958, pp7, 35

Nelson Algren, 'The Last Carousel', *Playboy*, February 1972, p72ff

'Are the Movies Teaching Us To Be Violent?', *New York Times,* June 30th 1968

Jerry Asher, 'This is Bogart', *Photoplay*, January 1944, p20ff

Martin Aston, 'Quentin Crisp's Ten Wonderful Gangster Movies', *Neon,* September 1997, p5

David Austen, Review of *Point Blank, Films & Filming,* March 1968, p25

_____, 'Out for the Kill', *Films & Filming,* May 1968, pp4 – 9

_____, 'Michael Caine Playing Dirty', *Films & Filming,* April 1969, pp4-10

Peter Barnes, 'Gunman No. 1', *Films & Filming*, September 1955, p12

'Barrow and Woman are Slain by Police in Louisiana Trap', *New York Times*, May 24th 1934

Peter Bart, "In Cold Blood' – On the Firing Line', *New York Times,* October 16th 1966

Robin Bean, 'Pinning Down The Quicksilver: Anthony Perkins', *Films & Filming,* July 1965, p44ff

_____, Review of *Catch Us If You Can, Films & Filming,* August 1965, p27

_____, 'Michael J. Pollard Talks About The Sexy Flying Machine That Burst From A Cloud And Other Movies', *Films & Filming,* November 1968, pp10-12

_____, 'Grand Gestures', *Films & Filming,* October 1977, pp44-45

J. Walker Bentley, 'Catch Us if You Can', *ABC Film Review*, August 1965, p26

Bigo., Review of *Little Caesar, Variety,* January 14th 1931

Josh Billings, 'Your Films', *Kine Weekly,* May 5th 1960, p14

Nicholas Blake, 'The Big Shots', *The Spectator,* March 31st 1939

Book review of *The Big Sleep, The New Republic,* March 15th 1939, p56

Book review of *The Big Sleep, The Times,* March 8th 1939, p8

Marcia Borie, 'Warren Beatty & Shirley MacLaine', *Photoplay,* January 1968, p18ff

'Box Office Champions' *Films & Filming,* January 1971, p43

Peter Brant and Ingrid Sischy, 'A Walk and Talk With Robert DeNiro', *Andy Warhol's Interview,* November 1993, pp90-95

Anwar Brett, 'Wigs make me look like I'm wearing a football helmet', *Neon,* May 1998, p93

Winifed Bristow, 'Charlie's New Leading Lady', *Picture Show & TV Mirror,* May 7th 1960, p2

_____, 'Filmland Gossip', *Picture Show & TV Mirror,* September 10th 1960, p3

Brog., Review of *The Postman Always Rings Twice, Variety,* March 20th 1946

____, Review of *The Big Sleep, Variety,* August 14th 1946

____, Review of *Kiss Me, Deadly, Variety,* April 20th 1955

John Lindsay Brown, 'Islands of the Mind', *Sight & Sound,* Winter 1969 / 1970, pp20-23

James M Cain, 'Postman Rings Thrice', *New York Times,* April 21st 1946

John Calendo, 'Robert Aldrich says: 'Life is Worth Living'', *Andy Warhol's Interview,* August 1973

Vincent Canby, 'Arthur Penn: Does His 'Bonnie and Clyde' Glorify Crime?', *New York Times,* September 17th 1967

_____ , 'M Is For The Mothers That She Gave Us', *New York Times,* July 7th 1968

Shirley Carrington, Review of *Psycho, Picture Show & TV Mirror,* September 3rd 1960, p13

Raymond Chandler, 'Writers in Hollywood' *Atlantic Monthly,* November 1945

Chatterbox, 'Clock Shock', *ABC Film Review,* January 1960, p3

Jay Cocks, Review of *The Getaway, Time,* January 8th 1973, pp33–34

_____, Review of *Dillinger, Time,* September 10th 1973, p64

Jean-Louis Comolli and André S. Labarthe, 'Bonnie & Clyde: An interview with Arthur Penn', *Evergreen Review,* June 1968, pp60–63

'Cool Beats' *Films & Filming,* August 1960, p17

'Crime, it's Awful', *Newsweek ,* July 13th 1959

Bosley Crowther, 'The Marvel of Lee Marvin', *New York Times,* September 24th 1967

John Culhane, 'In Capote Country', *Newsweek,* April 24th 1967

Paul Cullum, 'Waiting for G'Day', *Neon,* September 1997, p26

_____, 'The right-wing stuff', *Neon,* October 1997, p11

Will Cuppy, Book review of *The Big Sleep, New York Herald Tribune Books*, February 5th 1939, p12

Joe Curreri, 'What Makes Faye Dunaway Runaway?' *Photoplay*, June 1973, p34ff

Daku., Review of *Bonnie and Clyde, Variety,* August 9th 1967

Sanche de Gramont, 'Life Style of Homo Cinematicus', *New York Times,* June 15th 1969

Fred Dellar, 'It came as no surprise to Georgie Fame', *Mojo*, January 1998, pp36-37

'Dillinger Double' *Film Review*, May 1973, p18

'Dillinger Slain in Chicago' *New York Times*, July 23rd 1934

'Don't Sneer at Her', *Photoplay*, June 1956, p34

Keith Dudley, 'Hell Is a City', *Little Shoppe of Horrors*, No. 10/11, July 1990, pp32-33

_____, 'Val Guest', *Hammer Horror,* No. 3, May 1995, pp49-50

Paul Duncan, 'All The Way Home: Ted Lewis', *Crime Time*, Issue 9, 1997, pp22-25

Raymond Durgnat, 'Cupid v. the Legions of Decency', *Films & Filming*, December 1961, p46

_____, Review of *The Girl Hunters*, *Films & Filming*, September 1964, pp16-17

_____, Review of *The Killers, Films & Filming,* May 1965, p30

_____, 'TV's Young Turks' *Films & Filming,* March 1969, pp4-10

Roger Ebert, Review of *L.A. Confidential, Chicago Sun Times*, 1997

'Eleven Lay Dead', *Newsweek*, February 10th 1958

Allen Eyles, 'Edward G Robinson' *Films & Filming*, January 1964, pp13–17

_____, 'The Private War of Robert Aldrich' *Films & Filming*, September 1967, pp4-9

_____, 'Spillane's Violent World', *Films & Filming*, October 1968, p84

'The Fall Guys', *Neon*, July 1997, p71

Manny Farber, Review of *The Big Sleep, The New Republic*, October 23rd 1946

Stephen Farber, 'The Outlaws', *Sight & Sound*, Autumn 1968, pp170-176

_____, 'Coppola and *The Godfather*', *Sight & Sound*, Autumn 1972, pp217-223

'Farewell, Edward G', *Film Review*, July 1973, p47

Ken Ferguson, 'Expresso Bongo', *Photoplay*, January 1960, pp24-26

_____, 'From the Editor to You', *Photoplay*, June 1968, p4

_____, 'Is there too much VIOLENCE on the screen today?', *Photoplay*, June 1968, pp30–31

Fred Ferretti, 'Corporate Rift in 'Godfather' Filming', *New York Times,* March 23rd 1971

_____, 'TV's 'F.B.I.' to Drop 'Mafia'', *New York Times*, March 24th 1971

Bella Fiscal, 'It's complex, it's convoluted, it respects the audience', *Neon,* November 1997, p93

Guy Flatley, 'He Has Often Walked 'Mean Streets'', *New York Times,* December 16th 1973

Elizabeth Forrest, 'Michael J. Pollard', *Photoplay*, December 1968, pp18–19

Sally Francis, Record review of *The Truth About Bonnie & Clyde, Photoplay*, October 1968, p24

'Francois Truffaut', *New York Times,* September 27th 1970

Philip French, 'Incitement Against Violence', *Sight & Sound*, Winter 1967 / 1968 pp2–8

_____, Review of *Point Blank, Sight & Sound*, Spring 1968, p98

_____, 'French Connections', *Sight & Sound*, Autumn 1972, pp208-212

Nicholas Gage, 'The Godfather: A Few Family Murders, But That's Showbiz', *New York Times,* March 19th 1972

'Get Carter', *Neon*, May 1997, p39

'Gloria Grahame', *Picturegoer,* February 9th 1952, p18

Lionel Godfrey, 'Martinis Without Olives', *Films & Filming,* April 1968, pp10–14

_____, Record review of *The Truth About Bonnie & Clyde, Films & Filming,* September 1968, pp48-49

Michael Goodwin, Review of *Kiss Me, Deadly, Rolling Stone,* October 1st 1970, p37

Gordon Gow, Review of *Bonnie & Clyde, Films & Filming,* October 1967, pp20-21

_____, 'Metaphor: Arthur Penn', *Films & Filming,* July 1971, pp16–21

_____, 'Playboy in a Monastery', *Films & Filming,* February 1972, pp18–22

_____, Review of *Dillinger, Films & Filming,* August 1974, pp45–46

_____, 'Anything But Passive', *Films & Filming,* August 1975, pp8–15

Susan Granger , 'Guy Pearce – There goes the neighbourhood', *Neon,* November 1997, p10

Milton Grant, 'Hollywood's 'Love in the Afternoon' Girls', *Vice Squad*, Vol 1, No. 1, December 1960, p24 ff

Joel Greenberg, 'Robert Aldrich', *Sight & Sound*, Winter 1968 / 1969, pp8-13

Len Greener, 'Len Greener's Runaround', *Picturegoer*, October 10th 1959, p5

_____, 'Len Greener's Runaround', *Picturegoer*, April 23rd 1960, p8

Val Guest, Letter to *Picturegoer*, October 17th, 1959, p2

_____, Letter to *Films & Filming*, February 1972, p4

Leslie Halliwell, 'Merely Stupendous', *Films & Filming,* April 1967, p47

Aljean Harmetz , 'Man Was a Killer Long Before He Served a God', *New York Times,* August 31st 1969

Philip T. Hartung, Review of *The Big Sleep, The Commonweal,* September 6th 1946

Jean-Francois Held, 'A Car for Bonnie', *Evergreen Review,* September 1968, pp62–64

'Hell is a City', Hammer Films' synopsis sheet, 1960

Charles Higham, ''Little Caesar' is Still Punching', *New York Times,* November 5th 1972

Mike Hodges, 'Getting Carter', *Crime Time,* Issue 9, 1997, pp20-21

'Hollywood Crime and Romance', *New York Times,* November 19th 1944

Kirk Honeycutt, 'Milius the Barbarian', *American Film,* May 1982, p32 ff

'House of Horror Stuns the Nation', *Life*, December 2nd, 1957, pp24-31

Penelope Houston & John Gillett, 'Conversations with Nicholas Ray & Joseph Losey', *Sight &*

Sound, Autumn 1961, pp182-187

'Hugh and Pauline Harlow', *Little Shoppe of Horrors*, No. 12, April 1994, pp112-117

Tom Hutchinson, 'Tom Hutchinson's Runaround', *Picturegoer*, October 17th, 1959, p5

Raymond Hyams, 'Why I Turned Down a Fortune by Stanley Baker', *Photoplay*, January 1960, p35

'I was born in an area full of seedy characters', *Neon*, April 1997, p90

'Inside The Mind of a Villain', *Club*, January 1971, pp40-45

Item: *Badlands* preview, *Continental Film Review*, Vol 22 No 2, December 1974, p28

Item: *Bonnie & Clyde* Golden Globe nominations, *The Daily Cinema*, 31st January 1968, p2

Item: '*Bonnie and Clyde* the most tremendous thing I have ever seen.', *The Daily Cinema*, 20th September 1967, p3

Item: 'Bonnie and Clyde were here', *The Daily Cinema*, 29th December 1967, p4

Item: 'Bonnie critics', *Films & Filming,* December 1967, p36

Item: 'Life in Chicago', *New Yorker,* February 23rd 1957

Item: *Motion Picture Herald's* Top 10 Stars of US Box Office, *ABC Film Review*, April 1968, p12

Item: *Point Blank* 'doing well', *The Daily Cinema*, 29th December 1967, p7

Item: Promotional stunts for *Bonnie and Clyde*, *The Daily Cinema*, 29th December 1967, p12

Item: 'Should we ban *Bonnie & Clyde?*', *Films & Filming,* September 1968, p18

Item: Warren Beatty 'could so easily retire', *Photoplay*, June 1968, p7

Item: Warren Oates to play Dillinger, *Films & Filming* November 1972, p80

Item: Warner-Pathe West End successes, *The Daily Cinema*, 12th January 1968, p4

Adam Jezard, 'Hell Is a City', *Hammer Horror*, No. 5, July 1995, pp12–15

_____, 'Reel Life', *Hammer Horror*, No. 7, September 1995, pp8-13

Howard Junker, Review of *Point Blank, Newsweek*, September 25th 1967

Kahn., Review of *Double Indemnity, Variety*, April 1944

Stefan Kanfer, 'The Shock of Freedom in Films', *Time*, December 8th 1967, pp52-56

Bruce F. Kawan, 'A Faulkner Filmography', *Film Quarterly*, Summer 1977, pp12-21

Arthur Knight, 'Cold Blood, Calm Reflection', *Saturday Review*, December 30th 1967

_____, 'Nearer, My Godfather, to Thee', *Saturday Review*, March 25th 1972, p16

Max Kozloff, 'In Cold Blood', *Sight & Sound*, Summer 1968, pp148-150

'L.A. Confidential', *Neon,* September 1997, p26

'Les Mickeyrables', *Newsweek*, February 20th 1950

Letter, 'Adolf and Eva', *Films & Filming,* March 1968, p57

Letter criticising shades of nail polish used in *Bonnie and Clyde*, *Photoplay*, June 1968, p10

Letter to the editor, *Evergreen Review,* August 1968, p95

Letters to the editor, *Time*, December 15th 1967, p11

Letters to the editor, *Time*, December 22nd 1967, p5

Letter, ' Sex in Films', *Photoplay*, June 1968, p10

Jerry Lewis, Letter to the editor, *Time*, October 13th 1967, p12

Grace Lichtenstein, "Godfather' Film Won't Mention Mafia', *New York Times,* March 20th 1971

Malcolm MacPherson, 'John Milius, The Macho Kid,' *Newsweek*, February 5th 1973, p51

Joseph McBride & Michael Wilmington, 'Do I Get to Play the Drunk This Time – An Encounter with Howard Hawks', *Sight & Sound*, Spring 1971

Andrew Male, 'Kevin Spacey – from bowling-alley comedian to Walken impersonator', *Neon,* September 1997, p10

Ken Mate & Pat McGilligan, 'Burnett', *Film Comment*, January/February 1983, pp58-70

James W. Merrick, 'Hitchcock Regimen For A 'Psycho'', *New York Times,* December 31st 1959

'Michael Winner', *American Film,* July-August 1978, p24

'Mickey Spillane', *Esquire*, December 1972

John Milius, 'Guilty Pleasures', *Film Comment*, May/June 1982, pp24-26

Henry Miller, 'Make Love Not Gore', *Penthouse*, Vol 4, No. 7, 1969

Tom Milne, Review of *Bonnie and Clyde, Sight & Sound*, Autumn 1967, pp203–204

_____, Review of *Get Carter, Sight & Sound*, Spring 1971, pp107-108

_____, Review of *Dillinger, Sight & Sound*, Summer 1974, pp179-180

Joseph Morgenstern, Review of *In Cold Blood, Newsweek*, December 25th 1967

Brian Mosley, Letter, *Movie Collector,* Vol 1 Issue 4, March 1994, p73

Mosk., Review of *Tirez Sur le Pianiste, Variety,* August 31st 1960

Murf., Review of *Point Blank, Variety*, September 6th, 1967

____, Review of *In Cold Blood, Variety*, December 13th 1967

____, Review of *Bloody Mama, Variety,* March 18th 1970

____, Review of *Get Carter, Variety*, January 20th 1971

____, Review of *The Godfather, Variety*, March 8th 1972

____, Review of *The Getaway, Variety*, December 13th 1972

William Cotter Murray, 'Returning to the Scene of the Crime', *New York Times,* April 16th 1967

Peter Noble, 'Warren Beatty', *Cinema & TV Today*, 26th April 1975, p8

'Our Cover Girl', *Picturegoer*, January 2nd 1960, p3

'Partners in Realism', Press Book for *The Day the Earth Caught Fire*, 1961

Sian Pattenden, 'Danny DeVito Q&A', *Neon,* December 1997, p86

Arthur Penn, 'Arthur Penn Objects', *New York Times,* February 20th 1966

Malcolm D. Phillips, 'Embarrassing', *Picturegoer,* July 27th 1935, p7

Nicholas Pileggi, 'The Making of 'The Godfather' – Sort of a Home Movie', *New York Times,* August 15th 1971

Mario Puzo, 'The High Cost of Fame', *Playboy,* January 1971, p123

'The Question Box', *Screen Stories*, July 1959, p69

'Ugly', *Films & Filming,* August 1968, p20

Record review of Serge Gainsbourg and Brigitte Bardot's *Bonnie and Clyde, Films & Filming,* March 1969, p75

Rex Reed, 'Penn: And Where Did All The Chase-ing Lead?' *New York Times,* February 13th 1966

Bert Reisfeld, 'Dillinger is Back!', *Photoplay*, June 1973, p43,

Review of *Bonnie and Clyde, Time,* August 25th 1967, p25

Review of *In A Lonely Place, Newsweek*, June 5th 1950

Review of *In Cold Blood, Time*, December 22nd 1967

Review of *Kiss Me, Deadly, Newsweek*, April 25th 1955

Review of *Little Caesar, Time*, January 19th 1931

Review of *Point Blank, Time*, September 22nd 1967, p49

Review of *Ring of Fear, What's On in London*, January 14th 1955, p37

Review of *The Valachi Papers, Playboy*, January 1973, p30

Rich., Review of *Hell is a City, Variety*, May 18th 1960

'Richard Brooks', *American Film,* October 1977, pp33-48

Carole Robbins, 'Faye Dunaway: The Girl Who Wouldn't Say Yes To Warren Beatty', *Modern Screen*, February 1968, p38ff

William V. Shannon, 'The Godfather', *New York Times,* August 1st 1972

Hugh Samson, 'They All Want To Slug Baker', *Picturegoer*, January 2nd 1960, p12

Andrew Sarris, 'The World of Howard Hawks', *Films & Filming,* July 1962, p21ff

Lloyd Shearer, 'Crime Certainly Pays on the Screen', *New York Times*, August 8th 1945

'Sicily Gets Hollywood Version of *The Godfather*', *New York Times*, October 13th 1972

Paul Simper, 'Swearing can be wonderful if it's done with humour', *Neon,* September 1997, p99

'So Refreshing', *Photoplay*, July 1960, p5

F. Maurice Speed, Review of *Hell Is a City, What's On in London*, April 29th 1960, p12

Gloria Steinem, 'Maurice Joseph Micklewhite – What's 'E Got?', *New York Times,* December 4th 1966

Philip Strick, 'Bonnie and Warrendale', *Films & Filming,* November 1967, p28

Margaret Tarratt and Kevin Gough Yates, 'Playing the Game: Stanley Baker', *Films & Filming*, August 1970, pp30–34

Al Taylor, 'Val Guest', *Little Shoppe of Horrors,* No 7 (aka No. 3), December 1982, pp34-39

Norman Taylor, 'Spotlight On Stanley Baker', *ABC Film Review*, January 1960, pp26-27

'There Are Devils Inside Me says Michael Caine', *Photoplay*, May 1972, p19ff

Howard Thompson, 'How To Succeed By Trying To Be Bad', *New York Times,* May 23rd 1965

David Thomson, 'The Discreet Charm of the Godfather', *Sight & Sound*, Spring 1978, pp76-80

_____, 'In a Lonely Place', *Sight & Sound,* Summer 1979, pp215-220

John Toland, 'Sad Ballad of the Real Bonnie and Clyde', *New York Times,* February 18th 1968

'Trade Show Offers – March 1960', *Kine Weekly*, April 7th 1960, p30

'Val Guest', *Little Shoppe of Horrors*, No. 4, April 1978, pp49-52

Malvin Wald, Letter, *Sight & Sound*, Summer 1968, p160

Irving Wallace, 'He Makes Murder Pay', *Pageant Magazine*, July 1946, pp126-129

'Warner-Pathe Premieres *Hell Is a City*', *Kine Weekly*, May 5th 1960, pp12-13

'Warner-Pathe Trio in the Money', *Kine Weekly*, June 23rd 1960, p12

'Warners Drop Out of the Hays Office', *New York Times*, June 1st 1945

'Warners Lead Again With 21 1967 Oscar Nominations', *The Daily Cinema*, 21st February 1968, p1

Wear., Review of *In a Lonely Place, Variety*, May 17th 1950

Richard Weaver, Review of *Get Carter, Films & Filming,* May 1971, pp88-89

John Webster, 'Graduating...With Honours', *Showtime*, July 1968, p7

Bernard Weinraub, 'Director Arthur Penn Takes on General Custer', *New York Times,* December 21st 1969

Colin Westerbeck, Jr., 'Good Company', *Sight & Sound*, Autumn 1973, pp222-224

Whit., Review of *Dillinger, Variety*, June 13th 1973

Mel Whitcomb, 'Have the Hoods Put a Hex on Mickey Cohen's Moll?', *Vice Squad*, Vol 1, No. 1, December 1960, p16ff

Richard Whitehall, Review of *Hell Is a City, Films & Filming*, May 1960, p24

_____, Review of *Dr. No, Films & Filming,* November 1962, p36

_____, 'Crime Inc.,' *Films & Filming,* January 1964, pp7-12

Dan Yakir, 'Painting Pictures', *Film Comment*, September / October 1984, pp18-22

Dan Yergin, 'Peckinpah's Progress', *New York Times,* October 31st 1971

DVD

Get Carter - Audio commentary – Michael Caine, Mike Hodges, Wolfgang Suschitzky Warner Home Video, 2000

L.A. Confidential - Cast / Creator interviews, production notes etc, Warner Home Video, 1998

Index

237